GENERAL MANAGEMENT IN LATIN AND IBERO-AMERICAN ORGANIZATIONS

This book provides an examination of the general manager, which encompasses their roles as strategist, organizational designer and institutional leader. Instead of exclusively focusing on the economic aspect of general management, this book explores a humanist perspective based on the conviction that maintaining high ethical standards is a precondition to the healthy, long-term prosperity of firms and, more importantly, the development of employees.

Bringing together a team of contributors from several prestigious business schools in Spain, Portugal, and Central and South America, this book develops the field of general management through academic thinking, research and practical experience in the form of original and relevant case studies from the perspective of Ibero-American business communities. After explaining the foundations of its call for humanist general management practices, the authors focus on themes inherent to strategy and organizing such as sustainability, business model innovation, strategy in emerging markets, strategic alliances, digital strategy and organizational learning. They conclude by focusing on institutional leadership, and provide a fresh look at boards of directors, risk management, family businesses, stakeholder management and the work of CEOs.

General Management in Latin and Ibero-American Organizations is an invaluable resource that will be of great interest to practitioners and students in the field of international business, management, organization studies, strategy in emerging markets, leadership and corporate governance.

Adrián A. Caldart is a senior lecturer of strategic management and the academic director of the Food & Beverage Industry Meetings at IESE Business School (Barcelona, Madrid, New York, Munich and São Paulo). He is also professor of strategic management at AESE Business School (Lisbon and Porto, Portugal), where he is director of the Business Policy Academic Area and president of the Academic Council and of the EMBA Committee. His research interests include corporate-level strategy, international strategy and the work of the CEO, topics on which he has published several academic articles, book chapters and teaching materials, including over twenty teaching case studies. He coauthored the book *The Dynamics of Strategy: Mastering Strategic Landscapes of the Firm*.

Joan E. Ricart, fellow of the Strategic Management Society (SMS) and the European Academy of Management (EURAM), is the Carl Schrøder Professor of Strategic Management at the IESE Business School, where he was, from 1993 to 2016, chair of the Strategic Management Department, University of Navarra. He was the founding president of EURAM, president of the SMS and vice president of the Ibero-American Academy of Management. He was the academic director of the European Institute for Advanced Studies in Management (EIASM) and member of the research committee of the European Foundation for Management Development (EFMD). Ricart holds a PhD in managerial economics, Northwestern University; a PhD in industrial engineering, Universitat Politècnica de Catalunya; and a PhD in economics and business administration, Universitat Autònoma de Barcelona.

Alejandro A. Carrera is a professor of business policy at IAE Business School. He has been the founder, chair and director of the PWC Cátedra de Gobierno de las Organizaciones since 2009. He was, from 1986 to 2006, chair of the Business Policy Department at the IAE Business School, Austral University. From 2006 to 2012, Professor Carrera was a board member at this institution, fulfilling the role of vice-dean from 2008 to 2012. His research interests include corporate governance, entrepreneurship and the work of the CEO, topics on which he has published several academic articles, book chapters and teaching materials, including over thirty teaching case studies.

GENERAL MANAGEMENT IN LATIN AND IBERO-AMERICAN ORGANIZATIONS

A Humanistic Perspective

Edited by Adrián A. Caldart, Joan E. Ricart and Alejandro A. Carrera

Routledge
Taylor & Francis Group

LONDON AND NEW YORK

First published 2020
by Routledge
2 Park Square, Milton Park, Abingdon, Oxon OX14 4RN

and by Routledge
52 Vanderbilt Avenue, New York, NY 10017

Routledge is an imprint of the Taylor & Francis Group, an informa business

British Library Cataloguing-in-Publication Data
A catalogue record for this book is available from the British Library

Library of Congress Cataloging-in-Publication Data
A catalog record for this book has been requested

ISBN: 978-0-367-23433-1 (hbk)
ISBN: 978-0-367-23435-5 (pbk)
ISBN: 978-0-429-27982-9 (ebk)

Typeset in Bembo
by Apex CoVantage, LLC

MIX
Paper from
responsible sources
FSC
www.fsc.org   FSC™ C013985

Printed in the United Kingdom
by Henry Ling Limited

CONTENTS

PART 5
Cases   **259**

FIGURES

TABLES

CONTRIBUTORS

Rafael Andreu is a professor of information systems and strategic management at IESE Business School, University of Navarra. His interests include organizational learning and capability building; idiosyncratic knowledge and compensation; the management profession, with an emphasis on its ethical foundations connected to spontaneous learning and associated implications for management practice; and non-economic value management.

Africa Ariño is a professor and head of the Strategic Management Department at IESE Business School, where she holds the Joaquim Molins Figueras Chair of Strategic Alliances. Her research focuses on structural design and management processes of strategic alliances.

Pascual Berrone is a professor of strategic management and holder of the Schneider Electric Sustainability and Business Strategy Chair at IESE Business School. His award-winning research has focused on corporate sustainability, corporate governance and smart cities.

Adrián A. Caldart is a senior lecturer of strategic management and the academic director of the Food & Beverage Industry Meetings at IESE Business School (Barcelona, Madrid, New York, Munich and São Paulo). He is also Professor of Business Policy, Head of the Business Policy department and President of the Academic Council at AESE Business School (Lisbon and Porto). His research interests include corporate-level strategy, international strategy and the work of the CEO, topics in which he has published several academic articles, book chapters and teaching materials, including over twenty teaching case studies.

Luis Manuel Calleja is currently a senior lecturer at the Department of Strategic Management at IESE Business School and a professor of business policy at IEEM Business School (University of Montevideo). He also teaches in other places, such as AESE (Lisbon), San Telmo (Seville), AMS (Luanda), INALDE (Bogotá), ISE (São Paulo), MDE Business School (Abidjan) and MABS (Canary Islands), among others. He has developed management programs for politicians, public leaders, healthcare and fashion.

Alejandro A. Carrera is a professor of business policy at the IAE Business School, Universidad Austral (from 1980 to date). He has developed the discipline of entrepreneurship at the IAE Business School. Professor Carrera has been a member of the advisory board of the Center for Entrepreneurship of IAE since its foundation, in 1999. He has been chair and director of the PWC Chair in Corporate Governance since 2009.

Enrique Chamas currently teaches several courses in executive programs at IAE Business School and Torcuato Di Tella Business School. His actual areas of specialization and research include business models and their innovation, digitalization and platformization.

Magdalena Cornejo is a researcher at CONICET and professor at the Universidad Turcuato Di Tella in Argentina. Her publications have appeared in the *International Journal of Forecasting Agricultural Economics* and *Harvard Business Review*.

Iván Díaz-Molina is the director of the Center for Entrepreneurship and Innovation Studies and head of the Strategy Department at the ESE Business School in Santiago, Chile. His areas of interest include innovation systems, innovation-induced risk management and risk-based decision-making at upper management level within the organization.

Marta Elvira is the Puig Chair Professor of Global Leadership Development, with appointments to the departments of strategic management and managing people in organizations, at IESE Business School. Professor Elvira's work examines the political and economic processes involved in designing organizational reward structures, and the joint effects of incentive pay and promotion systems on employee earnings and performance.

Alfredo Enrione is the director of the Center for Corporate Governance and Society at ESE Business School and director of the Senior Management Program (PADE). Professor Enrione has pioneered the teaching and diffusion of corporate governance in Latin America through the oldest executive program for boards of directors while collaborating in the creation of similar initiatives in the region.

Jaume Llopis is a senior lecturer in the Department of Strategic Management at IESE Business School. He has served as CEO at prominent companies and a member of the board of directors at several multinational companies, as well as family-owned businesses in Europe and Latin America.

Jorge Iván Gómez Osorio is a professor in INALDE Business School University of La Sabana, and an expert on strategy, corporate governance and general management. He has held managerial positions in both the public and private sectors and worked as a professor at various universities in Colombia and Spain.

Joan E. Ricart, fellow of the Strategic Management Society (SMS) and the European Academy of Management (EURAM), is the Carl Schröder Professor of Strategic Management at IESE Business School. He was the founding president of the European Academy of Management (EURAM), president of the Strategic Management Society (SMS) and vice president of the Ibero-American Academy of Management.

Héctor Rocha is a professor of business policy and entrepreneurship at IAE Business School. For the past twenty-five years, he has been devoted to identifying and realizing the positive impact entrepreneurs and managers have on the integral development of their organizations and the communities where their strategies are implemented.

Mike Rosenberg is an associate professor in the Strategic Management Department at IESE Business School, where he lectures on strategy, geopolitics and sustainability in IESE's MBA programs. Professor Rosenberg is the author of *Strategy & Sustainability* (Palgrave Macmillan, 2015) and *Strategy & Geo-politics* (Emerald, 2017) and is coeditor of *Managing Media Businesses* (Palgrave Macmillan, 2017).

Horacio Rousseau is an assistant professor of management in the College of Business at Florida State University. Professor Rousseau focuses on studying how organizations such as nonprofits, corporations and community banks shape the sustainable development of their local communities.

Ángel Sevil is an entrepreneur and strategy consultant. His research in strategic management has focused on how entrepreneurship fosters ecosystems, competitive strategy in turbulent macroeconomic environments and competition dynamics in natural resources industries.

Josep Tàpies is a professor in the Department of Strategic Management and holder of the family-owned business chair at IESE Business School. He earned a PhD in industrial engineering at the Polytechnic University of Catalonia (UPC) and an MBA at ESADE. His areas of specialization include strategic management, corporate governance, family-owned firms and their development and governance structures.

Roberto Vassolo is a professor of business policy and strategy at the IAE Business School, Universidad Austral. He is also a visiting professor at Universidad Católica de Chile in the School of Engineering. He currently leads research in competitive strategy in turbulent macroeconomic environments, competition in natural resources industries and strategic leadership.

FOREWORD

The role of the CEO has become a Herculean task. Over the past two decades, a combination of radical changes in the global economy and society, including the changing preferences of a new generation of young professionals who have recently joined the business world, has exponentially increased the levels of uncertainty and ambiguity that CEOs face.

The very nature of the CEO's job – in large and small companies alike – is holistic, interdisciplinary and cross-functional. It requires a diversity breadth of knowledge, capabilities and values in the exercise of this important social function. This multidimensional nature makes it particularly difficult for scholars to capture the CEO's role in a few clear functions and tasks. In a world shaped by technology transformation, globalization and a new generation of employees and customers, CEOs need to reflect on the changing expectations of their role and social function and to learn to adjust their capabilities and commitment to new contexts and goals.

The increasing role of finance and technology in business and society has paved the way for a growing number of senior executives with highly specialized knowledge and expertise. Extensive expertise in a certain area is an excellent quality for senior executives to have, but its exclusive nature can become a shortcoming when they face new challenges. The missteps of CEOs can have a major impact on both their companies and wider society. A number of CEOs unwittingly led their companies toward disaster – particularly those in banking, professional services and high-tech, among other industries – during the 2008 financial crisis. However, this outcome did not derive from a lack of specialized knowledge. Rather, it was because they did not possess the indispensable integrative capabilities and attitudes of good CEOs.

In the current changing business context, three capabilities are particularly relevant for good CEOs. The first is taking a cross-functional, holistic view of the company, which helps lead a business beyond its technological or financial dimension.

More importantly, this holistic view is one that should be centered on the customer, whose needs the firm should serve. Unfortunately, in too many industries, customers are considered mainly sources of revenue to be maximized rather than stakeholders to be served. This attitude can easily lead to the misselling of products, price abuses and serious breaches in the use of private data.

The second capability is developing the company's purpose, which explains why a company actually exists and what it wants to achieve in the long term. There is often terrible confusion between the company's long-term goals and its short-term objectives, namely solid financial performance. This reflects a serious weakness in senior managers who are unable to articulate a long-term view of the firm that is compatible with the delivery of short-term performance. There are always quarters or years when corporate performance may be affected by unexpected events or an unanticipated market weakness. But the lack of clarity about what a company wants to achieve in the long term becomes a formidable obstacle to delivering in the short term. Moreover, a company that has a well-defined long-term purpose has a clear north that helps inspire and develop new options for future growth.

The third capability is recognizing that the CEO needs to develop and engage a team to be truly effective. A high-quality management team is a must for any company. Some investors and scholars still view the CEO as a stand-alone senior manager equipped with special capabilities to see into the future to set company strategy. Some CEOs may in fact have those abilities. But even those who have them need to consider that good companies are inherently social institutions. They are organizations that develop personalities, internally and externally, through the cooperation of many people. Unfortunately, prevalent notions of leadership – ranging from charismatic to autocratic, for instance – are more frequently focused on than the quality and diversity of expertise in the senior management team and that of the whole organization.

The fact that CEOs have the final word on certain decisions before the board is not reason enough to think they should make these decisions in isolation. Developing an effective team of senior managers who work with the CEO is vital. A good team adds different perspectives, offers specialized knowledge about different business functions, has a better understanding of customers and businesses in different geographies and includes different sensitivities to personal and cultural issues. Moreover, a strong management team helps engage people on lower levels of the organization. Unfortunately, the cult of the CEO that seems so dominant today is a serious deadweight on the shoulders of many CEOs.

Professors Adrián A. Caldart, Joan E. Ricart and Alejandro A. Carrera and their coauthors have done a great job of editing this most interesting book on general management. In particular, I would like to highlight three key attributes regarding the nature of the job of CEOs present in many of the chapters. The first is that they emphasize the interdisciplinary and integrative nature of the work of the CEO. They make an excellent adaptation of the classical work on the role of the general manager that was developed, among others, by leading scholars and thinkers such as Chester Barnard, Peter Drucker, C. Roland Christensen, Ken Andrews, Jay Lorsch,

Peter Lawrence, Henry Mintzberg, Joe Bower and Jeff Pfeffer. It is a pity that the research on the nature of the job of the general manager has lost relevance in the field of strategy and strategic management. There is a serious need to take it seriously once again, and this book makes a strong contribution to this effort.

The second attribute of this book is that it offers a variety of institutional and cultural settings where CEOs work and develop their mission and functions. Most of the chapters combine theory with cases and data related to specific European and Latin American countries. Moreover, it includes an institutional dimension of the job of a CEO: its role in the context of the firm's ownership structure and governance model. More often than not, a CEO's activities and performance are considered in isolation of this type of context, but experience shows that this context is more influential than many other factors in the long-term development of firms. This is a quality that makes this book special and provides perspective on the challenges that CEOs face.

The third dimension highlighted by this book is that the nature of the CEO's job be focused on people: good CEOs do things with other people, develop other people and have a positive influence on other people. Their performance depends largely on their ability to engage colleagues and collaborators professionally. In this way, a CEO's job has a relational dimension that goes beyond networking capabilities. In their work, CEOs help people grow while also growing themselves, by working with and learning from other people. In a business world dominated by financial criteria and technology-based solutions, this is a useful and much-needed quality.

All these factors make this book relevant in the strategy and organization literature. The different chapters provide a range of institutional contexts, conceptual frameworks, detailed analyses and approaches, making it crucial for management scholars. Moreover, it will inspire CEOs and general managers to consider broader dimensions of their work while encouraging scholars to ask new questions about the nature of the CEO's role.

Jordi Canals

Professor of Strategic Management, IESE Business School

Dean of IESE Business School (2001–2016)

28 July 2018

INTRODUCTION

The practice of general management

Adrián A. Caldart and Joan E. Ricart

This is a book about general management: the work of the chief executive officer (CEO) and their inherent sphere of responsibility. In this role, the CEO is the *strategist*, who sets the long-term direction of the organization and the goals to be achieved; the *leader*, who inspires and organizes the people in pursuit of these goals; and the *politician*, who harmonizes the interests of the different stakeholders to ensure long-term continuity and development. In light of these important roles, CEOs are arguably the most influential members of any organization. They not only influence the way that employees carry out their professional lives but also safeguard and shape the values the company embraces as a community.

But why do we need another book about general management *now*? The topic is hardly original: it has been the focus of a host of pioneering voices, including Henri Fayol, David Ulrich, Chester Barnard and John Kotter, among others. The highly acclaimed management thinker Peter Drucker devoted extensive attention to the subject in *The Practice of Management*, his most influential book. Henry Mintzberg's doctoral dissertation focused on the agenda of the general manager, a remarkable work that eventually became the core of the book *The Nature of Managerial Work*, a landmark contribution that, even forty years after its publication, remains an essential reference.

While these theorists have contributed important insights to general managers, we believe that the development of fresh "food for thought" on the work of CEOs is not merely important but urgent. Unfortunately, an abundance of classic and often-cited general management works has resulted in what we see as a dangerous lack of ongoing reflection about the topic. This has led to a decline among academics to reflect comprehensively on the work of the CEO. Currently, work on general management oscillates mainly between (1) anecdotal accounts of prominent general managers' work in the mainstream business press and (2) academic literature, which offers in-depth studies of specific aspects of the CEO's agenda but which lacks scope.

Joseph Bower observed that general management scholars must master a variety of topics related to strategy, structure and people (and the complex link among these). While such mastery might make them "wildly successful teachers, effective consultants and well-read authors . . . if they had no refereed journal articles, they could not be promoted (Bower, 2008, p. 274)." Bower partly attributes the abandonment of general management as a focus of the academic curriculum to a focus on competitive strategy – a narrower field that is more rigorously grounded in a single academic discipline (economics) and thus better suited for academic publication.

In addition, the emergence of the academic field of organizational behavior, which focuses on structure, power and the human side of the enterprise, has also contributed to the fragmentation of the general management curriculum. There is a growing misperception that these issues don't fall within the topic of general management. Yet, a global survey conducted by Harvard Business School professors Srikant Datar and David Garvin indicates that business school deans and executives appreciate the need for an integrated view of the work of general managers in the MBA curricula: a "solution-centric point of view, often from the vantage point of a CEO . . . who is steward of a complex organization, oversees multiple functions and is evaluated on an integrated P&L" (Datar, Garvin & Cullen, 2010, p. 91).

Certainly, there are "timeless" topics in a CEO's agenda, such as the need to form and develop a competent top team and delegate tasks. However, the agenda has changed significantly since Drucker, Mintzberg or Kotter carried out their research. Executives today are exposed to new forces that were clearly absent in previous decades. For instance, CEOs now benefit from – and contend with – almost unlimited access to information and have computer technology at their disposal to analyze data in ways not even dreamed of just a few years ago.

As leaders, they must manage the emergence of unprecedented attitudes toward work among the younger generations and deal with multicultural management teams and workforces. They also face competitive environments, in which business models change much more frequently than they did a generation ago. They must deal with consumers that increasingly value the use of goods over possession of them while demanding high levels of transparency in operations and governance. CEOs face international competition from firms coming from highly diverse cultures and capitalist traditions. Finally, society increasingly demands that CEOs deliver value socially and environmentally, in addition to financially (the "triple bottom line"). These elements were not alien to CEOs of previous generations, but they have become far more widespread and powerful in recent years.

If we understand the role of the CEO as the custodian and shaper of organizational values, as described previously, then the need for new perspectives becomes evident. Corporate failures stemming from scandalous malpractice and greedy behavior from top managers have led to an increasing loss of prestige among CEOs and large firms in general among the public in most developed countries. Cynical corporate statements about the importance of ethics and social responsibility have cast an understandable, yet not totally fair, shadow of skepticism over the ability of large firms to behave ethically.

The late Sumantra Ghoshal, a sharp observer and practitioner of management education, announced in a widely cited article that "by propagating inspired amoral theories, business schools have freed their students from any sense of moral responsibility" (Ghoshal, 2005, p. 76). In a similar vein, the previously mentioned study led by Datar and Garvin suggests that MBA programs have a worrisome lack of focusing on topics such as internal governance and socially responsible leadership (Datar et al., 2010, p. 80). Because businesses are implicitly tasked with helping improve society, it is critical that they recover moral credibility. Business schools have a central role to play in this process, which will require them to take a more lucid approach to business ethics and do away with glossy approaches based on PR (public relations) and often devoid of any substance.

High-quality general management education, based on a humanistic view of business affairs, was the raison d'être of IESE Business School when it was founded in 1958 in Barcelona. Antonio Valero, IESE's mastermind and first dean, always emphasized the need for "training students in criteria more than teaching techniques." In fact, a 1958 school brochure stated that "IESE will develop in its students ... *the desire and ability to understand human beings*" (Canals, 2009, p. 40).

Valero's path-breaking work, carried out when Spain was politically isolated from neighboring countries, eventually led to the creation of a vibrant network of international business schools, including AESE (Portugal), IAE (Argentina), IPADE (Mexico), ISE (Brazil), PAD (Peru), ESE (Chile), IEEM (Uruguay) and INALDE (Colombia). In fact, IESE's mission informed the founding principles of these schools.

Over the last four decades, these schools have played leadership roles in management education in their respective countries, educating thousands of top managers. Their leadership in the field of management education is the result of their success in providing high-quality programs with a deeply humanistic perspective.

In this human-centered view, the role of the general manager (and the business manager in general) is not just as an agent who decisively contributes to the efficient and innovative management of scarce social resources. Instead, CEOs are leaders responsible for creating organizations committed to the personal development of everyone in the company and to ethical business conduct. Thus, managers contribute to society by leading through example and proving that firms (and the professionals who run them) can do well by doing right.

In May 2015, AESE Business School in Lisbon hosted an academic conference that brought together a group of general management professors from the network of international business schools referred in this Introduction. The scholars discussed the need for contemporary academic work on the scope of the general manager, and they decided to put forward their views on the subject. This book is the result of that endeavor.

The contributing authors are senior academics who hold leadership roles in their respective schools. They have strong academic backgrounds, coupled with a deep involvement in their business communities as consultants, entrepreneurs and independent board members in business firms and NGOs (non-governmental

4 Adrián A. Caldart and Joan E. Ricart

organizations). The objective of this book is to present practical, down-to-earth insights for practicing senior managers, rooted in solid academic work.

The book is organized in five parts. In the first part (Chapters 1 to 3), we set the stage for the book by putting the focus on the anthropological foundations that inspire our shared humanistic approach to management education. In the second part (Chapters 4 to 9), we center on topics related to the content of strategic management and organizing practices, with a clear, yet not exclusive, focus on the realities of the Iberian Peninsula and Latin America. Issues covered in this section include, among others, strategic foresight, strategizing in Latin America, strategic coherence, sustainability, innovation management, organizational learning and business models. In the third part (Chapters 10 to 14), we focus on corporate governance. Importantly, in this book, we do not isolate corporate governance from ongoing management. Rather, we seek to emphasize the systemic nature of general management work and the need for harmony among strategy, organizing and governance, as a prerequisite for the long-term survival and healthy development of the firm. Contributions within this section explore topics such as the agenda of the Latin American CEO; the governance roles of the CEO as a creator of the internal context of the firm; the roles of boards of directors and top management teams; stakeholder management; the influence of ownership on the CEO; and risk management. The fourth part, Chapter 15, provides an integrative perspective of the chief executive's agenda. Finally, Part 5 contains a collection of case study abstracts developed within the business schools of the contributing authors as well as from other schools that integrate the network led by IESE. Such cases, many of which have been cited within different chapters, follow the general management perspective that permeates the whole book.

Our overarching goal is to shed new light on what it means to be a general manager in today's business environment, as seen through the lens of a humanistic view of management.

References

Bower, J. (2008). "The Teaching of Strategy. From General Manager to Analyst and Back Again?" *Journal of Management Inquiry*, 17(4): 269–275.
Canals, C. (2009). *Sabiduría Práctica. 50 años del IESE*. Barcelona: Planeta.
Datar, S., Garvin, D., and Cullen, P. (2010). *Rethinking the MBA. Business Education at Crossroads*. Boston: Harvard Business School Press.
Ghoshal, S. (2005). "Bad Management Theories are Destroying Good Management Practices." *Academy of Management Learning and Education*, 4(1): 75–91.

PART 1

The work of the general manager

Foundations

1

A GENERAL MANAGER'S AGENDA

What good managers do

Joan E. Ricart and Jaume Llopis

As management scholars and teachers, we often worry about a fundamental question: what do managers, especially good ones, do? It seems like a simple and easy-to-answer query. Just follow a few managers around and watch them. But this approach doesn't reveal essential information. Since managers spend most of their time in meetings, speaking with people both inside and outside the organization and addressing diverse issues, it's hard to tell between what is urgent, what is important and what is necessary. And distinguishing these is important.

We decided to try to answer the question by taking a different approach. We invited top managers from diverse types of firms and industries to attend our classes and explain their work to MBA students who were about to graduate. In addition to giving the students a chance to reflect on what they believed were the most important tasks for general managers, the discussion also forced managers to think about and identify them. Instead of merely describing how they spent their time, they were asked to identify their priorities. We encouraged them to focus on this idea when they prepared for the sessions, and in many cases, we followed up with separate interviews to clarify their views.[1]

Not surprisingly, managers' styles, and therefore their perspectives and in-class presentations, were quite varied. They reflected the characteristics of their firms, industries, histories, experiences and values. Despite these differences, clear patterns emerged. As we developed the framework to be explained in this chapter, and shared these with the executives in our executive education and alumni classes, we identified significant a convergence in key areas. We realized that our framework was not always explicitly articulated by executives, but it was a cogent reflection of their implicit understanding of the relevance and importance of their leadership task. In our framework, we identify three fundamental priorities: the future, the business model and people.

The first fundamental priority is creating a future for the organization and communicating this – something easy to say but so difficult to do. Top managers know that their essential responsibility, their true service to the organization they manage, is to make sure the organization has a future. And this requires playing the roles of entrepreneur, strategist and visionary. The CEO must act as a true integrator with a long-term perspective. Sometimes we call this the "strategizing" role of a general manager, to highlight the ongoing strategic thinking that is involved.

The second fundamental priority we identified was continuously adapting the business model. We consider the business model to be the instrument that creates value in a sustainable way. And this instrument requires constant renewal to deal with continuous changes in the environment, in competition, in the capabilities of the organization and in the learning of individuals. Renewal involves ongoing restructuring to boost efficiency, reengineering to be more effective and reinvention to sustain differentiation. We call this general manager role "renewal" to highlight the design perspective and the need to continuously reimagine the business model.

The third fundamental priority that emerged was people. We found that managers invest significant amounts of time and effort into attracting talent, developing people and helping them grow in their organizations. As one manager noted repeatedly, "My job is to get the best version of each person in the organization and focus them on our mission as a company." The general manager's role as "organizer"

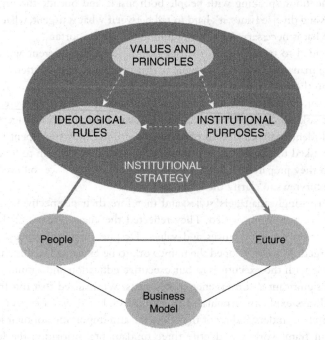

FIGURE 1.1   Priorities of a General Manager

Source: Authors.

emerged from these conversations but with a focus on people as a starting point rather than tasks.

In addition to these three fundamental priorities and roles, we identified another critical element. We found that managers frequently spoke about the mission, values and the contribution of their firms to society. Importantly, they discussed these issues as fundamental, rather than residual, aspects of their leadership roles. This led us to identify a fourth priority, which acts as an umbrella and gives meaning to general managers' work in their organizations. We called this priority institutional strategy.

In addition to giving meaning and direction to firms, particularly in highly complex and uncertain situations, this priority reflects the view of the firm as an institution with values, principles, norms and meaning in a broad sense. Serving as ambassadors for these attributes, on behalf of the organization, is perhaps the most important role that general managers play.

Figure 1.1 presents the framework we discuss in this chapter. It is a simple model that captures the complexities of leading organizations as they fulfill their missions in the world. It highlights the important aspects of a general manager's role, their important service to all stakeholders and the beauty of the profession of leading people to do extraordinary things for the good of society.

Search for the future

What could be more important than the future? The future is, of course, highly relevant and important for all stakeholders. There is no need for long discussions about this. So any leader should, before anything else, be aware of the future as a fundamental responsibility. They, along with everyone else, should be thinking about, working toward and imagining the future – a positive future – for everyone involved in this collective project. The creation of the future is the base for any strategy. It involves the analysis and identification of opportunities and is the starting point for the existence of the firm itself.

Consider the quote of one executive, José María Pujol, president of the Spanish multinational Ficosa International. Ficosa, which designs and produces components for the auto industry, was a small company back in the 1980s manufacturing mainly for Seat, the Spanish carmaker that now forms part of the Volkswagen Group. Over the years, it has undergone various transformations. Today, it is a small multinational with a turnover of roughly 1 billion euros selling to basically every car manufacturer in the world, with a leading position in retrovision systems.

Pujol said, "The future will come. The question is if you are going to have future. You have to anticipate it, make decisions and be right about your choices. Sometimes you even need to commit suicide to really innovate and lead the change that is coming."

Difficult choices have to be made, which are even more difficult in situations in which there are opportunities for creating a different future. Often the first choice to be made is whether one should anticipate the future or create it. Creating the future, in fact, is the best way to anticipate it, but can you also be a leader in it?

The starting point for the reflection about the future should always be the anticipation of the future needs of your clients (or future clients). One of Ficosa's main divisions is focused on retrovision systems, which feature mirrors. Today, cameras have become just as important in cars as mirrors are. And tomorrow, the industry may need no mirrors at all if cars become driverless. So what are the real needs to be satisfied in the future? Whose needs will the company satisfy? What should be done today to secure the firm's future tomorrow?

A culture of innovation

In a world of innovation, there is vast space for creating a new future. And it derives from needs that are not satisfied today and perhaps not yet known. Apple, for instance, showed people their great unmet need for smartphones and tablets. And today we can't live without them!

The second step in creating the future is to put forward a value proposition that satisfies the needs we are anticipating. The value proposition provides a clear vision that can inspire the whole organization. Rather than a "dream" projected onto the future, it manifestly satisfies customer needs through its value proposition.

Good managers are good entrepreneurs, who effectively carry out these fundamentally creative tasks with the support of their teams. They are also able to bring the vision to the present moment and put the necessary strategic building blocks in place to take the company into this future. Again, in this process, there are two fundamental steps.

First, managers should define the businesses in which the firm can create sustainable competitive advantage. It helps to focus on one fundamental question: where do we want to compete? Businesses are defined, in a practical sense, by the needs that are going to be served, the clients who have these needs, the geographic areas that will be served and the competencies required to carry all these actions out successfully.

In terms of competencies, a second fundamental question must be asked: how are we going to win? Both questions need to be explored simultaneously. We can't choose where to play without understanding how we're going to win. Both questions are equally important.

Most work in the strategy field over the last fifty years has centered on providing the answer to the second question, which is extremely difficult to answer. Consequently, countless methods have been developed to help general managers understand the competitive environment, a firm's capabilities and resources, competitive interaction, potential new players and radical change actors.

The analysis of these first two questions gives rise to a third: what capabilities are needed? As we carry out the process, we need to identify the core competencies and which of those associated with them are actually necessary.

Clearly, the answers to these questions will differ according to the industry, the firm, the interest of the owners and the geographical area. Ultimately, though, strategy is about being different, not doing the same things better. This first priority, the future, connects us directly to the second one in our framework: business model renewal.

Business model renewal

What is a business model? It's the set of choices that a company's leadership makes, taking into account the company's history, philosophy and the way it creates value for its stakeholders. The business model describes how the company generates value for society as it seeks to create the future it has envisioned.[2] As revealed in our discussions, general managers continuously renew the business model. Since clients' needs are constantly evolving, the vision of the future must evolve, too.

The Swedish furniture retailer IKEA acts as a useful example of both effective design and constant adaptation of a business model. In our sessions, Belén Frau – at the time general manager of IKEA Italy and previously a manager of a large retail store in Northern Spain – explained this to us in detail. IKEA's business model is determined through fundamental choices. When it first began, the company set out to "democratize" good Nordic design by making it widely accessible to customers through low prices obtained through large volumes and operational capabilities, especially logistics. But this basic value proposition has always evolved. Currently, IKEA sells unassembled furniture, which eases the logistics process and enables clients to transport merchandise themselves, cheaply and efficiently. But IKEA hasn't always done this. Instead, the company decided to embrace the idea at the suggestion of an employee as it sought to refresh the business model to better serve the needs of clients.

Similarly, IKEA is constantly adapting the buyer experience and business model by studying the habits of consumers in different countries. Changes are implemented either on a global or local level, based on ongoing experimentation, pilot tests and prototypes.

Traditionally, the business model – its design, configuration and adaptation – has been a priority for general managers. A more relevant issue today has become the increasing opportunity to do things differently.[3] For this reason, business model types are proliferating. In the past, discussions centered on the trade-off between differentiation and cost, or mass markets and focused segments. These differences are still important, and business models have to be carefully designed to ensure they are consistent with the choices made in these domains. But today, general managers must consider other factors too.

Numerous drivers of change – demographics, globalization and technology, among others – can help identify alternative ways of designing business models. As a result, value chains often become fragmented as value-added activities are distributed geographically and outsourced to other companies and as distribution systems grow. The key dimensions of business models have multiplied, providing increasing opportunities to create new and distinctive types.

As a consequence, there has been an explosion in recent years in the number of tools, models and proposals for redesigning, innovating and renewing business models. Meanwhile, designing, experimenting, rapidly prototyping and deploying new business models has become a daily task and priority of general managers. As new competencies are necessary, business model renewal has become an important element in management education, with systemic and design-thinking capabilities now emphasized.

A focus on people

We found that general managers firmly believe that people are the center of the organization and the key to execution. Everything is done by and through them. Following this view, good managers spend significant amounts of their time focused on people.

The first fundamental priority in the area of people is to manage talent. Firms use different procedures and processes, but good managers put a lot of their time into identifying talent, developing it, providing challenges and new tasks, offering training and planning careers and assignments. In other words, they provide opportunities for people to grow.

Jaime Aguilera – president of Unilever in Spain and at the time of writing in charge of Eastern Europe – told us that his main role was to make sure he had the optimal team and that each member was able to "bring the best version of herself or himself to the table every day." In fact, he actually stated that this was the *only* thing he did: simply get the best version of each person to work with others on the team to fulfill the goals of the company. This is a nice way to express what should be the first priority of the top executive of any firm, division or department, and not just the domain of the human resources (HR) manager.

Importantly, talent management is an individualized task and therefore one has to involve every manager in the organization as a mentor, trainer and/or coach. It's a fundamental duty to ensure that people are growing and able to bring out the best in themselves at work every day. Managing talent is also challenging on an individual level since most tasks are carried out in teams. This means that people need to be combined in ways that enable them to flourish and grow while producing positive results.

Yet another dimension is managing levels of challenges and risks by making people feel responsible and therefore accountable. This involves empowering people and providing the tools and processes for good decision-making, along with channels for measuring and evaluating performance and providing feedback. Doing all this in a fair way is not easy and requires an understanding of motivation and incentives. It also means providing recognition and rewards fairly while correcting what needs to be corrected.

In our discussions, Luis Cantarell, VP of Nestlé Global, Head of Zone EMENA (Europe, Middle East and North of Africa), asserted that in his company, everyone behaves as if people are the most valuable asset in the company. Over the years, his many mentors and bosses helped him develop his career at Nestlé and provided him with opportunities to thrive and grow. When we spoke with him, he was developing team members and mentoring people in units throughout the company. In addition, he kept his own list of potential talent within Nestlé.

In essence, good managers are strong believers in human capital being fundamental for good execution, believing that optimal productivity is obtained not by exploiting people but by helping them grow and develop. They understand that passion comes from commitment and empowerment, and they manage human capital carefully. The result is often extraordinary things carried out by ordinary people – the key to success.

Building an institutional strategy

We live in a world characterized by high uncertainty and risk. Companies struggle to create or at least anticipate the future; design and constantly adapt the business model; and develop talent that can execute effectively. In a world sometimes described as VUCA (volatility, uncertainty, complexity and ambiguity), providing direction for these priority tasks is tough. How can general managers provide sufficient direction and stability in a VUCA world?

Detailed planning, a conventional approach for dealing with this challenge, is simply unfeasible today. Of course, you need to plan, but you also need to keep in mind that you may have to change plans tomorrow. For this reason, detailed planning is essentially death. So what do good managers do? They map out a clear institutional strategy.

An institutional strategy has different complementary elements, which include values and principles; institutional purpose and mission; and a working philosophy or "rules of the game." Let's take a look at each of these elements in more detail.

Values and principles form the backbone of any corporate culture. We have described how various general managers express their organization's values and how these connect to action and performance. They serve as ambassadors for these values, and moreover, they seek to live them. The consistency between espoused values and actions of key managers is crucial, because good managers demonstrate how to live these values.

The origin of values can vary considerably, depending on the history and the ownership structure of the firm. Even in centuries-old companies, the founder has an important impact. We found that values tend to be simple, clear and with a few unique characteristics. Generic values are not useful for providing direction and focus. Finally, values need to be shared by the whole organization, which is why the ambassador role played by top management is so important.

The second important element is institutional purpose, sometimes used interchangeably with the word "mission." The basic question to be asked here is, what contribution does the company make to society? This goes deeper than just talking about needs, clients and geographic areas that the company serves.

The purpose should include the *external mission*, which defines the value proposition and/or segments of clients. It should also include the *internal mission*, the purpose of the organization on a deeper level. By connecting the inside and outside, managers can link managerial choices with the organization and its clients.

Many times, the values and principles, as well as the purpose or mission, become ingrained, not only in the organizational culture but also in what we call the working philosophy of the place. Often, these are artifacts derived from the culture of the place. Sometimes they are largely implicit: learned by doing and by following examples. Sometimes they are explicit: written down and communicated to everyone even before they start working in the organization.

Two elements stand out when defining the working philosophy since they condition the behavior of people in the organization. The first centers on excellence, or what it means do things well in the company. The second point relates to merit. Does the company recognize excellent work? If so, how is this done? How effective is this recognition?

A relevant example for understanding the role of institutional strategy is La Fageda, a Catalan cooperative founded by Cristóbal Colón. The company was started to provide dignity through jobs to mentally impaired people in the region of La Garrotxa, Spain. La Fageda produces, as Colón likes to say, the best yogurts (also ice creams and marmalades) in the world. Although the company competes with Danone and Nestlé in the marketplace, its driving force is its internal mission to generate employment for the mentally impaired. Driven by the combined external and internal missions and supported by strong values, the company competes successfully while providing tremendous social value.

Many companies with sustained long-term success have strong cultures based on intrinsic values, a clear purpose and a specific working philosophy. The world outside is changing fast, so the company has to adapt, change and learn. But the institutional strategy gives the company stability, a sense of direction and focus for everyone in the organization.

The institutional strategy is, therefore, an umbrella that provides direction to the other three fundamental priorities: future, business model and people. Without this umbrella, the VUCA world can become a turbulent, unmanageable place. The institutional strategy provides order amid chaos and agility when adapting the business model.

Conclusion

The priorities of top managers that emerged from our study, which are summarized in Figure 1.1, are consistent with other studies on the normative behavior of top management. They are also aligned with the principles of IESE Business School, as articulated by the founding dean, Prof. Antonio Valero, and the emeritus dean, Prof. Juan Antonio Pérez López.[4]

By integrating academic work into our empirical observations, we can categorize the areas of responsibility for general managers in four interdependent elements that together make a system.[5] The role of the general manager (GM) is to work on each of the areas in a balanced and coordinated way, as presented in Figure 1.2.

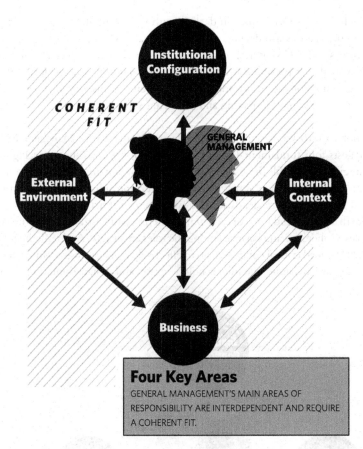

FIGURE 1.2   General Management Main Areas of Responsibility

Source: IESE Insight, No. 23, Fourth Quarter 2014, pp. 15–21.

Institutional configuration: The role of the GM is framed by the ownership, governance and stakeholders of the firm. The GM makes decisions relating to issues such as laws, regulations, government intervention, fiduciary law, as well as social norms. The GM never has total freedom, nor is totally constrained, since he or she can always manage or influence to some degree.

External context: GM actions are conditioned by the external context, which includes customers, channels and competitors. Again, the GM can sometimes greatly influence such parameters. But even when the degrees of freedom are limited, the GM has to manage the external context in a coherent way with the other elements while also considering the company's idiosyncratic dynamics.

Internal context: GM actions are also conditioned by the internal context, particularly people inside the organization. Consequently, the purpose should include an external mission dealing with the external environment but also an internal mission dealing with the internal context.

Business: The GM is responsible for the development of a business model that makes it possible to fulfill the internal and external mission within the constraints of the institutional configuration. In this way, they can follow a consistent logic for creating and capturing value.

It's not easy to work with this system in a balanced way. Management literature suggests four fundamental roles for the GM or CEO, as shown in Figure 1.3: (1) strategizing, to fulfill the external mission; (2) organizing, to fulfill the internal mission; (3) business model renewal; and (4) governing. The empirical observations gathered in our work are clearly aligned with these abstract tasks.

Note that the gerund form of each word is used to emphasize that these are continuous roles. Coherence and balance among the roles are crucial. And remember – it is a system! GMs need critical competencies to effectively manage this system, such as having an open and dynamic systemic or holistic vision and design-thinking capabilities.

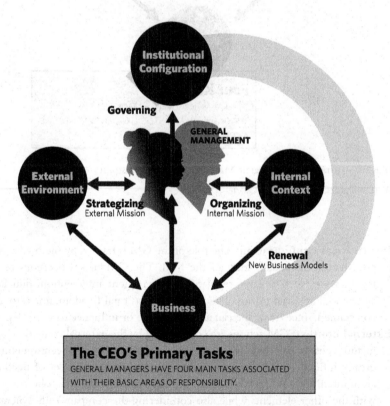

FIGURE 1.3 General Management Main Tasks Associated with the Areas of Responsibility

Source: Authors.

When GMs manage a system, they need to have a systemic or holistic vision. They need to see the forest beyond the trees. They also need to understand that a system is more than the sum of the parts, so aspects such as proper fit, consistency and reinforcement are vital. Furthermore, in a world of swift evolution, GMs need to understand systemic change. They may need to modify many things at the same time and, of course, will face many difficulties doing this.

But the system is open and dynamic. It's open because it constantly interacts with diverse stakeholders, many of them outside the organization itself. And it's dynamic because such relationships and interactions are constantly changing: sometimes steadily evolving, other times undergoing punctual change.

In summary, the role of the GM is the configuration and management of an open and dynamic system in a complex context with myriad stakeholders. So managers need to be careful when using tools that simplify and specialize, since their task is essentially integrative. For this reason, they should always maintain a systemic perspective.

The Japanese imaging and electronics company Ricoh provides an example of this transformational role of the GM.[6] In the wake of the economic crisis and the onset of the digital economy in Spain, Ricoh Spain needed to create new opportunities in the marketplace. As general manager of Ricoh Spain Ramón Martín explained to us, the firm decided to move beyond the introduction of new products launched by the corporation and embrace a new business model based on digital services. The deployment of the new business model is still in progress, requiring adjustments in all dimensions of this system.

GMs face the challenge of understanding complex situations and excelling in difficult roles. Management literature points to three criteria for judging the quality of a GM's decision-making:

1 **Discipline**. This refers to the managerial competencies to make rigorous decisions using the available information and the right managerial tools. Essentially, GMs should be competent and well trained, work hard and understand the complexities of the world today.
2 **Innovation**. We can also call this creativity or imagination. The complexity of the problems today requires novel solutions and innovative formulas to respond to the external, internal and governance context.
3 **Responsibility**. It may seem obvious, but an intrinsic sense of responsibility is associated with the work of a GM. The GM manages systems that affect stakeholders in many ways. And behind each stakeholder group, there are people affected by choices, either in positive or negative ways. GMs leave their fingerprints on every decision they make, a fact they are keenly aware of.

The GMs in our sample demonstrated these criteria and sought to transmit them to our students, each in a different way. They viewed the criteria as important for making choices during their careers.

As we got to know the person behind the GM role, we were able to identify several common character and personality traits and lifestyle patterns. In total, we pinpointed eight personal characteristics associated with good managers:

1   Hard work
2   Knowledge and competence
3   Shared values
4   Integrity
5   Spirit of service
6   Conflict management
7   Personal balance
8   Passion in their work

Being a general manager has always been difficult, never more so than today. Beyond the authority, status and power that we usually associate with the role, general managers perform a service that is ideally carried out by well-prepared professionals who possess integrity, competence, passion and a deep sense of responsibility for the well-being of all stakeholders. Ultimately, GMs are leaders of institutions that serve society and are agents of change and prosperity in a quickly changing world.

Notes

1   This research has been collected in two books published in Spanish: J. E. Ricart, J. Llopis and D. Pastoriza. *Yo Dirijo: La Dirección en El Siglo XXI Según Sus Protagonistas.* Deusto Ediciones, 2007; J. Llopis and J. E. Ricart. *Qué Hacen los Buenos Directivos: El Reto del Siglo XXI.* Madrid, Spain: Pearson, 2012. A summary was published in J. Llopis and J. E. Ricart, "What Good Managers Do: Management Priorities for the 21st Century," *The European Business Review,* September–October, 2013.
2   See R. Casadesus-Masanell and J. E. Ricart. "How to Design a Winning Business Model." *Harvard Business Review,* 100–107, January 2011.
3   See technical note: Strategy in the 21st Century: Business Models in Action, SMN-685-E, December 2012.
4   Some classical references here are
      S. Finkelstein and D. Hambrick. *Strategic Leadership: Top Executives and Their Effects on Organizations.* Minneapolis/St. Paul: West Publishing Company, 1996; J. Kotter. *The General Managers.* New York, NY: The Free Press, 1982; H. Mintzberg. *The Nature of Managerial Work.* New York, NY: Harper & Row, 1973; J. A. Pérez López. *Fundamentos de la Dirección de Empresas.* Madrid: Ediciones Rialp, 1993. Forthcoming in English as *Foundations of Management.*
      A. Valero and J. L. Lucas. *Política de Empresa: el Gobierno de la Empresa de Negocios,* 2nd ed., Pamplona, Spain: EUNSA, 1991.
5   What follows comes from R. Andreu and J. E. Ricart, "The Genuine Responsibilities of the General Management," *IESE Insight,* 23, Fourth quarter, 15–21, 2014.
6   See case 5.2: Ricoh Spain. Transforming the Business (María Eugenia Pascual, Miquel Lladò and Joan Enric Ricart).

2

BUSINESS POLICY

Historical evolution and epistemological roots

Héctor Rocha and Jorge Iván Gómez Osorio

Introduction

Business policy as a field of study was originally conceived as an endeavor to develop the practical skills of managers and establish management as a profession focused on the role of CEOs and guided by an ethos of service to society (Khurana, 2007). Today, however, the field is no longer able to address the social, environmental and ethical challenges currently facing business enterprises (Pfeffer & Fong, 2004; Ghoshal, 2005; Adler, 2013; Hollensbe et al., 2014). In fact, the newer academy of management areas of research, such as social issues in management and critical management studies, as well as new business education courses like ethics, sustainability and corporate social responsibility, have increasingly gained traction to adequately respond to new social, environmental and ethical demands (Christensen et al., 2007; Rocha, 2008; Cavico & Mujtaba, 2009; Murcia, Rocha & Birkinshaw, 2016).

In our view, the lack of fit between business policy as a field and current societal and ethical challenges may be partially explained by the progressive dilution of the field of business policy resulting from an enhanced focus on strategic management. As a result of this process, core research areas like ethical leadership, the role of business in society and a holistic approach regarding the roles of the CEO and enterprise which transcend the scope of the strategic management field became neglected as central spheres of action of CEOs and their teams.

This chapter offers a historical and epistemological review of the business policy field to illustrate this shift. The historical review centers on Harvard Business School (Gómez Osorio, 2015) and other schools that follow its model, whereas the epistemological review spotlights the intuitive and practical contributions of Sumantra Ghoshal (Ghoshal, 2005; Rocha & Ghoshal, 2006; Rocha, 2008).

In this chapter, the section "The historical evolution of business policy" surveys the historical evolution of business policy; the section "Business policy and strategic

management: epistemological roots" outlines the epistemological backdrop underlying the historical change in the field; and section "Conclusions" ties these ideas
together.

The historical evolution of business policy

Strategic management as a field of study evolved from a subject called "business
policy," imparted at Harvard Business School (HBS) and later at other US business schools. The subject first appeared in Harvard's curriculum in 1910 and was
taught until 1986. This evolution generated unintended consequences, not only in
the teaching of the subject itself but also in the conception of general management
within business education and the concept of business strategy.

Business policy as an academic topic first appeared in 1910, two years after the
founding of the HBS. It was a compulsory course for second-year students of Harvard's master of business administration program(MBA), which aimed to develop
skills like problem-solving and decision-making (Copeland, 1958).

First period: 1910–1965

The subject of business policy emerged as an initiative of the first dean of HBS,
Edwin Francis Gay, and the entrepreneur Arch W. Shaw, who together designed
the course syllabus based on three premises. In the absence of study materials, the
first premise was to invite business leaders from Boston and the surrounding areas
to share their experiences and challenges in the exercise of their management activity (Khurana, 2007). The second premise was to offer a course with an integrative
nature to teach MBA sophomores about the main corporate functional areas, taking
a holistic approach. The third premise was to train CEOs from the perspective of a
company as a whole (Copeland, 1958). Thus, in the beginning, the course sought
to rely on managerial experience and training practical skills for the development
of managerial activity.

The primary teaching method entailed using real-life cases (Arden, 1997) in
which general managers presented specific business challenges to students. Students then prepared a report with their proposed solution and participated in class-
room discussions on the causes and implications of each of the problem variables,
together with the executive and the subject professor. Since the establishment of
HBS, Dean Gay intended to employ a teaching system initially referred to as the
laboratory method. This method pursued a business pedagogy focused on real and
practical experiences and reflected a significant influence from the experimentalist
philosopher John Dewey and his practical approach to education (Gómez-Osorio
2015). Similarly, Harvard Law School began to develop its courses using the case
method, which Dean Gay considered as a model for teaching business (Khurana,
2007). In this way, business policy evolved in parallel with the case method in HBS.

For the promoters of business policy, the concept of enterprise thought of the
company as an "agent of civilization" (Gay, 1927), meaning that the company

should go beyond economic gains and additionally fulfill duties and responsibilities toward society. Likewise, the concept of leadership held that management must be considered a profession, like medicine or law. For Gay, the professionalization of business management served to legitimize it (Heaton, 1952) and provide a channel to promote technology and values. With this approach, Gay intended to prevent business education from becoming merely a platform to teach techniques to make money.

In summary, the core elements of business policy studies during this initial period were focused on the role of the CEO, a teaching method based on managerial practices (which later became the case study method) and an organizational and managerial approach that advocated management as a profession and, in particular, the role of the enterprise as a social transformation agent.

Second period: 1965 and 1975

In 1965, professors Kenneth R. Andrews and C. Roland Christensen were forerunners on the subject of business policy following the publication of the first edition of *Business Policy: Text and Cases* (Christensen et al. 1965 [1978]), written in collaboration with Edmund Learned. During this period, the course had a broad description of its objectives and methodology while offering a pioneering concept of business strategy. As in the previous period, the roles and responsibilities of the CEO held center stage.

Andrews and Christensen believed that a CEO should master certain qualities and take on certain responsibilities, in particular those pertaining to defining the business's course of action and monitoring its journey [(Montgomery, 2012(2015)]. This approach emphasized the manager's ability to strategize and set goals for the organization's future and, at the same time, the capability to mobilize corporate resources and personnel toward the proposed objectives. In general management education, this model was coined the strategy-structure-performance (SSP) paradigm (Bower, 2008).

Both professors, particularly Andrews, were highly influenced by the humanities (Arden, 1997). In fact, Andrews had a PhD in English literature, and his doctoral dissertation was on Mark Twain. Although Andrews was trained in liberal arts and humanities, his academic interests focused on practical problems. Andrews defined himself as "a man whose career as professor and researcher has always been oriented toward the pragmatic training of executives, . . . to focus their attention on the need to define a purpose for their lives and their organizations, based on the fact that this purpose had to be valuable in terms of economic performance and social responsibility" (Moulton, 1995).

In this regard, both professors bridged a gap between their academic interests in general management and the case methodology by designing a course centered on the *practitioner's* experience, practical guidance and the analysis of the company as being unique and singular, since they conceived management as matter-of-fact that was linked with reality and based on each company's distinct characteristics

(Grant, 2008). As a result, the research generated by business policy professors became a written body of evidence on real-life cases of companies that originated from their consulting work or from related work done by company executives who participated in academic programs.

Andrews and Christensen's concept of business viewed the company as an institution with both economic and non-economic objectives. Both authors stressed the notion of management's duties and responsibilities to society (Learned et al., 1965). For this reason, Andrews believed that business strategy had to be linked to four elements: what the company *can* do in terms of capabilities; what the company *could* do in terms of opportunities; what company managers *want* to do in terms of their preferences; and what the company *should* do in terms of its duties and responsibilities to society (Andrews, 1971).

Third period: 1975 and 1986

By 1975, business policy had become a recognized field of studies thanks to its prominence at HBS and other US business schools. In fact, the AACSB (Association to Advance Collegiate School of Business) highlighted the importance and relevance of the course in business school curricula due to its inclusive nature (Gordon & Howell, 1959).

During this period, a young professor named Michael Porter was completing his PhD in the Department of Economics at Harvard University. Porter joined the HBS faculty and focused part of his research on merging the industrial economics concepts of professors like J. S. Bain (1912–1991) and E. Chamberlin (1899–1967) with general management (Martínez-Echevarría, 1983). Initially, Porter's major achievement was to connect economic fundamentals and business policy concepts.

After joining the business policy group, Porter became a source of internal tension, since his approach diverged from that of Andrews and Christensen (Kiechel, 2010). Notwithstanding, Porter continued his research work in management and industrial economy and went on to publish "Note on the Structural Analysis Industries," which received numerous accolades. Similarly, he launched an elective course called Competition and Strategy, which was highly regarded by students (Kiechel, 2010). In this way, Porter ventured further away from the business policy mainstream and began to form different conceptions about general management, business strategy and the notion of enterprise. This tension ultimately resulted in dividing the course in two: business policy into strategy and strategic management.

Around the same time, Dan Schendel, a former professor of business policy, organized a conference called Business Policy Planning and Research to analyze the state of affairs of the field. Held at the University of Pittsburgh, the conference gathered eighty-two academics primarily from Harvard, Yale, Princeton, and Purdue, of which 35 percent were trained in the HBS case study method (Evered, 1980).

During the conference, the future of the research on the business policy course was discussed, and other criteria were defined since, according to faculty participants, "business policy" had a distinct emphasis on pedagogy and case discussion.

Participants were critical of the "Harvard case paradigm" (case study method), claiming it relied too heavily on simple descriptions of facts and subjective analyses of the enterprise's realities.

This conference centered mainly on the professors' complaints regarding business policy research. For example, Professor William Guth communicated his discomfort regarding a 1970 Committee on Business Policy in Chicago, whose agenda focused mainly on pedagogy affairs and overlooked topics pertaining to theory and research. During the Pittsburgh meeting, Prof. Guth claimed there was a gap between business policy and the respective functional fields, quoting the opinion of a colleague which concluded that the field combined the two core characteristics of religion: lots of faith and no empirical knowledge (Hambrick & Chen, 2008).

The main objective of the meeting convened by Schendel focused on defining guidelines for a course that included the basic parameters of a normal science – that is, quantitative rigor and empirical evidence. As a result, participants at the meeting agreed that that strategy would be the target of research on business policy. Likewise, the participants considered the name "business policy" too strongly linked to the Harvard case paradigm (case study method) and agreed that "policy" did not convey the features of a specialized discipline, scientifically rigorous research or pedagogical methodologies. Motivated by these conceptual divergences, participants agreed to create a new field of study, called strategic management, to better reflect the parameters of a science. According to Hambrick and Chen, this was the creation of a new scientific paradigm.

After the meeting, Schendel promoted an academic movement aimed at developing the new specialty. Now that he had achieved consensus among the professors in attendance in Pittsburgh, he took further steps to obtain broader consensus among educators, managers and company consultants from all over the world. He carried out a series of different actions toward this purpose.

First, Schendel published *Strategic Management: A New View of Business Policy and Planning* with Charles W. Hofer, which summarized the conclusions of the meeting and aimed to develop a framework of this new field of study. For example, the book presented the model called *Strategic Management Process*, outlining the necessary steps to formulate and implement the strategy process.

In 1980, he organized a meeting in London with professors, entrepreneurs and others who supported his ideas. The Strategic Management Society (SMS), an entity dedicated to the research, development and practice of strategic management, emerged from this meeting. SMS aspired to attract academics, entrepreneurs and stakeholders interested in the study and development of ideas on strategy. People from all over the world joined the SMS and formed a board of directors with renowned scholars, including SMS presidents Dan Schendel (1982–1985), Henry Mintzberg (1988–1991) and Carlos Cavallé (1991–1994). The society proposed the creation of a movement, led by academics, to promote the study of strategy.

The SMS spearheaded several initiatives to reach their objective: they launched a specialized magazine called the *Strategic Management Journal*, which published books on strategy (*Book Series*), organized meetings and annual conferences and scouted for new members (*Membership*). Published by Schendel, the *Strategic Management Journal* became the official magazine of the SMS. Four years after its inception, it was included in the Social Science Citation Index, an important entity in the academic field since it collects the most noteworthy articles in the social sciences and provides information on the most frequently cited ones. In brief, the momentum generated by the SMS and the magazine to disseminate their ideas triggered a paradigm shift in the academic community: strategy as a new field of knowledge. In this way, this new paradigm emerged from the consensus and acceptance in the academic community. In short, Michael Porter and Dan Schendel both played critical roles in the advent of a new field of knowledge called strategy and strategic management.

Accordingly, the field migrated toward a strong focus on to economics, empirical analysis, mathematics and statistics. This evolution lessened the importance of the role of the CEO, because there was now greater emphasis placed on strategy formulation and development that uses models and analytical schemes (Mintzberg, 2004).

The underlying business concept adhered to an approach supported by the neo-classical theory of enterprise (Martínez-Echevarría, 2001), according to which the enterprise's main purpose is to capture and create value, framed by a theory of profit centered on a maximizing criterion regarding corporate economic performance (Grant, 2008; Chamberlain, 2010). Similarly, Porter's initial understanding disregarded elements like business ethics and social responsibility, which were present in the first and second periods. On the contrary, the central element of his enterprise model was competitive strategy, grounded on economic forces inherent in the environment and the industry in which every company moves (Porter, 1980).

Similarly, Porter's concept of management was geared more toward preparing the company for the competitive scenario: creating and capturing value by developing a competitive advantage contingent on differentiation and costs. Porter's model neglected the CEO's function and preferences in strategy formulation; the role of the organization and structure; and the importance of the government and company stakeholders (Kiechel, 2010).

Ethics within the business policy paradigm

In addition to its focus on developing practical skills, a salient feature of business policy was its attempt to legitimize business activity by transforming management into a profession (Khurana, 2007). In this context, the profession was a concept with Christian roots that intended – in Max Weber's terms – to rationalize ethical conduct through a secularization concept of the divine vocation by means of the profession's rationalizing concept (Múgica, 1998). In light of this study, introducing the professional concept to business policy stems from an educational project with deep Christian and religious roots, yet expressed in a rational manner and with scarce religious connotations. Consequently, the ethical and philosophical foundations of business policy are grounded on an ethical corporate project and its relationship with higher social purposes.

The aforementioned was possible thanks to the Calvinist and Protestant ethic that prevailed in Boston and in Harvard at the time, which gave a "high estimation to ethical order" through the sanctification of good deeds such that the holiness of the act turned into a system, an individual ethos characteristic of this community (Weber, [1922(1997)]). This entailed a streamlining of behavior through a special asceticism premised on frugality, hard work and helping others (Múgica, 1998) as the way to salvation. In brief, this doctrine ultimately pursued "to convert all Christians into monks for the rest of their lives" (Weber, [1922(1997)] through the Methodism of their behavior and the Christianization of their existence in the professional work scene (Weber, [1922(1997)].

Following the lead of Andrews and Christensen, business policy before 1965 showed a strong conceptual inclination toward entrusting directors with ethical matters, the notion of professionalization and the enterprise's duties and responsibilities to society (Learned et al., 1965). Authors like Chester I. Barnard (1886–1991) and Philip Selznick 1919–2010) also influenced Andrews and Christensen, since they placed greater emphasis on issues such as the organization, policies and, most importantly, the conception of the enterprise as an institution. Likewise, they raised the concept of an integral enterprise based on four dimensions: organizational capabilities, opportunities in the environment, management leadership and social responsibility. However, one of the core elements of Andrews and Christensen's framework was the interdisciplinary perspective of general management, in which no particular discipline prevailed, sparking the convergence of other fields such as history, economics, politics, psychology and philosophy, among others.

As in the period of 1975, business policy turned toward economic theory, particularly the enterprise's neoclassical model (Gómez-Osorio, 2015). Consequently, business policy and its replacement – strategy – created a concept of the enterprise in which the director is an agent who makes decisions based on market analysis, competition and industry forces. In this approach, the essential elements of the classic business policy course, including the ethical vision of the company, social responsibility and, especially, the role of the CEO in the organization's management and structure, were overshadowed.

In this way, the new field of strategic management sought to overcome the criticisms to business policy by implementing an academic approach based on quantitative research and mathematical models to explain and prove the business strategy assumptions. This approach is sustained on economic science, a discipline then deemed to resemble physics in terms of the causality of natural phenomena (Bennis & O'Toole, 2005). Consequently, parallel to the evolution of business policy as a field, business education began to emphasize the rationality of natural sciences and overlook the fact that businesses, and particularly organizations, are human realities whose object of study is human action. This naturally implies the consideration of ethics and politics as central features of its expressions.

The transformation of business policy opened a chasm in the academic world, as courses on general management with an integrative, generalist and humanist content are no longer imparted. As a result, management courses converted into

TABLE 2.1 A Comparison between Business Policy and Strategic Management

	Business Policy	*Strategic Management*
Characteristics	Integrative and holistic	Functional
Orientation	Generalist	Specialized
Nature	Practical	Theoretical
Object of Studies	The CEO/general manager	The competition
Skills Developed	Decision-making	Analytical
	Problem-solving	
	Political skills	

Source: Prepared by the authors.

strategy courses, which are vastly different areas given that management is a complex phenomenon that requires a broad pool of knowledge depending on circumstances and context, whereas strategy is knowledge based on analysis, forecasts and techniques.

A new scenario arose when management turned into strategy. First, practical lessons on management were replaced by theoretical lessons on competition analysis and the environment. Second, the comprehensive business policy content was disregarded in favor of specialized knowledge. Third, greater emphasis was placed on quantitative research to the detriment of qualitative research. Lastly, a management approach inspired by the enterprise's neoclassical model was adopted (Martínez-Echevarría, 2005). Table 2.1 summarizes the comparison of the business policy and strategic management approaches.

At the same time, the field of economic theory gained force in the general management field to such a degree that strategy courses increasingly incorporated economics and econometric and statistical models into their curricula. As a result, the teaching of strategic management was entrusted to economists with academic interests in the business world.

Despite the aforementioned shifts, the evolution also had some positive consequences on the study of general management by adding rigor and depth. Yet, the field lost its identity, essence and original spirit as general management transformed into strategy and distanced itself from the CEO's functions and responsibilities and from the company's ethical vision. Ultimately, what was won in analysis was lost in practical relevance (Montgomery, [2012(2015)]).

Business policy and strategic management: epistemological roots

The previous section explored the historical evolution of business policy and its metamorphosis into the current field of strategic management. History – with its focus on events – illustrates the visible part of this evolution. Behind the metamorphosis, however, lie profound epistemological roots that act as invisible drivers. We rely on Sumantra Ghoshal's intuitive and practical vision as a guide in this section, which inquiries about these epistemological triggers by defining the philosophy of science as the branch of philosophy that studies the nature, scope and goals of science and the methods through which these goals are achieved (Rothbart, 1998).

The core argument is as follows: the methodological demands imposed by the new field of strategic management in terms of quantitative rigor and empirical evidence diminished the original phenomenological scope of business policy, over-looking technical aspects, the holistic view of the CEO and the role of the company in society. These phenomena cannot be quantified by following the studies of physical science, although they were then taken by neoclassical economics and, finally, by the strategic management field (Ghoshal, 2005). This reductionism is based on three conceptions intrinsic to the field's epistemological roots: first, the conception about what constitutes a theory of management; second, the conception about the appropriate methods in line with the theory of management; and third, the conception formed by individuals and companies necessary to ensure coherency among theoretical, methodological and phenomenological conceptions.

Assumptions on management theory

A review of the management literature on theory building shows two dominant paradigms (Rocha & Ghoshal, 2006). The first focuses on theory as a prescription or as an a priori explanation (Smelser & Swedberg, 1994) and points to simplicity or parsimony as a crucial element of a good theory, which would explain why mainstream economics uses mathematical models as its main method of inquiry. This approach is often criticized as an end unto itself by leading to either prescriptions without explanation or data without theory (cf. Leontief, 1971; Nelson & Winter, 1982; Sen, 1997, 2002; Solow, 2000).

The second paradigm alludes to description and explanation based on realistic assumptions as the overriding aims of theory. This view derives from sociology (Etzioni, 1988) and political science (Mansbridge, 1990), although it also has strong advocates in the field of economics (Sen, 2002). For its part, it is frequently reproached as description without theory, description without prescription or an after-the-fact explanation of events, as in "placing the bet after the race is over" (Coase, 1983; Etzioni, 1988, p. 12; Singleton & Straits, 1999, p. 25).

These views have been the source of numerous debates (Ferraro et al., 2005) on trade-offs, which impedes building bridges between them. Following an Aristotelian-Thomistic approach, it could be argued that the main goal of theory building is understanding (Aristotle, 1984a, Book I, p. 1). The latter encompasses the goals of description, explanation and prescription, or control (Singleton & Straits, 1999). In fact, explanation and prediction are interdependent theoretical goals that aspire to facilitate knowledge or understanding (Aristotle, 1984a–b; McMullin, 1988; Singleton & Straits, 1999; Rocha, 2013). The historical evolution of the field, as examined in this section, shows that the original concept of business policy focused more on understanding, whereas the current notion of strategic management clearly emphasizes explanation and prescription.

Assumptions on methods for theory building in management

A review of the literature on management demonstrates that the dominant research paradigm for theory building is reductionism (Rocha, 2013). Reductionism is either an assertion that phenomena are real only at the individual level – i.e., ontological reductionism – or a research strategy to explain phenomena or build theories from only one level – methodological reductionism in general (Rocha, 2013; cf. Artigas, 2000, pp. 153–155, 163; Curd & Cover, 1998, p. 1305).

In the field of strategic management, the dominant types of reductionism on the methodological level are methodological reductionism applied to phenomena and methodological individualism. The former occurs when a phenomenon at one level is explained from a phenomenon at the same or different levels, whereas the latter is a research strategy that asserts that "all social phenomena (their structure and their change) are, in principle, explicable only in terms of individuals" (Blaug, 1992, p. 42; Elster, 1982, p. 453) or from individual units of analysis (Rocha, 2013). For example, the strategic management field uses methodological reductionism applied to phenomena when it reduces the scope of business policy to strategy and competition. In the same vein, it applies methodological individualism when assuming that profit maximization at the firm level automatically translates into national growth and development (Friedman, 1970; Baumol, 1990).

Methodological individualism is currently the main research strategy applied in neoclassical economics (Becker, 1976; Friedman, 1953), which explains why it is one of the main research approaches in the field of strategic management. However, a good management theory should use methods that are adequate to the formal objects of study, which in the case of the business policy field are individuals (CEOs) and business organizations rather than strategy and competition. This feature leads to the use of theory-building methods appropriate for the study of human behavior, characterized by intentional and moral modes of research as opposed to methods borrowed from mathematics, physics and/or biology (Ghoshal, 2005). In fact, according to Ghoshal, the basic unit of explanation in social sciences is individual action guided by some intention.[1] This spotlights the relevance of the moral foundations of management theories,[2] in which the distinction between good and evil (which goes beyond what is correct or incorrect) or the distinction between right and wrong make sense.[3] This argument is clearly reflected in Figure 2.1, which represents an adaptation of the scheme presented in one of Ghoshal's posthumous articles.[4]

Figure 2.1 highlights two aspects. First, human nature requires theories that study it to rely on different premises and methods. In particular, good management theories consider the nature of their object of study: human action directed by a specific intentionality. This affects personal (organizational managers), organizational and social planes since management, as a human and social discipline, cannot fail to consider human intentionality at these three levels.[5]

This feature is more a variable than a given constant – that is, a well-founded questioning of whether intentionality is reduced to one's interests[6] – which is

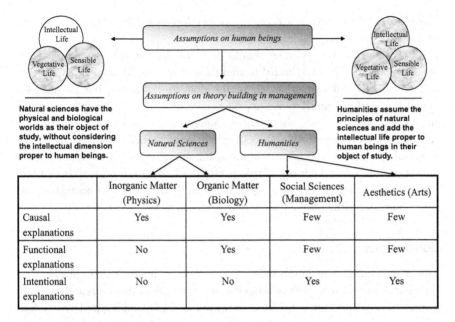

FIGURE 2.1   Assumptions on Theory Building

Source: Adapted from "Beyond Self-Interest Revisited" by H. Rocha and S. Ghoshal, 2006, Journal of Management Studies 43: 585–619.

detailed in the following section. Consider, for example, Ghoshal and Bartlett (1997), Moran and Ghoshal (1999) and Rocha and Ghoshal (2006). For a more in-depth look at the impact of human intentionality on the three levels highlighted in Figure 2.1, see Rocha (2008), Ghoshal and Moran (1996), Birkinshaw (2006) and Rocha and Ghoshal (2006).

Assumptions on people and organizations

The previous section shows that strategic management borrowed two key assumptions from neoclassical economics: "homo economicus" on the individual level and profit maximization on the organizational level (Rocha & Ghoshal, 2006). However, given that the objects of study in management theories are individuals and organizations, a good theory should be guided by realistic and more positive assumptions. At the personal level, these assumptions are related to human nature, human intentionality and human relationships, and at organizational level, these assumptions relate to the nature of organizations and their goals.

In particular, Ghoshal, Bartlett and Moran formulated what they called a "managerial theory of the firm."[7] This stream of research was based on the classical tradition of management research, similar to that of Barnard, Selznick and Mayo, in which theory was developed in close collaboration with businesses and entrepreneurs. This manner of implementing theory contrasted with the dominant tradition derived from the neoclassical economy of developing theories from incomplete premises on the company and the CEO.

These more positive premises should be highlighted in three areas: personal, organizational and social. Ghoshal treated these three aspects simultaneously and with a radically different approach to the dominant theories, but his nucleus stemmed from the personal sphere, as evidenced in his work with his colleagues,[8,9,10] emphasizing the premises about nature, intentionality and human relations.[11] Regarding the organizational and social sphere, good theories consider three fundamental premises: our economy is an organizational economy as opposed to a market economy, in which organizations play the leading role in wealth creation and economic progress.[12] This progress is not only social but also organizational, and it depends mainly on the quality of management.[13]

Conclusions

The field's historical evolution indicates that business policy was originally conceived as an endeavor to both develop the practical skills of managers and establish management as a profession, focusing on the role of CEOs and inspired by an ethos of service to society (Khurana, 2007). However, its evolution toward the current strategic management field and resulting focus on strategy, competition and a quantitative approach to management have disregarded core areas of research, including the ethical behavior of leaders, the role of business in society and a holistic approach to the role of the CEO and enterprises.

A review of the epistemological roots of business policy demonstrates that the methodological requirements imposed by the new strategic management field – particularly its focus on empirical evidence and quantitative rigor – diminished the original phenomenological scope of business policy and disregarded other aspects, such as business ethics, the comprehensive vision of the role of the CEO and the function of enterprise in society.

As noted, these phenomena cannot be quantified following the canons of physical science and then integrated into neoclassical economics and ultimately into the field of strategic management (Ghoshal, 2005). This epistemological reductionism occurred in three conceptions: good management theory; the most appropriate methods with respect to a good management theory; and finally, the necessity of individuals and companies to ensure coherence among theoretical, methodological and phenomenological demands.

We hope that this historical and epistemological review serves to reinvigorate the field of business policy and provide a platform to creatively and rigorously navigate the current ethical and societal challenges facing global decision makers.

Notes

1 Ghoshal (2005, p. 78). As Professor Martínez-Echevarría asserts, Ghoshal had captured the sense of "telos," or ultimate end (Martínez-Echevarría, personal communication),

which asserts that the most important or essential aspect of reality cannot be captured by any type of formal language (Echevarría, 2005, p. 136).

2 Ghoshal (2005); Ghoshal and Gratton (2005).
3 Ghoshal (2005); Ghoshal and Gratton (2005); Rocha and Ghoshal (2006:597).
4 Ghoshal, (2005, Figure 2.1).
5 See for example Ghoshal and Bartlett (1997); Moran and Ghoshal (1999); Rocha and Ghoshal (2006). See Rocha (2007) for a deeper understanding of the impact of human intentionality on the three levels mentioned in Figure 2.1.
6 Ghoshal and Moran (1996); Birkinshaw (2006); Rocha and Ghoshal (2006).
7 Birkinshaw (2005, p. xvii).
8 Ghoshal and Moran (1996).
9 Ghoshal and Bartlett (1997).
10 Nahapiet, Gratton and Rocha (2005); Rocha and Ghoshal (2006).
11 The intrinsic relationship among these three levels can be seen in Ghoshal (2005) and is currently being developed by the author (e.g., see Rocha [2007, 2019]).
12 Ghoshal and Bartlett (1997); Moran and Ghoshal (1999); Ghoshal and Gratton (2005); Rocha and Ghoshal (2006).
13 Ghoshal and Gratton (2005); Rocha and Ghoshal (2006, p. 613).

References

Adler, A. (2013). *The Practice and Theory of Individual Psychology* (Vol. 133). Oxford, England: Routledge.

Andrews, K. R. (1971). *The Concept of Corporate Strategy.* Homewood, IL: Richard D. Irwin, Inc.

Arden, P. (1997). "The Integrating Course in the Business School Curriculum, or, Whatever Happened to Business Policy." *Business Horizons*, 40(2): 65–70.

Aristotle (1984a). "Nicomachean Ethics." In: Barnes, J. (ed.), *The Complete Works of Aristotle, Revised Oxford Translation*. Princeton, NJ: Princeton University Press.

Aristotle (1984b). "Politics." In: Barnes, J. (ed.), *The Complete Works of Aristotle Revised Oxford Translation*. Princeton, NJ: Princeton University Press.

Artigas, M. (2000). *La Mente del Universo*. Pamplona, Spain: EUNSA.

Baumol, W. J. (1990). "Entrepreneurship: Productive, Unproductive, and Destructive." *Journal of Political Economy*, 98(5): 893–921.

Becker, G. (1976). *The Economic Approach to Behavior*. Chicago, IL: University of Chicago Press.

Bennis, W. and O'Toole, J. (2005). "How Business Schools Lost Their Way." Harvard Business Review, 83(5): 96–104.

Birkinshaw, J. (2005). *Sumantra Ghoshal on Management: A Force for Good*. New York: Pearson Education.

Birkinshaw, J. (2006). Introduction to 'Beyond Self-Interest Revisited' by Hector Rocha and Sumantra Ghoshal. *Journal of Management Studies*, 43(3), 583–584.

Blaug, M. (1992). *The Methodology of Economics, or How Economists Explain*. Cambridge, England, Cambridge University Press.

Bower, J. (2008). "The Teaching of Strategy: From General Manager to Analyst and Back Again." *Journal of Management Inquiry*, 17(4): 269–275.

Cavico, F. J. and Mujtaba, B. G. (2009). "The State of Business Schools, Business Education, and Business Ethics." *Journal of Academic and Business Ethics*, 2(1): 1–7.

Chamberlain, G. (2010). *Understanding Strategy*, Charleston, SC: CreateSpace.

Christensen, C. R., Andrews, K. R. and Bower, J. [1965 (1978)]. *Business Policy: Text and Cases*, 4th ed., Homewood, IL: Richard D. Irwin, Inc.

Christensen, L. J., Peirce, E., Hartman, L. P., Hoffman, W. M. and Carrier, J. (2007). "Ethics, CSR, and Sustainability Education" in the Financial Times Top 50 Global Business

Schools: Baseline Data and Future Research Directions." *Journal of Business Ethics*, 73(4): 347–368.

Coase, R. H. (1983). "The New Institutional Economics." *Journal of Institutional and Theoretical Economics*, 1: 229–231.

Copeland, M. (1958). *And Mark an Era: The Story of the Harvard Business School*, Boston, MA: Little, Brown and Company.

Curd, M. and Cover, J. A. (1998). *Philosophy of Science: The Central Issues*. London, England: W. W. Norton & Company Ltd.

Elster, J. (1982). "Marxism, Functionalism, and Game Theory." Theory and Society, 11(4): 453–482.

Etzioni, A. (1988). *The Moral Dimension: Toward a New Economics*. New York, NY: Free Press.

Evered, R. (1980). "A New View of Business Policy and Planning by Dan Schendel and Charles Hofer." *Administrative Science Quarterly*, 25(3): 536–543.

Ferraro, F., Pfeffer, J., et al. (2005). "Economic Language and Assumptions: How Theories Can Become Self-Fulfilling." *Academy of Management Review*, 30(1): 8–24.

Friedman, M. (1953). *Essays in Positive Economics*. Chicago, IL: University of Chicago Press.

Friedman, M. (1970). "The Social Responsibility of Business Is to Increase Its Profits." *New York Times Magazine*, 13 September: 32–33, 122–126.

Gay, E. F. (1927). "The Founding of the Harvard Business School." *Harvard Business Review*, 5(4): 397–400.

Ghoshal, S., and Moran, P. (1996). "Bad for Practice: A Critique of the Transaction Cost Theory." *Academy of Management Review*, 21(1): 13–47.

Ghoshal, S. and Bartlett, C. A. (eds). (1997). *The Individualized Corporation: A Fundamentally New Approach to Management: Great Companies Are Defined by Purpose, Process, and People*. New York, NY: Harper Business.

Ghoshal, S. and Gratton, L. (2005). *Integrating the Enterprise. S.G.O. Management*. London, England: Pearson Education Limited.

Ghoshal, S. (2005). "Bad Management Theories Are Destroying Good Management Practices." *Academy of Management Learning and Education*, 4(1): 75–91.

Grant, R. M. (2008). "Why Strategy Teaching Should Be Theory Based." *Journal of Management Inquiry*, 17(4): 276–281.

Gómez-Osorio, J. I. (2015). "La Evolución de la Asignatura Business Policy en Harvard Business School." *Cuadernos de Empresa y Humanismo*, 127: 9–128.

Gordon, R. A. and Howell, J. E. (1959). *Higher Education for Business*. New York, NY: Columbia University Press.

Hambrick, D. C. and Chen, M. C. (2008). "New Academic Fields as Admittance-Seeking Social Movements: The Case of Strategic Management." *Academy of Management Review*, 33(1): 33–54.

Heaton, H. (1952). *A Scholar in Action: Edwin Francis Gay*. Cambridge, MA: Harvard University Press.

Hollensbe, E., Wookey, C., Hickey, L., George, G. and Nichols, C. V. (2014). "Organizations with Purpose." *Academy of Management Journal*, 57(5): 1227–1234.

Khurana, R. (2007). *From Higher Aims to Hired Hands: The Social Transformation of American Business Schools and the Unfulfilled Promise of Management as a Profession*. Princeton, NJ: Princeton University Press.

Kiechel, W. (2010). *The Lords of Strategy: The Secret Intellectual History of the New Corporate World*, Boston, MA: Harvard Business Press.

Learned, E., Christensen, R., Andrews, K. R. and Guth, W. D. (1965). *Business Policy: Text and Cases*, Homewood, IL: Richard D. Irwin, Inc.

Leontief, W. (1971). "Theoretical Assumptions and Nonobserved Facts." *American Economic Review*, 61(1–7): 1–7.

Mansbridge, J. J. (1990). "The Rise and Fall of Self-Interest in the Explanation of Political Life." In: Mansbridge, J. J. (ed.), *Beyond Self-Interest*, Chicago, IL: The University of Chicago Press.

Martínez-Echevarría, M. A. (1983). *Evolución del Pensamiento Económico.* Madrid, Spain: Espasa.

Martínez-Echevarría, M. A. (2001). "Teorías de la Empresa y Crisis de la Modernidad." *Cuadernos de Empresa y Humanismo*, 83: 4–84.

Martínez-Echevarría, M. A. (2005). *Dirigir Empresas: De la Teoría a la Realidad.* Madrid, Spain: Ediciones Internacionales Universitarias.

McMullin, E. (1988). *The Goals of Natural Science: Scientific Knowledge Socialized*, edited by I. Hronszky, M. Feher and B. Dajka. Dordrecht, England: Kluwer.

Mintzberg, H. (2004). *Managers, Not MBAs: A Hard Look at the Soft Practice of Managing and Management Development.* San Francisco, CA: Berrett-Khoehler Publishers.

Montgomery, C. [2012 (2015)]. *El Estratega.* Bogota, Colombia: Aguilar.

Moran, P. and Ghoshal, S. (1999). "Markets, Firms, and the Process of Economic Development, Academy of Management." *The Academy of Management Review*, 24(3): 390–412.

Moulton, H. W. (1995). "Profiles in Executive Education: Ken Andrews." *Business Horizons*, 38(5): 75–79.

Múgica, F. (1998). "La Profesión: Enclave Ético de la Moderna Sociedad Diferenciada." *Cuadernos de Empresa y Humanismo*, 7: 3–63.

Murcia, M. J., Rocha, H. O. and Birkinshaw, J. (2016). "Business Schools at the Crossroads? A Trip Back from Sparta to Athens." *Journal of Business Ethics*, 1–13.

Nahapiet, J., Gratton, L. and Rocha, H. O. (2005). "Knowledge and Relationships: When Cooperation Is the Norm." *European Management Review*, 2(1): 3–14.

Nelson, R. and Winter, S. (1982). An Evolutionary Theory of Economic Change. Cambridge, MA: Harvard University Press.

Pfeffer, J. and Fong, C. T. (2004). "The Business School 'Business': Some Lessons from the U.S. Experience." *Journal of Management Studies*, 41(8): 1501–1520.

Porter, M. [1980 (2013)]. *Estrategia Competitiva: Técnicas Para el Análisis de la Empresa y Sus Competidores*, 3rd Spanish ed. Madrid, Spain: Pirámide.

Rocha, H. O. and Ghoshal, S. (2006). "Beyond Self-Interest Revisited." *Journal of Management Studies*, 43: 585–619.

Rocha, H.O. (2007). Intrinsic Alignment Between Personal Interests, Firm's Goals and Societal Needs. A Fresh Lens for Doing Good and Well. Academy of Management Annual Meeting, Philadelphia (Best CMS Paper Nominee and William H. Newman Award Nominee).

Rocha, H. O. (2008). "Las Teorías y la Práctica de la Dirección Son una Fuerza Para el Bien: La Contribución de Sumantra Ghoshal." *Empresa y Humanismo*, 11(2): 171–217.

Rocha, H. O. (2013). *Entrepreneurship and Regional Development: The Role of Clusters.* Basingstoke, England: Palgrave Macmillan.

Rocha, H. (2019). Enlightening the Future with Wisdom from the Past: Revisiting the Intrinsic Alignment Between Personal Motives, Organizational Purpose, and Societal Development. 35th EGOS Colloquium 2019, Edinburg, 4–6 July.

Sen, A. (1997). "Economics, Business Principles and Moral Sentiments." *Business Ethics Quarterly*, 7(3): 5–15.

Sen, A. (2002). *Rationality and Freedom.* Cambridge, MA: The Belknap Press of Harvard University Press.

Singleton, R. A. and Straits, B. C. (1999). *Approaches to Social Research.* Oxford, England: Oxford University Press.

Smelser, N. J. and Swedberg, R. E. (1994). *The Handbook of Economic Sociology.* Princeton, NJ: Princeton University Press.

Solow, R. M. (2000). "The Nature of Economies." *New Republic*, 222(20): 34–36.

Weber, M. [1922 (1997)]. *Economía y Sociedad.* Mexico City, Mexico: Fondo de Cultura Económica.

3

THE ORGANIZATION CENTERED ON ITS PEOPLE

Alejandro A. Carrera

The rising role of people in companies

> He was always committed to making a positive contribution in every community in which he participated. He was a revolutionary in redefining the mission and the purpose of the corporation. In this sense, he was The Real Che.

In 2009, Oscar Alvarado was thus described by Joe Carvin, head of Altima, one of the world's leading farming funds and an investor in El Tejar Ltd. Oscar Alvarado had led this organization through a transformation process that, in little more than twenty years, turned it from a small association of Argentine cattle farmers into the world's largest agribusiness firm, with nearly 1 million hectares planted in the MERCOSUR region.

Alvarado built the organization on the idea that a business should stand as a long-lasting, relevant project focused on people, driving its expansion efforts with trust-based organizational networks. El Tejar boasted the reputation of a reliable, innovative and entrepreneurial company, with commendable growth and a people-centric approach. The firm relied on the potential of its people, who sought to forge long-term relationships. It was a networked, trust-based business, with a shared vision for the future and a strong set of values – notably joy, humility and professionalism – with trust serving as a linchpin. These values all served as levers for El Tejar in overcoming uncertainty and growing exponentially.

Why have human beings earned such a prominent role in corporate settings? How did the largely mechanistic, economics-focused views of the early 20th century gave way to the 1950s approach focused on human relations and professionalism, eventually leading to today's unchallenged view that differences among companies lie in "people matters," as professor and author Dave Ulrich puts it?

The common thread underlying this evolution is the *increasing uncertainty* that permeates throughout business environments. Uncertainty became a mounting thrust stemming from the dynamics of ongoing change that steadily grows more unpredictable, sudden and rapid. Exponential change dynamics blur the big picture, making reality seem overwhelming and threatening. This in turn leads to perplexed paralysis. It also forces companies to come up with immediate, spontaneous and, more importantly, consistent responses if they intend to continue operating. How should this perfect storm be navigated?

Against this backdrop, out of necessity rather than virtue, CEOs have gradually realized that they need to delegate decision-making to their subordinates, granting people more autonomy to act. In other words, they have granted people more freedom of action – a key driver for the innovation required by companies to join this new reality and continue in business. Among the many and complementary definitions of management, one proves especially noteworthy: "Managing is creating room for freedom" (Lucas Tomas, 1995). Today and in the future, the companies that want to last must rely on people and their key distinctive feature: freedom. Freedom is the human dimension that enables creativity, the mother of innovation, the source of differentiation – the true driver of competition.

This reality seems to reveal a Copernican sort of paradigm change in effective management. Yet upon further analysis, it becomes clear that this trait has always been present in successful companies, albeit not widespread. What is essential – what seems to be invisible to the eye, as Saint-Exupéry (1943) noted in The Little Prince – has blossomed in some outstanding business organizations, particularly long-established companies (Arie de Geus, 1997). These organizations have been able to put people front and center, becoming true working communities and surviving over time. Such firms feature behavioral patterns that should be further explored and imitated.

It is increasingly clear that the "secret ingredient," the key to business success, resides in the role afforded to people in companies. A company's sound performance stems from its commitment to the quality of life of its people and their all-around growth – construing quality of life not only as the availability of greater and better goods but, first and foremost, as "the respect for human beings and their dignity, as well as the attention to their higher endeavors: the advancement of knowledge and the effective use of freedom" (C. Llano, 2000, 2010). Along with the effective use of freedom, "the predominance of good and the personification of trust-based relations" (Bruni & Zamagni, 2003) have driven radical changes seen lately in business management styles. Trust-based relations have proven to be most effective when seeking to fulfill the multiple purposes required for companies today (J. Canals, 2008).

Trust – the primary force to reduce uncertainty in general – is the "currency" that needs to be exchanged when building ties between the company and its diverse stakeholders. There is no commitment without trust, particularly since the rationale to cooperate comes from the rationale of trust.

This new reality expands companies' boundaries beyond classic employment relationships, pushing them into other dimensions associated with the quality and commitment of ties. These should be based on cooperation rather than on pure "hierarchy or market" trade-offs (O. Williamson, 1975). Increasingly, we find legally independent companies collaborating with each other and competing as a single organization. This new reality may be putting the role of people in the spotlight, where they should have been all along.

What is a people-centric company like? What does it mean for managers? Where and how does this view and understanding of the human organization known as "a company" translate into practice? What are their practical consequences? Are people-centric companies (PPCs) even possible in the real world? This chapter will explore these questions.

What is a people-centric company like?

Every business management theory draws from a specific view of what a company is (nature and key traits), what it does (its purposes, what is expected of it) and on a specific notion of human being. Philosophical and anthropological bases are required, including a specific theory on human action, life and, particularly, the work carried out by the company.

This topic requires an in-depth examination, but first I must summarize the anthropological paradigm on which I base my observations and proposals. It is drawn from the work of J. A. Pérez López (1993), Antonio Argandoña (2006) and Domènec Melé (1996, 2012), all of them academics that developed their work at IESE Business School of the University of Navarra in Spain, as well as Tomás Melendo (1990), Aranguren Echevaerría (2003) and Echeverría (2016) of the University of Navarra; Carlos Llano (1994, 1997) from IPADE Business School, Mexico; and Ricardo Crespo (2005) and Hector Rocha of IAE Business School, Universidad Austral Argentina, working in collaboration with Sumantra Ghoshal (2006) and from de Pope John Paul II (1991).

Schools associated with IESE have disseminated this approach to the study of business organizations around the world, diffusing it through thousands of executives that attended to their management programs, who then roll it out in their companies.

The following are some of the underlying premises of this anthropological paradigm:

1   **It views companies as human organizations, regarding them as communities of people**. A company is not just a technical system or an ecosystem with life: it is something more encompassing that includes and integrates both. This concept is known in cybernetics as a Freely adaptive system (FAS), where people, as free agents, play a central role (Domènec Melé, N. Nuria Chinchilla & Marta López-Jurado, 2018).

2   **To serve people constitutes the primary purpose of every company**. Companies are economic organizations that need to be effective and efficient (according to C. Barnard, 1938). They exist to serve people and contribute to

their betterment. PPCs prioritize human beings, with their dignity, which is absolute in nature (Carlos Llano, 2010). They recognize that their ultimate end focuses on the development of all the people within them. As a specific type of human organization, a company must fulfill the "root" purpose shared by all human organizations by managing its own economic ends.

This primary purpose – the only one that can serve as an ultimate or higher end – can be summarized in just a few words: contributing to the personal betterment of the people associated with the company. In addition to the specific goal of creating and distributing wealth, companies play a clear role in serving and transforming reality – especially human reality. This is done by developing people associated with them to meet some of their actual needs – whether these people are direct collaborators, customers, suppliers, shareholders or members of surrounding communities.

3   **The mission of all companies – their guiding principle – is to make a specific contribution to society, meeting an actual need, creating and distributing wealth for the common good**. Based on this key purpose, companies, as social institutions, play an increasingly broad and complex role in society. From their early days in the 19th century until the present, the purpose of the company has evolved, acquiring new nuances.

As a human organization, a company's reason for existence has consistently been sparked by the need to satisfy the real needs of people in society. This origin has also consistently led to one requirement: the creation of genuine wealth, which, in turn, companies must manage and distribute. Thus, they serve an exceptional social role.

Firms have become increasingly regarded as working communities, where people associated with them expect a positive environment for human development. However, society's growing interest in companies and the broadening purposes in firms do not give them carte blanche. For instance, companies are expected to care for the environment – for present and future generations – and to incorporate this responsibility into their wealth creation and distribution schemes. Clearly, it is no longer as easy as it was a century ago for companies to secure a "social license" to operate.

4   **If people really "make a difference,"** if they are truly the distinctive factor from which competitive advantage is derived, then the elements that set organizations apart will depend on their most inherent attribute: **the spirit of its members**. As noted by Carlos Llano (2010), drawing from Thomas Aquinas (1265), the spirit is the human reality that gives individuals their unique abilities to do the following:

a   Conceive abstract ideas (opening their scope)
b   Think about non-material entities/come up with these realities (establishing ends that are higher than themselves)
c   Ponder upon themselves with the ability to self-examine themselves (realizing that they exist and acknowledging their competencies)

    d   Act freely (having complete self-control)[1]
    e   Reach their highest development potential (unlimited progressive growth)

Human beings' growth comes from an inherent trait – the spirit and its faculties, relying on the following:

    Freedom, which spurs initiative
    Decision-making, which grounds and fuels all actions
    Will, which drives action and seeks goodness
    Intelligence, which creates knowledge and gravitates toward the truth
    Creativity, which promotes and guides innovation
    Potential, which prompts continued improvement and constitutes the core of
        organizational learning

Given that the ideas of initiative, action, knowledge, innovation, continued improvement and learning have become daily staples in the business world, relying on the human spirit to compete is important. To illustrate that these notions have always been present, albeit not with complete or extensive validation, here are two definitions by business leaders from the past century – one of them made at age 90:

> An organization is a community of human beings that is in business – any business – to stay alive.
>
>   – *Arie de Geus, 1997*

> The goodwill of the people is the only enduring thing in any business. It is the sole substance. . . . the rest is shadow.
>
>   – *H. F. Johnson, 1927*

What does it mean for managers?

Based on this anthropological paradigm, it follows that good corporate managers need to *know* about human sciences, which serve as irreplaceable guidelines, in addition to management sciences. Human sciences include philosophy, which helps to "learn the fundamental nature of things," particularly philosophical anthropology; ethics, which teaches "the art of living and acting as human beings," indicating "the inner rationale of free actions – the actions that, if human beings fail to perform, lead to the loss of freedom" – and serving as a true operating manual for free individuals; and political science, the discipline that covers how government service work and how leadership can guide people toward common ends.

    Leadership has become more demanding, difficult and complex today. For managers to effectively fulfill their responsibilities, they clearly need more and broader training. Most importantly, they need the set of human virtues required to lead. Executives' notion and use of power prove key since, ultimately, top managers set the tone for corporate actions.

"Power is service" is the definition of power that underlies PCCs. This goes hand in hand with a return to basics regarding governance, with power used as an opportunity to serve others, creating a context that facilitates freedom and that is grounded in justice and truth.

Building a genuine working community where everyone is aware of a shared, common destiny is the core responsibility of CEOs and their management teams. These individuals should first and foremost focus on fostering a sense of community. An institutional setting of this kind will make it easier to promote people's commitment to the company's purpose.

This idea is hardly new. Prominent business leaders such as Sony chair Akio Morita, as well as HP's founders David Packard and William Hewlett, expressed that the success of their companies stemmed from a people-oriented philosophy. In the realm of academia, Peters and Waterman (1982) addressed this issue in their bestseller *In Search of Excellence*, and Christopher Bartlett and Sumantra Ghoshal (1999) explored it in *The Individualized Corporation: A Fundamentally New Approach to Management*. David Ulrich (1997) proclaimed that "people matter" in his renowned book *Human Resource Champions*.

Yet there is a crucial difference between our view and that of these authors, who accurately realized that people are the key motor for sustained corporate success. The difference is that while they deem people as organizations' (in this case, companies') primary "assets," we take a step further and regard people as the organization itself, as the main purpose of its multiple ends. People's supremacy in corporate ends should not be temporary or specific to a single group of stakeholders (employees, shareholders, customers, surrounding communities, etc.). It should prevail as the guiding principle for everyone, since all stakeholders have the same dignity. This means always regarding people as ends in themselves and not as mere assets, instruments or resources.

Clearly, purely economic results are not and should not be the primary driver for the virtuous cycle of wealth creation. Rather, paraphrasing the father of liberal capitalism, Adam Smith, profits should stem from the good work carried out by the entire organization. As Johnson & Johnson's credo states, "at last, but not least, if we do well everything that needs to be done, profits will come" as a necessary but definitely not a sufficient condition.

If people, treated with dignity and building a true working community, are the source of success for business organizations, we should gain a deeper understanding of *what people are*, their specific traits and what it means to build a working community to elaborate a better approach regarding the role of to business and leadership. This is where politics, defined as the leadership required to guide people in pursuit of common ends, and ethics, as an operating manual for free individuals, play vital roles.

How does an understanding of the human organization translate into practice?

Companies leave clear traces of what they are and what their purpose is in everything they say and do, as well as in how they carry out their activities and organize themselves. Based on more than thirty years of collaborations and research on global companies, I have reached the following conclusions regarding the overriding actions of PCCs:

- They expand their mission statements

    - to elaborate on what they have set as their purpose and how they intend to accomplish it
    - to outline the business philosophy that they have embraced when establishing their axiological values (those safeguarding people's human nature), their operating values (those promoting their efficacy to achieve their goals) and the role played by people. At PCCs, people have a central role.

- They indicate the stakeholders they recognize and their commitment to these groups. PCCs have multiple stakeholders, and they typically maintain open, explicit and candid cooperative relationships with these groups.
- They use control and reward systems that focus on

    - facts, not people
    - contributions and value added.

- They build formal structures that

    - feature dedicated departments for human development
    - revolve around learning
    - promote networking and teamwork.

- They pursue expansion policies that ensure they operate as multiple local firms, adopting the traits of local companies in every country/region.
- They make sure that their organizational climate hinges on trust.
- They foster a business model based on networks.
- They provide training programs that

    - address all human dimensions and are available to everyone
    - drive an ongoing learning culture
    - become a true school for leaders.

- They feature highly engaging, open and consensus-based decision-making processes.
- They ground knowledge management and innovation processes on people's freedom and build formal spaces and practices that promote it.

Finally, PCCs display the characteristics of a working community, where freedom plays a key role and where people can grow, bound by clearly established and shared values. The CEO's role proves increasingly significant in this context: they need to create and maintain elements that will ensure the firm's continuity. These freely adjusted systems require political management and leadership grounded on shared values and a service calling. If these conditions are not provided, PCCs will fail over time, tumbling down like a house of cards, and eventually vanish.

What are the practical consequences?

PCCs tend to experience above-average growth, coupled with and spurred on by their superior organizational development capability, leveraged by their learning ability – their distinctive quality that characterizes their organization. It comes as no surprise, then, that the DNA study of long-lasting companies, introduced by Arie De Geus in *The Living Company*, shows many of the common characteristics of PCCs:

- Attractiveness: by building trust, they attract many stakeholders who are interested in working with them.
- Expansion: as a result of their great appeal, they grow at a faster pace.
- Strength: they become stronger because of the quality ties they forge.
- Openness to learning: they are true "learning organizations," and this makes them willing to change and facilitate change processes.
- Innovativeness: their ability to innovate comes as a result of the freedom and trust they have in their operations.
- Leadership development: they provide an environment that supports leadership at every level.
- Working community nature: they gradually turn into working communities.
- Long life: as long as they maintain these traits, they strengthen their ability to endure, and it becomes likely that they will last for decades.
- "Last but not least": the ability to steadily create enough wealth for everyone over time, meeting the most essential requirement for survival.

Are people-centric companies even possible in today's world? A real-life example

The cases "El Tejar SA" (Carrera & Quiroga, 2004) and "El Tejar Ltd." (Carrera & Quiroga, 2014) describe an organization with the distinctive traits of PPCs, as well as other novel features. Led by Oscar Alvarado ("Emprender con valores," FISOA, 2012), in under twenty-five years, El Tejar transformed from a small association of cattle business owners in Argentina's prime farming region, holding 700 hectares (1,730 acres), to the world's largest grain and oilseed planting and producing company. The association encompassed nearly 1 million hectares (2.5 million acres) devoted to agricultural farming in MERCOSUR and investments in other Latin American countries.

El Tejar's PCC characteristics and innovative practices include the following:

1 Providing an environment conducive to personal and family growth for everyone associated with the company. This entails "a notion of company construed as an organization fully centered on people; a virtuous, long-lasting and transcendent project centered on people; a place where people can grow as individuals . . . regarding people as the end of business operations, making all the difference" (Carrera and Quiroga, 2004).

2 Making El Tejar a place where everyone can realize their personal dreams.
3 Becoming an economically, emotionally and ethically responsible company, where people's lives are enhanced as the end of all business operations. Business and profit are construed as necessary but not sufficient conditions.
4 Relying on values that are based on professionalism (pragmatic value), joy (emotional value) and humility (ethical value). In addition, integrity serves as a guarantee for transparent management that seeks enrichment for all, including community and society, resting firmly on the pledged word.
5 Viewing business leaders as community leaders, with a true calling for service – "legitimate business leaders, who raise the demand for capitalism" (Carrera and Quiroga, 2004).
6 Prioritizing cooperation over competition, and therefore sharing everything, listening, communicating and helping. Focusing on transparency and the ability to listen stand as drivers for improvement and trust-building. The aim is to build a common history that promotes unity and harmony. CEOs guarantee the trust needed for everyone to contribute to the common project.
7 Standing as a large group of people who, based on common values, share a dream that will hopefully last at least 700 years – "a company conceived for transcendence and long-term continuity" (Carrera and Quiroga, 2004).
8 Believing in building a better world for everyone, with El Tejar as our current and future best contribution.
9 Building a network of networks. This business model has created enough trust to consolidate long-lasting alliances and achieve growth, securing funds and rallying people in pursuit of a common venture.
   "Network trust: a relational rationale that hinges on trust-based, long-term ties grounded on shared values, as opposed to the transactional rationale based on the mere exchange of goods or services and short-term profitability" (Carrera and Quiroga, 2004). This preference characterizes networking companies, where every individual builds long-term relationships at their level for their company.
10 Hoping that the work area shows that it values itself and values us. "Being multi-local, operating in every chosen country or region as a local company, committed to investing locally, offering work and encouragement to local service companies, and supporting the social projects that local communities view as important. Pursuing a clear, strong community integration philosophy."
11 Changing the paradigm: the company intends and proposes to "turn the pyramid upside down," using the organization to serve customers and viewing management work as a means to serve others.
12 Embracing a quality public policy, owning up to mistakes by

- acknowledging them
- apologizing for them
- analyzing them
- making amends to customers/others.

People at El Tejar enjoy ample freedom but are at the same time held accountable for their behavior and are expected to honor their responsibilities. The company's key quality assurance policy zeros in on people's behavior rather than on products or processes.

13 Changing the name of the HR department to "people's development area," which focuses on "training leaders and not viewing people as resources."

14 Providing overall, inclusive training (for everyone, with no exceptions) and creating an environment that fosters people's well-being and growth while promoting the company's goals. Turning boundaries into improvement opportunities.

15 Basing the company on the notion of *eutopia* – a good, happy, adequate place that we wish would exist and a possible *utopia* – El Tejar states that it works on the concept of the "Eutopian company: a place where people come together and grow – a business utopia that can come true."

Conclusions

Taking a fresh look at the role of companies and business leaders in society from an anthropological standpoint opens up a promising path to follow. A company is both an economic institution and a social good, a human reality that holds interest for society. Companies are expected to rise to the status of true working communities by creating and distributing wealth efficiently, providing useful goods and services to people, contributing to their well-being and building an environment conducive to human development for everyone interacting with them. Companies are also expected to do all this consistently and fruitfully over time.

The new outlook introduced by this approach certainly leads to "revolutionary and hard" conclusions for companies' lives and ends and particularly for managers' roles and tasks. To move in this direction, I now outline a number of recommendations that I believe to be useful for managers – especially CEOs – to lead their companies amid today's exponential change and high uncertainty:

- Viewing organizations as open, freely adapted systems with an identity of their own.
- Personalizing relationships, building cooperative ties that respect and value people. Focusing on building true working communities.
- Focusing on building true working communities.
- Managing people by making room for freedom by encouraging collaborators to live up to their full potential. Sharing and disseminating information, delegating decision-making power, training, building trust and rewarding contributions.
- Embracing some virtues and leading by example – transparency, truthfulness, loyalty, humility, discretion and some boldness.
- Relying on proximity and specific criteria rather than generalizations.
- Assessing the consequences of decisions that will affect every stakeholder, consistently trying to satisfy their legitimate interests.
- Satisfying and harmonizing rather than maximizing and balancing.

- Bearing in mind the organization's continuity at all times, following the principle of "all-term" and merging viability (short-term demands) with sustainability (long-term outlook) based on common good tenets.
- Pursuing and underscoring efficacy via cooperation and service rather than through power and competition.
- Fostering strategic thinking, learning, innovation and the development of leaders.
- Stopping to regard quantitative growth as a goal in itself. The new paradigm focuses on having the right scale to ensure continuity and remain strong.
- Finally, as a legacy of sorts, making sure to leave potential successors who will be able to ensure their organizations' continuity.

Note

1 Human beings differentiate themselves from all other beings based on their ability to make decisions. Decisions are, as Herbert Simon (1946) adroitly put it, the key to understanding organizations – and rightly so, as organizations consist of people, and the ability to decide is their unique attribute. Human beings do not set the rules of their nature; they are not autonomous. They can act freely according to their nature, increasingly earning more humanity, or even against their nature, dehumanizing themselves by losing some of their freedom. Depending on their decisions, which fall within the "praxis" realm, the good can be served or not.

References

Aquinas, T. (1265). *Summa Contra Gentile*.

Aranguren Echevarría, J. (2003). *Antropología Filosófica*. Madrid: McGraw-Hill.

Argandoña, A. (2006). "La Identidad Cristiana del Hombre de Empresa." Barcelona, *OP Nbr*. 07/7. IESE.

Barnard, C. (1938). *The Functions of the Executive*, Harvard University Press.

Bartlett, C. and Ghoshal, S. (1999). *The Individualized Corporation*. New York: HarperCollins.

Bruni, L. and Zamagni, S. (2003). *Persona y Comunión*, Buenos Aires: Ciudad Nueva.

Canals, C. (2008). *En Busca del Equilibrio*. Madrid: Prentice Hall.

Carrera, A. and Quiroga, J. (2004). *El Tejar SA*. Buenos Aires, IAE Publishing, Universidad Austral.

Carrera, A. and Capillo, A. (2014). *El Tejar Ltd*. Buenos Aires, IAE Publishing, Universidad Austral.

Crespo, R. (2005). "¿Es Verdad que Ser Ético es un Buen Negocio?" Buenos Aires, *IAE Business School Alumni Magazine*.

De Geus, A. (1997). *The Living Company*. London: Longview Publishing Ltd.

Echeverría, J., et al. (2016). *Dirigir Empresas con Sentido Cristiano*. Pamplona: EUNSA.

FISOA. (2012). *Oscar Alvarado. Emprender con Valores*. Buenos Aires: RHM.

Lucas Tomas, J. L. (1995). *El Fomento de la Libertad*. Barcelona: EUNSA.

Llano, C. (1994). *El Postmodernismo en la Empresa*. Mexico: McGraw-Hill.

Llano, C. (1997). *Dilemas Éticos de la Empresa Contemporánea*. Mexico: FCE.

Llano, C. (2000). *Sistemas versus Persona*. Mexico: McGraw-Hill.

Llano, C. (2010). *Viaje al Centro del Hombre*. Madrid: Rialp.

Melendo, T. (1990). *Las Claves de la Eficacia Empresarial*. Madrid: Rialp.

Melé, D. (1996). *Ética en el Gobierno de la Empresa.* Pamplona: EUNSA.

Melé, D. (2012). "The Firm as a Community of Persons," *Journal of Business Ethics,* 106.

Melé, D., et al. (2018). "The Freely Adaptive System: Application of This Cybernetic Model to an Organization Formed by Two Dynamic Human Systems," *Philosophy of Management,* 18(1): 89–106.

Pérez López, J. A. (1993). *Fundamentos de la Dirección de Empresa.* Madrid: Rialp.

Peters, T. and Waterman, B. (1982). *In Search of Excellence.* New York: Harper & Row.

Pope John Paul II. (1991). *Centesimus Annus.* Buenos Aires: Ediciones Paulinas.

Rocha, H. and Ghoshal, S. (2006). "Beyond Self-Interest Revisited." *Journal of Management Studies,* 43(3): 585–619.

Simon, H. (1946). *Administrative Behavior.* New York: Free Press.

Ulrich, D. (1997). *Human Resources Champions.* Boston: HBS Press.

Williamson, O. (1975). *Markets and Hierarchies.* New York: Free Press.

PART 2

Strategizing and organizing

4

THE ROLE OF THE CEO IN BUSINESS MODEL RENEWAL

Joan E. Ricart

As outlined in Chapter 1, we conceptualize the fundamental task of general management as the design, management and renewal of a complex system within the framework of the organization's *institutional configuration* (owners, stakeholders, governance bodies), its *external environment* (and by extension, its external mission), its internal context (and therefore its internal mission) and its *business* (as observed in Figure 4.1). Senior-level executives have influence and limitations in each dimension, but perhaps the business realm is where they can exercise the greatest influence and help balance the demands of others.

Top management should naturally use all levers in a consistent, coherent and balanced fashion, taking into account the holistic and systemic nature of the CEO's role. A focus on the business itself is a good way to integrate all of these tasks, since it responds to the real needs of customers (external mission) and the expectations of employees and other internal stakeholders (internal mission). Consequently, overseeing the constant renewal of the business should be considered a central task of the CEO.

Shaped by drivers such as technology, globalization and demographic change, our fast-paced business climate generates new opportunities to do things differently and design business models that better respond to current needs This constant state of flux undoubtedly increases the significance of business model innovation in the role of the CEO.

Recent changes in Ricoh Spain exemplify this shift. The economic downturn, coupled with digital transformation, triggered an important crisis in the company's Spanish business. The world was digitalizing, so printing and copying were losing ground, and the crisis was leading clients to reduce unnecessary expenses. Ricoh's business in Spain was shrinking and all indications suggested that the change would be permanent. The general manager was faced with the formidable challenge of redefining the company's strategic course. Moreover, the corporate solution of

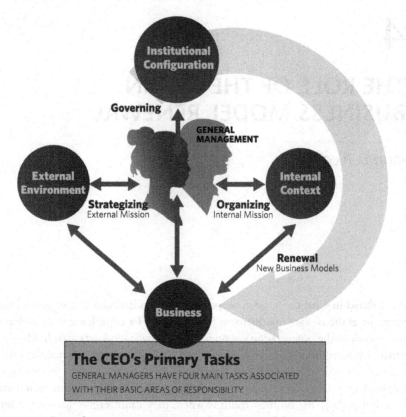

FIGURE 4.1 General Management Main Areas of Responsibility

Source: Andreu and Ricart (2014). IESE Insight, No. 23, Fourth Quarter 2014, pp. 15–21.

expanding the business to close extensions of current offerings was needed, but not enough. To survive, the company had to develop a new business model.

The new business model entailed entering into a lateral business of information technology (IT) applications, which meant expanding the consulting arm of the company, an area that differed significantly from Ricoh's selling organization. This shift took time but was accelerated by an acquisition and the necessary cultural change that it provoked. In this time of turbulence, it is important to emphasize the need for the CEO to develop a business that aligns with the corporation while supporting the current and future organization.

General managers rely on business models to address the business realm. Business models identify the firm's underlying logic and how it creates and captures value for stakeholders. A business model is simply a model of a business, one focused on the firm's essential "strategic elements": value creation and capture for all stakeholders. As the environment's growing complexity incites novel ways of doing things, business models have become increasingly important to discover, innovate, design and renew businesses and essentially transform the *business* dimension into a central task of the CEO.

This centrality has important consequences for the leadership competencies and capabilities required in today's global organizations. The "old" task of a CEO now has "new" components. A new brand of leader is emerging based on their capacity to design and deploy new business models, which will ultimately transform the competitive landscape.

A new world

The context in which CEOs operate is changing dramatically. Think about the most significant trends currently disrupting global markets: the tremendous impact of technology and digital transformation; global urbanization and the associated demographic consequences; the complexity of issues relating to the globalization of products and services, people and jobs, power and politics; the environmental impact of human activities and global warming; social demands in the face of global inequalities, security concerns and gender differences. The list goes on. But what are the impacts?

I highlight three core consequences that emerge from this "perfect storm" of global trends:

1 *The context in which firms operate grows in complexity.* Local problems are now global problems, paradigms quickly transform, new players enter the arena and innovation continues to surprise us on a daily basis. Without a doubt, complexity is increasing at breakneck speed.
2 *As uncertainty increases, so does risk.* Greater uncertainty makes it more difficult to anticipate change, plan and deploy strategies. In the face of uncertainty, we see more experimentation, trial and error and fast actions toward fast learning. In the midst of this rapid-paced, ever-changing and uncertain world, it's important for firms to reinforce their sense of mission, values and institutional framework to better navigate it. Firms also face more unexpected risks and therefore need to work on resilience strategies to ensure a sustainable future.
3 *Opportunities to do things differently also increase at a much higher frequency.* When firms speak of enhancing the malleability of their business model, it is just another way of saying that there are other ways to develop their business model. They are really referring to reconsidering the underlying logic for value creation and value capture of the firm.

Peter Drucker used to say that "change is a source of opportunities." Innovators create new opportunities by serving new and old needs with different and novel approaches. Innovation magnifies change in the world, increases complexity and uncertainty, opens the door to further malleability and reinforces the cycle of change and evolution.

This increase in complexity, uncertainty and malleability is referred to as a VUCA environment: volatility, uncertainty, complexity and ambiguity. We see an increasing number of studies about the impact of these factors on industry structures and the creation or transformation of competitive ecosystems. The typical discourse identifies important drivers of change and how they generate new or renewed industries. The mechanism seems to claim that "drivers" drive "industry change."

VUCA environments unleash new ways of doing things and inspire new business models, yet we sometimes overlook the real mechanisms that trigger change. The decision lies with management to adapt their businesses to the new context; try to influence the context; serve new or old needs with new approaches; or create effective business models in an environment shaped by other actors that are also developing alternative business configurations. The result of this interaction is a "new" ecosystem that we identify as industry change. So drivers do not directly change our environment. Rather, change results from the actions of change agents like CEOs who renovate (or invent) their firms' business model, as outlined in Figure 4.2.

This perspective provides a new view of strategy, in which business is the focus, the integrative element to strategize, organize and govern. More importantly, it again underlines the centrality of the role of the CEO in business (model) renewal.

One can easily claim that this has always been the case, and that claim would be true. The CEO's task has always been complex. But what is different today has to do with the combination of two core factors that reinforce each other: the acceleration of the drivers of change and the increasing malleability of business models. These factors merge to create a virtuous cycle in which change fuels opportunity for more change, and opportunities for developing alternative sources of competitive advantage heighten the VUCA dimension of the environment. In this context, new dominant business models (perhaps with transitory competitive advantages) will surely emerge. Greater variability among business model opportunities leads to greater competition among business models, which leads to the need for CEOs to focus on business model innovation.

Of course, this new paradigm doesn't affect all businesses at the same speed. Some industries are more entrenched, so change might take longer, but the drivers

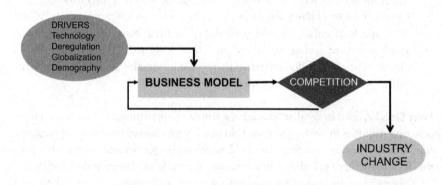

FIGURE 4.2 A New View of Strategy Focused on Business Model

Source: Author.

of change, fueled by the innovation of "new business leaders" and skillful designers of robust business models, are accelerating the pace of change *everywhere, in every industry* and *in every part of the world*. Since change can be quite disruptive, legacies can act as heavy burdens that hinder innovation.

BOX 4.1   BUSINESS MODEL RENEWAL IN IBERO-AMERICA: A TALE OF UNICORNS

Ibero-America has offered tremendous opportunities for savvy technology entrepreneurs who are willing to engage in business model innovation. Over the past decade, several Latin American technology firms were able to surpass a market capitalization of US$1 billion within their first year of existence by taking advantage of a relatively less-populated competitive environment and overcoming institutional voids inherent in the region ("tropicalization" of the value proposition). Referred to as unicorns, these firms are typically led by entrepreneurs highly attuned to the local ecosystem who leverage the decline of established sources of advantage – those associated with physical assets and positions – and capitalize on the emergence of new ones. A few unicorn examples include Mercado Libre, OLX and Globant.

Founded in 1999, Mercado Libre is a premier online business platform, with operations in eighteen Latin American countries and in Portugal. The firm has developed a unique, innovative and localized business ecosystem that integrates a virtual store (*mercados* or marketplaces), a payment system (*mercado pago*), an advertising business (*mercado libre publicidad*) and a logistic service (*mercado envíos*) around their shop, or *mercado libre*. By capitalizing on these strengths, Mercado Libre has been able to successfully keep other industry players like Amazon, eBay and Alibaba in check.

OLX (online exchange) has also effectively leveraged technological change. Among the world's leading free online classifieds platforms, OLX has attracted millions of people to purchase and sell goods, rent properties and seek employment opportunities.

Finally, Globant offers another example of a Latin American firm successfully competing against established industry players. The IT company offers software development and outsourcing and offshoring services to a global client base, avoiding price competition through a low-cost structure.

Chapter 7 will delve more deeply into these stories.

Business model innovation and renewal

Business model design and innovation are gaining importance in the CEO's scope of responsibilities. The growing body of literature[1] on these topics in the fields of strategic management, entrepreneurship and innovation undoubtedly reflects this evolution. In light of this shift, it seems fitting to examine the competencies necessary to execute this crucial task.

A business model explains the underlying logic of a business unit, namely how it creates and captures value for stakeholders. Although we could apply the same logic to different types of units, we generally refer to business units as those that meet the explicit needs of a customer group in a given geographical area. The firm then can define a specific value proposition and design a business model to deliver it. Hence, the approach is the logic behind the business model.

Why are business models useful? In addition to revealing the logic behind value creation and value capture, business models allow top management to assess the consistency and robustness of the firm's value proposition and use this information to make any necessary modifications. All the aforementioned tasks convey a design perspective: CEOs use business models to understand the logic, evaluate it and modify it to their advantage. This requires a focus from a *design perspective*: the CEO uses the model to better design, manage, execute and eventually renew the business model.

There are two other elements worth highlighting. First, the model sheds light on the dynamics of value creation and value capture, an important focus since CEOs address systems that are inherently open and dynamic. CEOs strategize, organize, govern and renew the business model (Figure 4.1). Change is continual, so the dynamics of any competitive advantage should be at the core of any modeling tool.

The second key element is perhaps obvious: the model should consider *interactions* in order to predict competitive dynamics (Ricart (2012). Referring back to Figure 4.2, it is not the design of the business model in isolation that matters; it is the resultant interaction that will ultimately survive. The tool, the model, should facilitate the dynamic interaction that defines a successful business model.

There are numerous ways to represent or model a business. Possibly the most established one is the "value chain" concept introduced by Michael Porter in 1985 in his book on competitive advantage. Porter argued that companies should design their value chain idiosyncratically to gain differential positioning and thus competitive advantage. It was at this point that the value chain transformed from an extremely useful tool into a ball and chain, and variations on this theme began to emerge. Even Porter decided to replace the value chain concept with the activity system, to make his concept more flexible (Porter, 1996). Despite its many offshoots, the field of strategy leans toward the consensus that the value chain and its variations must give way to a broader, more systemic concept like the business model.

Another famous business model representation is Osterwalder's "business model canvas."[2] His definition of a business model includes nine key components, which are organized similarly to the value chain (see Figure 4.3):

1 Value proposition
2 Customer segments
3 Customer relationships
4 Channels

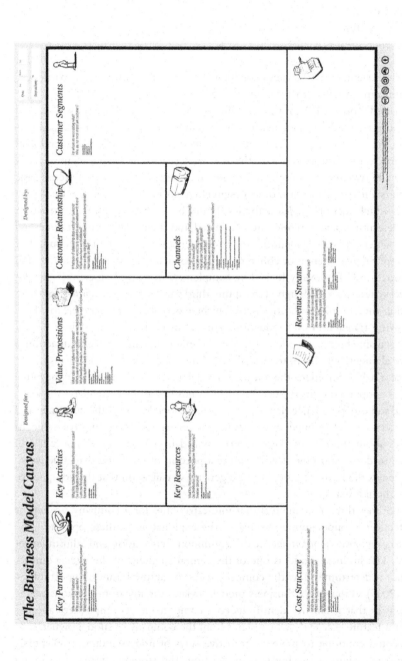

FIGURE 4.3 The Business Model Canvas

Source: www.businessmodelgeneration.com, December 2012.

5   Key activities
6   Key resources
7   Key partners
8   Cost structures
9   Revenue streams

The various elements of the canvas are interconnected, not independent. Moreover, the figure aims to reflect that the whole is greater than the sum of its parts.

Amit and Zott (2010) propose a definition derived from the study of several online business models. Their definition, therefore, clearly has a transactional orientation, but it is also a beneficial resource for entrepreneurs. In the Amit and Zott (2010) article, the authors start with the activity system as the central focus of activities and add two important aspects for reflection in the design of the system's basic parameters. First, they establish three design elements in the activity system: (1) the content, which identifies *what* activities should be carried out; (2) the structure, which determines *how* activities are connected and their relative importance; and (3) the ownership, which identifies *who* must perform each activity. Second, they identify four design themes or coherent settings for activity systems, summarized in the acronym NICE (novelty, locked in, complementarities and efficiency): *novelty*, for novel systems; *lock in*, designed to capture third parties; *complementarities*, for those exploiting the complementarities between these activities; and *efficiency*, for those emphasizing transaction cost reduction. This set of tools is tremendously helpful when discussing business models, especially in online domains, where transaction is the core element, but also in the initial stages of the entrepreneurial process.

Teece (2010) considers the business model to be a company's "conceptual model" – as opposed to its financial model: "A business model articulates the logic, the data, and other evidence that support a value proposition for the customer, and a viable structure of revenues and costs for the enterprise delivering that value. In short, it's about the benefit the enterprise will deliver to customers, how it will organize to do so, and how it will capture a portion of the value that it delivers." Teece deems the business model to be a generic visualization that the competitive strategy should then spell out.

He outlines three fundamental dynamic capabilities for a company: *sensing*, or the detection of opportunities; *seizing*, or the exploitation of these opportunities; and *managing threats/transforming*, or the continuous reinvention and adjustment of business. The business model is one of the central elements of the *seizing* dimension since it determines how the company seeks to capture business opportunities. Teece (2009) vision of the business model deviates slightly from previous representations in that if fails to identify its core components yet emphasizes another important feature – *design* – which stems from the company or model owner.

We could continue to present alternative ways of understanding, conceptualizing and representing the business model,[3] but the aforementioned are among the best known in a body of literature that reflects the unique perspectives of each author.

Following this overview, we would like to emphasize three main ideas. First, the business model is something that a company *designs*. Second, the business model consequently has a *high entrepreneurial* component, since it designs the essence of the entrepreneurial process: how we create and capture value. Third, the system of activities, perhaps supplemented with design elements and themes – a modernization of the nine elements included in the canvas – is extremely useful in identifying the core elements of entrepreneurial design. As we will see, however, today's executives need to look beyond this tool.

Casadesus-Masanell and Ricart (2011) propose representing the business model as a structure of choices and consequences. In this way, the connections between choices and consequences force the modeler to understand the dynamic logic and virtuous (or vicious) cycles that can emerge. Furthermore, by adding the impact of choices made of other entities and their effect on our consequences and vice versa, we can easily incorporate these interactions, which often reverse an action or generate unexpected consequences. Finally, by distinguishing between rigid and flexible consequences, we can better identify true and robust sources of competitive advantage. In sum, business model innovation requires identifying the interrelationships between the relevant choices and consequences that are new to the firm and the industry. It also requires a particular mindset to identify opportunities and design solutions to seize it.

The process of business model renewal starts with *sensing* an opportunity for a new value proposition by identifying underserved needs, anticipating changes in needs or "generating" new needs A world in constant evolution provides numerous possibilities to find such opportunities, including solutions linked with digital transformation, sustainability and new solutions to serve the base of the pyramid. In essence, using old or established business models to create new ones won't suffice. In this regard, collaborative approaches like design-thinking techniques can help. This method helps CEOs identify opportunities and find alternative ways to address challenges, which brings us to the second step: seizing the opportunity.

Seizing the opportunity boils down to designing a business model that supports the value proposition and turns it into a reality. The different representations mentioned earlier can help in this process, in addition to fast prototyping techniques and, to some degree, experimentation, which in some cases can lead to commitments that make it hard to backtrack and explore alternative options.

Sensing and seizing opportunities are the cornerstones of entrepreneurship. In the current context, it isn't surprising that so many opportunities have opened up for new start-ups, yet established companies have also sought to leverage new avenues for growth. More and more, businesses and corporations are creating new business through corporate venturing and acquiring promising start-ups early. In fact, large firms tend to have a stronger set of resources and broader capabilities than start-ups, which can give them an edge, assuming that they are able to cultivate an entrepreneurship mentality. Leveraging this advantage, however, requires CEOs to think like *entrepreneurs*.

Getting the CEO to don the hat of an entrepreneur is no easy feat. In fact, many entrepreneurship experts don't think it's feasible and claim that this function should be left to start-ups. In reality, we need to separate the innovator from the entrepreneur. To excel and ensure their firms' long-term survival, CEOs need to become *innovators* to reinvent their business models. To deploy the results of this process of innovation, CEOs can use corporate venturing if they believe changes should be made with an independent unit. Acquisitions are another option to accelerate the process. CEOs might also find a way to renovate an established business model by merging it with a new one or moving toward an integrated business model.

Legacies, procedures and established practices represent important roadblocks when firms embark on the path to organizational renewal, requiring the CEO to assume the role of innovator, entrepreneur and business model designer. But these competencies are not enough. CEOs also need to be *transformational leaders* since business model renewals are complex and entail upending an entire system.

The Spanish clothing design and manufacturing company Mango provides an interesting case study. For more than thirty years, Mango's affordable fashion, targeted at young women in urban areas, enjoyed considerable success in markets around the world. Unfortunately, its business hit a roadblock in 2008. The global economic crisis, a certain relaxation in the business model and the rise of its "fast fashion" competitor, Zara, created a "perfect storm" for Mango.

The firm reacted by spearheading incremental improvements, lateral diversification, better collections and additional expansion. These strategies ensured the company's survival, but the storm continued to brew. President Isaac Andic decided it was crucial to go back to Mango's roots to rediscover what had made the brand popular in the first place: experimenting, trying new things and creating novel formats while imitating others. After thirty years, Mango needed to reinvent its business model. Although the company is still en route to a safe harbor, they have so far weathered the storm thanks to this transformation.

Let's review the main reflections of the "new view of strategy" outlined thus far. The first key aspect is that "the business model is the focus of strategy." In my view, the overall scope of the CEO's functions, as described in Figure 4.1, hasn't changed dramatically, but the relative weight of its various elements has changed significantly. For many years, strategy was associated with the search for resources, but in time, the external environment and differential positioning necessary to secure a foothold in a hypercompetitive environment began to gain greater traction.

This shift away from resource-based strategies was also fueled as the internal context – knowledge and people – became more central. In all stages, the business itself, business design and business model innovation have been crucial, yet in today's world, the level of variability and the number of possibilities available to CEOs are far more powerful and diverse. Without a doubt, business model innovation opens countless new doors that were previously closed.

A second point is that "the business model is a reflection of the adopted strategy," which means that strategizing is still important. CEOs should center their strategy on changing the architecture of their industry to their advantage. Be the bottleneck; otherwise, value capture will be more difficult. The trade-off between creating value within the global ecosystem while capturing enough value is still present and should guide strategic choices.

In this dynamic environment, understanding how drivers of change affect the persistence of the business model is important. Robustness remains a core element, but CEOs should also anticipate business model competition by widening their scope beyond established players to consider emerging ones.

Another important reflection may be summed up as "cheap experimentation may be required." This means fast prototyping to learn and experiment at a low cost and verify the underlying assumptions that drive innovation. CEOs should embrace discovery-driven strategic planning and aim to avoid the entrepreneurial paradox of committing by trying and later being unable to leverage the acquired learning.

A new undertaking for CEOs

The role of a CEO has always been difficult, centered on managing a complex, open and dynamic system while balancing the requirements of the institutional configuration, external environment, internal context and the business. This integrative task requires a concrete skill set, attitudes and core values that translate into specific managerial competencies.

This chapter addresses the growing relevance of business model design and renewal for the CEOs of today and, more importantly, for those of tomorrow. Given this increasingly vital dimension, CEOs will need to develop new managerial competencies and strengthen existing ones.

Before exploring these competencies, it is worth highlighting that the growing collective and team-based dimension of the general management role. The level of complexity in some firms and their environments is such that general managers need to rely on their teams or governance bodies to ensure that these competencies form part of the decision-making process, as it would be difficult for one person to embody all of the needed capabilities. As a result, self-awareness and an understanding of the necessity of complementariness are crucial.

This chapter also stresses the essential roles of the CEO as an innovator (especially a business model innovator), an entrepreneur, a business designer and a transformational leader. In a previous publication (Ricart, 2015), I identified three fundamental competencies that CEOs should develop:

1 **Strategic thinking**: Organizations need to sense opportunities effectively and therefore require following processes to this end. To lead this process, CEOs need to act as entrepreneurs, framers of the future and strategic thinkers. They need to understand complexity and foster creativity to design this new future, which normally involves the collaboration of their teams.

2   **Design thinking**: Organizations need design-thinking capabilities to seize opportunities in today's market. As mentioned earlier, there are numerous tools, business model representations, procedures and methods to assist in this regard.

  Since novel business models are complex, their design often requires substantial experimentation. CEOs, as designers and architects of the business model, should have competencies to design creative experiments to quickly learn from the complex interactions with other existing and potential models. The key is *cheap and fast learning*, which is undoubtedly a difficult skill to develop.

  In addition, design thinking integrates elements of strategizing and organizing, and even governing. For this reason, CEOs need to have these aptitudes. Some elements may be relegated to the team, but leading the process in an integrative way clearly falls on the CEO.

3   **Systems thinking**: Organizations also need renewal and transformation competencies, which can be developed by promoting processes for continual learning and making efforts to gain a sharper understanding of the firm's impact on stakeholders. In short, organizations need to better manage their present reality while preparing for a different future. This shift often necessitates the development and implementation of a new system. To manage this system change, CEOs need to be proficient at system thinking.

The transformations associated with business model renewal are clearly systemic, calling for a view of the firm as a complex, open and dynamic system in interaction with many stakeholders. This has always been the case for CEOs, but the rising complexity in many markets and the emergence of new business models make this competency even more critical. System-thinking abilities are also difficult to develop.

Conclusions

The global marketplace is shaped by uncertainty, volatility, complexity and ambiguity, yet it also provides tremendous opportunities, especially those that offer new approaches to existing needs In this context, businesses can and should be reinvented. A new mindset is often needed.

  CEOs, in their new role as business model innovators, designers and entrepreneurs, must develop concrete capabilities to sustain performance in the long run. While this function is relatively new, CEOs in certain markets, particularly in Latin America, have been exercising it for quite some time.

  Although this new mindset is spreading to other parts of the world – in Asia and Africa, for instance – Latin America has a closer cultural proximity to the West and higher levels of education and urbanization. These factors give the region a head start and clear advantage when it comes to reinventing new business models and competing in global markets.

Notes

1 To learn more, please see D. Teece. (2010). "Business Models, Business Strategy and Innovation," *Long Range Planning*, 43; *R+D Management* (2014); *Strategic Entrepreneurship Management* (2015); and a book edited by Nicolai J. Foss and Tina Saebi titled *Business Model
Innovation: The Organizational Dimension*, Oxford University Press, 2015.
2 See A. Osterwalder and Y. Pigneur, *Business Model Generation: A Handbook for Visionaries,
Game Changers and Challengers* (Wiley, 2010) for a practical guide to its use.
3 Others can be found in the "Special Issue on Business Models," *Long Range Planning*, cited
previously.

References

Amit, R. and Zott, C. (2010). "Business Model Design: An Activity System Perspective,"
Long Range Planning, 43, 2–3 April/June: 216–226.
Andreu, R. and Ricart, J-E. (2014). "The Genuine Responsibilities of the CEO: A Frame-
work for Managing Today." *IESE Insight*, 23, Fourth Quarter: 15–21.
Casadesus-Masanell, R. and Ricart, J. E. (2011). "How to Design a Winning Business Model."
Harvard Business Review, 100–107.
Osterwalder, A. and Pigneur, Y. (2010). *Business Model Generation: A Handbook for Visionaries,
Game Changers and Challengers.* Hoboken, New Jersey: John Wiley & Sons.
Porter, M. (1985). *Competitive Advantage. Creating and Sustaining Superior Performance.* New
York, NY: Free Press.
Porter, M. (1996). "What Is Strategy?" *Harvard Business Review*, 74(6): 61–78.
Ricart, J. E. (2012). "Strategy in the 21st Century: Business Model in Action." IESE Techni-
cal Note SMN-685-E.
Ricart, J. E. (2015). "The CEO as Business Model Innovator." In: Canals, J. (ed.), *Shaping
Entrepreneurial Mindsets.* Basingstoke, England: Palgrave Macmillan.
Teece, D. (2009). *Dynamic Capabilities and Strategic Management: Organizing for Innovation and
Growth.* New York, NY: Oxford University Press.
Teece, D. (2010). "Business Models, Business Strategy and Innovation," *Long Range Planning*,
43: 172–194.

5

STRATEGIC MANAGEMENT IN EMERGING MARKETS

Roberto Vassolo and Ángel Sevil

Today's organizations coexist in increasingly open markets, characterized by the globalization of products and services and management practices. Yet, competitive contexts vary depending on region-specific geographical and current economic and social features, including local historical developments. This makes it difficult to pursue the same strategic choices in different regions, even when in pursuit of the same goals. To address this challenge, this chapter outlines the key theoretical frameworks that CEOs should bear in mind when making strategic decisions and the specific traits of emerging markets, with a special focus on Latin America.

The starting point for a sustainable successful strategy

Strategic analysis is all about current and potential changes, inside and outside of organizations. Organizations determine their individual action priorities in the form of strategic initiatives based on the observation and interpretation of the context and their own internal capabilities. In a nutshell, a strategy amounts to a set of initiatives intended to accomplish an organization's success. Where should companies competing in different environments look for these priorities?

A first step to satisfactorily explore this question hinges on examining the sources of organizational success for companies competing in different contexts over time. Organizational success is a broad term that, in a more restricted sense, can be defined as the ability to meet the needs of all stakeholders – people or institutions – somehow involved with an organization, which is a rather difficult task. Extraordinary corporate results constitute a proxy commonly used to establish whether a strategy is successful. Despite its bias in favor of a specific stakeholder (shareholders), this indicator allows for broad, worldwide comparisons.

Upon analyzing these results, we first notice that there are companies sharing a similar profitability level that differs from that of other groups of companies. These groups largely match industries. In general, different industries systematically display different profitability levels. Organizations choosing to compete in one industry or another are heavily conditioned by the developments in their respective industry. Changes in buyer-supplier leverage driven by mergers and acquisitions, a competitor's seizing a key resource or the existence of a special tax scheme that benefits one industry alone are among the factors that can shape industry performance. Figure 5.1, for instance, shows average profitability levels for ten industries in Argentina over a five-year period.

Industry isn't all that matters; the country where organizations operate proves influential as well. The same industry shows systematic profitability differences across countries – due to varying regulatory pressures, tax burdens and labor costs, for instance – as well as comparative advantages from one country to another. These advantages may result from an abundant natural resource, special infrastructure or more qualified HR. Figure 5.2 illustrates this, showing the average profitability of telecom companies across five Latin American countries from 2000 to 2005.

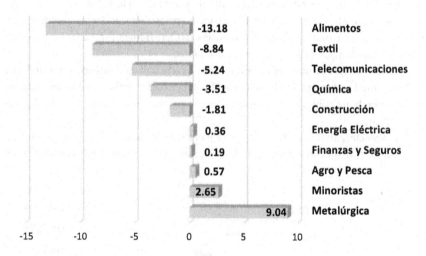

FIGURE 5.1 Average Profitability across Ten Industries in Argentina, 2000–2005

Source: Authors.

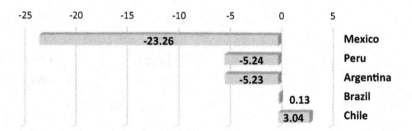

FIGURE 5.2 Average Profitability for Telecom Companies, 2000–2005

Source: Authors.

Finally, in addition to industry- and country-based influences, companies show systematic profitability differences within an industry. This means that environmental conditions are compounded by what companies do and how they do it. For example, Figure 5.3 shows the dispersed profitability average among Chilean retailers from 2000 to 2005.

Of course, the question is, which element – industry, country or company – has the most influence over an organization's profitability? One way to answer this question is to use the variance decomposition statistical technique, breaking down the variance among organizations' results and establishing the share of the variance determined by what an organization does, the industry where it competes and the country where it operates. Specific years are also a factor.

These four effects are known as permanent, because their influence on corporate profitability is sustained, year after year. Permanent effects do not include the exogenous shocks that change every year and prove hard to anticipate. In everyday terms, these shocks may be characterized as strokes of luck or misfortune; they are viewed as transitory or random effects, and they are not included in our core analysis.[1] Table 5.1 illustrates the relative impact of permanent and random effects on return variance, based on Return On Assets (ROA) figures for 12,000 companies across 448 industries and seventy-eight countries.

The first observation worth noting is that nearly half of companies' profitability is determined rather randomly, whereas the other half is influenced by permanent effects, which are subject to companies' intervention – albeit with varying degrees of freedom.

It is also clear that the company effect weighs more heavily than the decision to compete in one industry over another or in a specific country. The company effect

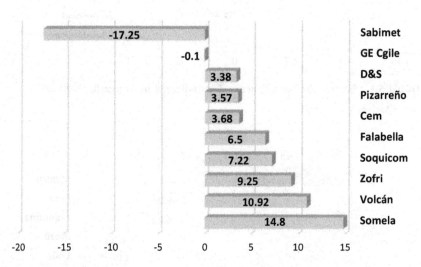

FIGURE 5.3 Average Profitability of Chilean Retailers, 2000–2005

Source: Authors.

TABLE 5.1 Breakdown of Permanent Effects on Industry Returns

Effects	Percentage
Permanent Effects	
Organization	26.58
Industry	3.15
Country	6.08
Industry-Country	12.49
Year	1.08
Random Effect	50.62
TOTAL	100.00

Source: Author.

encompasses everything an organization systematically does in a unique way – that is, the distinctive capabilities it has been able to create. Next comes the country-industry interaction effect, also known as the cluster effect (Porter, 1998). Separately, the relative weight of the industry and country effects on return composition varies from one industry to another. The industry effect is associated with the competitive isolation mechanisms in an industry, making it more or less attractive.

Some of the best-known competitive isolation mechanisms include economies of scale (lowering costs by increasing output levels), economies of scope (reducing costs by diversifying product portfolios), learning economies (lower production costs as experience increases), consumers' switching costs, product differentiation and network externalities (users' benefit upon acquiring a product increases since more users already have it). In turn, the country effect is associated with the consequences of economic cycles and the institutional context faced by every organization.

While interesting, the data provided by Brito and Vasconcelos (2006) has two significant limitations: first, they make no distinction between developed and developing countries, and second, they do not differentiate companies with higher profitability rates from those with lower profitability rates. These issues will be tackled in the next section.

The relative weight of the country effect changes when we consider profitability rates for companies in the developed world and their counterparts in the emerging world. A study on Japanese multinational affiliates found that the country effect weighs twice as much in emerging countries as it does in developed nations (Makino, Isobe & Chan, 2004). Does this mean that differentiation proves harder to accomplish in emerging countries? Does it mean that strategic formulation is carried out with less freedom in emerging countries than in developed countries? Our answer to both questions is a resounding no.

Rather, these data suggest that strategic formulation has different nuances in emerging economies but has the same or more likelihood of success if those nuances are acknowledged adequately. To delve into these issues, Díaz-Hermelo and Vassolo (2010) conducted a study on extraordinary return sustainability in

Latin America, comparing returns with those in similar studies carried out in the United States and Europe. The empirical evidence in developed economies shows that only 5 percent of companies that achieve extraordinary results manage to maintain them at the top of their industries for more than ten years. If extraordinary results are considered proof of a successful strategy, they indicate that success is possible but difficult to sustain – at least in the developed world.

What happens in emerging economies? After examining the returns of companies listed in stock exchanges in Latin America from 1990 to 2006, the authors established that, on average, 8.5 to 16 percent of companies that reached the top managed to stay at the top for longer than ten years. This finding leads to a valuable conclusion: having a sustainable successful strategy seems more likely in Latin America than in developed countries. In other words, there seems to be less mobility among leading companies in Latin America than in the developed world. Companies that reach the top in Latin America appear to be more likely to remain there for long periods of time.

Díaz-Hermelo and Vassolo also found extraordinary returns to be more sustainable in certain countries, like Chile, Mexico and Peru, and less sustainable in Brazil, the largest economy in Latin America, where extraordinary return sustainability rates proved similar to those in the United States. A number of key questions surface as a result: Why does this happen? How do Latin American companies operate to secure sustainable extraordinary returns? What factors should be taken into account when formulating strategies in Latin America?

In a later study, Díaz-Hermelo, Vassolo and Rodríguez (2012) examined the performance of companies competing in Latin America and divided their sample into subsamples to separate companies with superior results from those with results below their industry's average. They found that permanent effects prove more significant for high-performing companies than for those with lower performance. That is, companies with poor results in Latin America seem to be more affected by random factors established by the environment than companies with higher performance. At the same time, the element that seems to provide more stability to corporate profitability is the company effect more so than country and industry effects.

In the following sections, we offer several frameworks to analyze the strategic impact of the two variables – industry and country – which are external to the organization and shape the competitive environment.

Industry strategic analysis

An industry or sector determines the immediate context within which a company must perform and within which it is possible to find similar organizations. Although these organizations are not identical, they satisfy similar needs with similar business models. Their similarities support the notion of an industry and enable the rigorous incorporation of the competitive environment into strategic analyses. An industry or competitive environment features a life cycle, with clearly established stages, as shown in Figure 5.4.

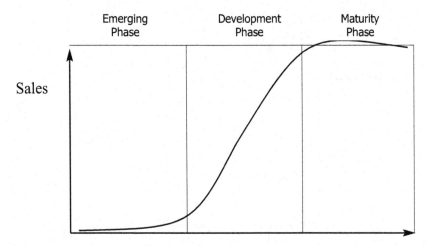

FIGURE 5.4 Industry Life Cycle Stages

Source: Author.

These stages unfold in every industry in a similar fashion and stem from the breakthrough innovation–imitation dynamics, which are triggered in the market when an organization manages to supply a product or service that meets a need in a novel manner. This innovation may relate to a new technology or a modified business model. The innovative nature of the product or service, or its production or distribution, sharply increase its value in the market. When its viability and success are proven, the innovation brings extraordinary returns for the organization and drives competitors to imitate it. New competitors join the market, trying to replicate the innovating company's capabilities, as shown in Figure 5.5.

The first stage, known as the emerging phase, is characterized by significant technological and market uncertainty: the industry's future structure is unknown. Organizations operating in this stage do not yet fully understand the need they have to satisfy, nor do they know what product or service standards will be like, and their business model remains unclear. Emerging phases in industries can last years. Within the innovation–imitation dynamics, this stage unfolds before the breakthrough. From a strategic formulation standpoint, businesses in emerging states will translate into corporate exploration initiatives. The priority in this stage zeros in on searching, learning and finding.

At some point, those searches bear fruit, and thus, a radical innovation emerges. The industry's development phase starts. The need to be filled becomes more clearly defined; standards are established, and business models are finalized. One of the most hectic, beautiful races in industries' life cycles starts at this juncture, with booming demand and a resultant wave of imitations. This time holds a rare charm, as everything seems to grow without any boundaries. With a huge unsatisfied demand, the pressure exerted by imitators (the so-called competitive pressure) does not take too heavy a toll: margins are healthy, and profitability is high.

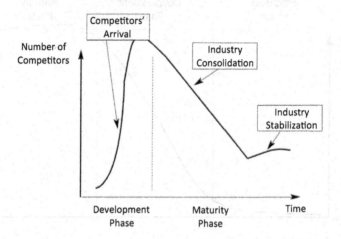

FIGURE 5.5 Number of Competitors in an Industry across Its Life Cycle Stages
Source: Author.

During the development phase, it is necessary to set a course (variables to drive growth swiftly) and focus the entire organization's attention in the pursuit of that goal. The ability to do this will determine the competitive position that the organization will hold and enjoy in its maturity. The development phase comes with an imperative: grow. As a result, strategic initiatives at this point underscore actions that enable quick market coverage, even at the risk of creating some efficiency issues for the sake of accomplishing that goal.

How fast should a company grow when a company is competing in a developing industry? That will depend on the consolidation expectations for maturity, which will hinge on building competitive isolation mechanisms. At this stage, the greater the ability to put these mechanisms in place, the greater the need for speedy market coverage, with companies running the risk of failing to become large enough and secure a sustainable positioning by the time growth starts to slow down.

When an industry becomes mature, competitive pressures reach their full intensity. Low market growth rates prove insufficient to support profitability for all the companies competing in the previous phase. Prices and margins drop. Mergers and acquisitions become commonplace, and the number of companies leaving the market increases. The companies that remain in the race turn their attention to enhancing their production performance (cost management, productivity, process improvements) and marketing practices (promotions, customer loyalty) – that is, the primary activities in their value chains. It comes as no surprise that mature industries largely feature oligopolies, characterized by a few large competitors dominating the market and greater risks of collusion. In this phase, strategic initiatives generally focus on cost efficiency, customer retention and rather sophisticated formal organizational processes.

Niche strategies deserve a dedicated note. Some competitors specialize in serving specific needs – which is theoretically unappealing for large companies. Usually, niche strategies prove sustainable when pursued in mature businesses, but they may turn out to be extremely risky for sustainability if they are pursued during an industry's development phase.

How the country environment influences strategies

Industries develop within countries, which in turn feature their own rich and complex realities and unique evolution patterns. Two country environmental factors influence industry development and, as a result, the competitive context where companies operate. The first refers to a country's economic evolution – or, more precisely, the changes in macroeconomic conditions. An industry or sector grows in the midst of an economy, and what happens in that economy fully impacts that industry. The second factor is linked to a country's institutional setup: institutions establish the rules of the game that industries and companies must follow. The ability to sway these playing rules leads to a set of strategies known as "non-market" strategies.

Industry life cycle in an emerging context

To analyze the impact of a macroeconomic cycle in emerging countries on industry life cycles, we will use the example of Argentina's mobile telephone sector, as depicted in Figure 5.6.

To explain these phenomena, we use terms coined by the economist Guillermo Calvo: *sudden stop* and *phoenix miracle*. A sudden stop is a sharp downturn experienced by a country's gross domestic product (GDP), caused by a marked decline in foreign capital inflows. In turn, a phoenix miracle occurs when an economy reemerges from the ashes, just like the mythical bird, shortly after suffering a severe crisis. It appears that the sudden stop in 2001–2002 brought Argentina's development to a halt, followed by a speedy recovery to make up for the "lost time."

In other words, sharp GDP downturns apparently do not thwart industries' core evolution process (their life cycle); rather, they seem to slow them down and later strengthen their development. Thus, it may be safe to expect a sustained industry life cycle evolution pattern in emerging countries, even if their behavior is not as smooth as it is in the developed world (see Figure 5.7).

Nonetheless, even if an industry's aggregated demand follows the pattern shown in Figure 5.4 that characterizes its life cycle, recurring crises may structurally upset the rivalry among industries. Particularly, a temporary shift in demand may permanently alter an industry's structure, especially when its impact proves so strong that it forces financially weaker companies out of business. Recovering lost territory might be impossible for companies with lower funding capability in times of economic growth. As a result, industries may consolidate more than their counterparts in stable macroeconomic contexts (Garcia-Sanchez, Mesquita & Vassolo, 2014).

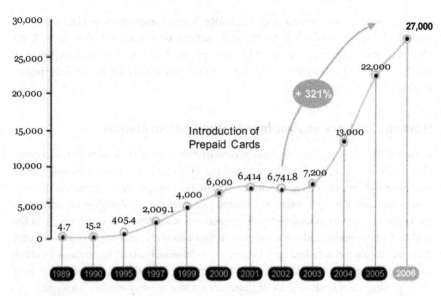

FIGURE 5.6 Argentina's Mobile Phone Life Cycle

Source: "De la estrategia a la comunicación," CCR Group, based on data from Argentina's Census and Statistics Bureau (INDEC), August 2006. Figures in thousands.

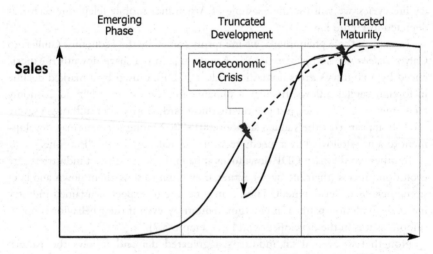

FIGURE 5.7 Effects of a Macroeconomic Crisis on an Industry's Life Cycle

Source: Author.

A complex phenomenon surfaces here. On one hand, we know that mature industries undergo a consolidation period that depends on its competitive isolation mechanisms. On the other hand, economic crises can also unleash consolidation processes, for different reasons and at different times. Strategists have to properly distinguish between these processes to avoid incoherent strategic choices, responding as if it were one process when it is actually another. Thus, there are at least two types of misconstructions that can be made when interpreting an industry's situation in emerging environments.

The first is confusing the consolidation driven by industry dynamics with one actually caused by a macroeconomic shock. The second error is mistaking the growth stemming from a macroeconomic bounceback for the characteristic growth expected in an industry's development phase. As a result, a company operating in an environment with characteristics of emerging economies will face the following conditions:

1   Temporary demand curve displacement
2   Increased competitive rivalry resulting from demand curve displacement
3   Transitory lack of credit during recessions
4   Changes in relative prices for production factors
5   Potential relative industry consolidation compared to similar industries in developed countries

Such a context generates a number of strategic formulation recommendations that incorporate macroeconomic cycles into industry life cycles, avoiding the need for an arbitrage strategy based solely on macroeconomic cycles.

First, because we are in an emerging environment, we are likely to face sudden aggregated changes in demand, which will warrant planning installed capacity (and therefore fixed costs) accordingly. While it may seem trivial, this has proven to be difficult, especially when an economic bounceback unfolds and expansion seems never-ending. There is also tension between the need to minimize fixed costs and holding the company's market share. Balancing these needs requires a lot of creativity for anticipating installed capacity requirements.

Indebtedness also adds rigidity. Generally speaking, companies in emerging environments should have lower financial leverage than their counterparts, within stable contexts. Also, companies should aim to maintain a balance between foreign trade and the domestic market to shield it from abrupt price changes and to exploit the opportunities that these changes confer. In other words, it is imperative to diversify country risks within these contexts.

Finally, organizational unity and talent management are crucial. Companies that foster these aspects will fare far better and react with greater clarity during macroeconomic storms than their competitors. Indeed, a cohesive management team may be the best defense in the face of a crisis, which also ties into the critical aspect of corporate social responsibility. In times of crisis, top management teams may be inclined to address economic problems by firing employees straightaway. But this decision is particularly harmful to those affected since during recessions, the unemployment rate grows, so finding new employment is extremally difficult. Managers faced with this challenge would be wise to retain their talent pool during downturns and avoid taking the easy way out, namely firing employees as a means to curtail losses. Moreover, recessions are often a good time to hire talent that would be more difficult to attain during periods of stable economic growth.

Recessions: a window of opportunity for leapfrogging

We have already described macroeconomic shocks as events that affect industry as a whole due to lower aggregated demand and that drive weaker competitors out of business. Companies with greater experience and productive and financial flexibility that have leveraged their industry's competitive isolation mechanisms will be better positioned to weather recessions.

However, macroeconomic events can significantly affect order-of-entry advantages, enabling newcomers to leverage an economic downturn, even in industries with high barriers to entry. As an example, Hyundai commanded successful upturns in financial performance and market share during the 2008 economic depression (see Figure 5.8). Having entered the US automobile industry later than most of its rivals, it lagged behind incumbents in expertise, process technologies, market space and other path-dependent assets. Remarkably, it overcame these weaknesses by playing up old skills that temporarily became more valuable.

What skills are important within this context? What characteristics must a new entrant possess, and what strategies must it deploy to maximize its chances for success in a recession? In what instances will new entrants succeed in displacing an incumbent during a macroeconomic shock?

First, we must acknowledge that when demand is more heterogeneous, we can classify it into two broad categories: high-end users and low-end users. Innovators view the customer from a social cognitive perspective, focusing on users' experience as the primary need to be fulfilled and creating a cultural imprint. Therefore, innovators ground their strategy on the uniqueness of their value proposition for users, serving high-end markets and creating new disruptions (Christensen & Raynor, 2013).

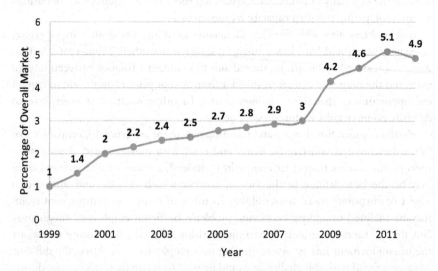

FIGURE 5.8 Hyundai's US Market Share Growth, 1999–2012

Source: Automotive News Data Center.

On the other hand, new entrants build their strategy on sharp decreases in price performance. They consider the customer as a rational, economic being, offer the customer affordability and thus address a low-end mass market. Economic shocks exogenously induce industry discontinuities that shift customers' required value from enhanced experience to affordability, affecting the competitive advantages associated with non-turbulent contexts. As a result, recessions prevent incumbents' advantages while giving new entrants the opportunity to catch up and even over-take incumbents (Sevil, Murcia & Vassolo, 2016). Importantly, these changes can affect the long-term competitive landscape, so they differ from typical downturn effects, as shown in Figure 5.9.

A recent example of a new entrant leapfrogging an incumbent was in the smart-phone operating system industry, when Android was able to seize a window of opportunity created by the 2008 financial downturn to overtake iOS.

In 2007, Apple launched the iPhone with its iOS operating system, unveiling the convergence of traditional mobile telephony, internet services and personal computers. A year later, Apple introduced the Apple Store, a virtual store for all sorts of applications, creating a dynamic software-based platform ecosystem – a disruptive innovation that completely changed the competitive landscape of the entire smartphone operating system industry. In 2008, Google launched the first Android-based mobile phone, offering moderate, affordable performance to target

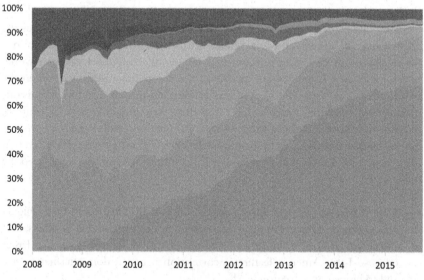

FIGURE 5.9 Smartphone Operating System Industry Market Share Evolution (Worldwide)

Source: Statcounter 2016. http://gs.statcounter.com/#mobile_os-ww-monthly-200812-201609, accessed in October 2016.

a huge underserved market. The appealing value proposition that Android offered was boosted by the global crisis, allowing it to leapfrog iOS and reign as the leading operating system by 2010.

The cases of Hyundai and Android illustrate that under the effects of a recession, an installed base advantage does not provide a safety net for incumbents. This challenges two prevailing beliefs: first, industry endogenous variables suffice to understand market dynamics, and second, as a result, incumbents are better prepared than new entrants to face slump economic conditions.

The second belief is that new entrants overtake incumbents because of higher functionality or technology. On the contrary, managers in turbulent macro-environments should take into account potential demand shifts and threats from new competitors that ground their strategy on improved price-performance propositions.

Non-market strategies

Emerging economies feature environments that are in many ways far more complex than those found in developed economies. In the developed world, businesses – and therefore strategic analyses – center on technological developments and market changes, while in emerging countries, the institutional context represents the main source of uncertainty. The fact that institutional context stands as a central factor does not preclude other sources of uncertainty. Rather, it compounds them, which makes leadership in these environments particularly complex.

When we speak of institutions, we refer specifically to the legal framework that regulates companies' introduction into markets and societies and that shapes the relationships among stakeholders. Unlike what occurs in the developed world, a salient feature in emerging economies is frequently changing legal frameworks, which add a new source of uncertainty in the competitive landscape. When the government does not assure institutional stability, institutions turn into a decision-making and operating variable for companies. Strategies that aim to confront industry dynamics stemming from institutional environment changes are known as non-market strategies. A 1978 study (Meller, 1978) on concentration levels at eighteen manufacturing industries in ten Latin American countries concluded the following:

- Latin American countries share a similar concentration structure – that is, highly concentrated industries in one country tend to be concentrated in others.
- Industries tend to be more concentrated in smaller countries than in larger ones, so Latin America features a correlation between domestic market size and industry concentration levels.

In turn, the ownership of large companies is also more concentrated in Latin American than in developed countries. When this concentration comes hand in hand with imperfect instruments to shield off competitors, the ability of large business groups to lobby and sway power in their favor can prove unusually strong.

For large companies, the creation of business groups often provides a means to mitigate institutional instability and at the same time boost organizational size and relevance.

Business groups are holdings of companies controlled by a single family or investor group that don't necessarily have interlinking operations. The prevalence of large business groups in a country is depicted in the ownership concentration data in Table 5.2, which shows the share of large companies owned by family business groups in a selection of countries across three continents. Countries with highly developed capital markets and low institutional turmoil – such as the United Kingdom, the United States and Germany – feature low ownership concentration levels. On the contrary, countries with a history of economic and institutional instability – like Argentina, Brazil and the Philippines – display high ownership concentration levels.

Ownership concentration across several industries and businesses brings benefits and costs. On the upside, companies are capable of influencing the institutional framework to protect themselves from changes that might impact their operations. Large conglomerates draw advantages from their power over financial and labor sectors, accessing key resources at lower rates than other companies and transferring resources from one business unit to another when necessary. By building a favorable reputation in emerging markets, these business groups become the most appealing partners for foreign investors. Finally, business groups can achieve economies of scale via lobbying efforts, which enables them to exercise more leverage when facing strong negotiating agents, such as unions.

On the downside, these groups experience inefficiencies from several sources. First, managing unrelated companies adds operating costs to each business. Second, taking advantage of synergies may prove elusive since the requirements to compete in different businesses tend to be quite dissimilar. Finally, from a dynamic standpoint, belonging to the same owners may jeopardize or limit the businesses' ability to innovate.

The institutional context must be factored into strategic formulations through specific initiatives. In other words, if a strategic plan does not contemplate specific

TABLE 5.2 Percentage of Large Companies Owned by Family Business Groups in Selected Countries

Europe		Americas		Asia	
Denmark	6	Argentina	85	Hong Kong	43
France	38	Brazil	91	Taiwan	73
Germany	7	Canada	42	South Korea	61
Spain	47	United States	19	Philippines	100
United Kingdom	16	Mexico	100	Singapore	16

Source: Adapted from Morck, R., Wolfenzon, D., and Yeung, B., Corporate Governance, Economic Entrenchment and Growth, presentation for the World Bank, January 2005.

efforts to deal with the institutional environment, it is likely to lead to blind spots that could put the company at risk. Non-market strategies should be considered by factoring in the institutional weakness in emerging economies and the need for companies to do something about it. Strategic plans must explicitly address this issue when establishing long-term efforts.

Also, the actions of large corporations directly affect the long-term institutional health of their countries of operations. The dark side of institutional weaknesses is that they provide an opening for big firms to leverage their power for corporate gain, at the expense of society as a whole. On the other hand, large ethically managed firms are in a unique position to spearhead positive change for the common good.

In the exercise of leadership at top management levels, an important facet of the CEO's agenda is to contribute to the overall improvement of the institutional contexts within which their organizations operate. This might imply sacrificing short-term benefits for the sake of sounder, long-term conditions. Such actions might imply coordination with other large corporations. Including institutional improvements should be a must on the agendas of top-tier executives who lead large Latin American firms.

Conclusions

Opportunities stem from change, which emerge from different sources and with dissimilar frequencies. Understanding current changes and, most importantly, anticipating future changes are critical for strategy formulation. Organizational success depends on having a set of processes that meet current demands. These processes are not acquired immediately – hence the need to read and anticipate scenarios. In turn, context has its own rules, and companies can't do whatever they want. Their respective context will provide the options for the potential positioning that organizations will choose.

Context and organizations interact, and as a result, there are organizations with high, moderate or poor performance. For this reason, CEOs should, first, gain a solid understanding of what happens in their industry; second, examine how macroeconomic volatility affects those dynamics and offers opportunities that would otherwise be unattainable; third, analyze what the non-market framework says; and, finally, review the organizational capabilities required to adapt to that context. The result will be a strategy, understood as the strategic priorities or initiatives that will guide the organization in coming years.

Note

1 Some random effects present regular or foreseeable behavior. These are known as self-regressive effects. Recent studies seem to indicate that they take up most of the profitability, but we have omitted them for the sake of simplicity and because they do not change relative sizes.

References

Brito, L. A. and Vasconcelos, F. C. (2006). "How Much does Country Matter." In Cooper, A., Alvarez, S., Carrera, A., Mesquita, L. and Vassolo, R. (eds.), *Entrepreneurial Strategies: New Technologies and Emerging Markets*, pp. 95–113. Oxford: Blackwell.

Christensen, C. M. and Raynor, M. (2013). *The Innovator's Solution: Creating and Sustaining Successful Growth*. Boston, MA: Harvard Business Review Press.

Díaz-Hermelo, F. and Vassolo, R. (2010). "Institutional Development and Hypercompetition in Emerging Economies." *Strategic Management Journal*, 31(13): 1457–1473.

Garcia-Sanchez, J., Mesquita, L. F. and Vassolo, R. (2014). "What Doesn't Kill You Makes You Stronger: The Evolution of Competition and Entry-Order Advantages in Economically Turbulent Contexts." *Strategic Management Journal*, 35(13): 1972–1992.

Makino, S., Isobe, T. and Chan, C. (2004). "Does Country Matter?" *Strategic Management Journal*, 25(10): 1027–1043.

Meller, P. (1978). "The Pattern of Industrial Concentration in America." *The Journal of Industrial Economics*, XXVII.

Porter, M. (1998). "Clusters and the New Economics of Competition.". *Harvard Business Review*, 76(6), November–December: 77–90.

Sevil, A., Murcia, M. J. and Vassolo, R. (2016). "Platform Competition in Unstable Contexts," Presented at the Academy of Management Annual Meeting, Anaheim, California.

Vassolo, R., Díaz-Hermelo, F. and Rodríguez, I. (2012). "How Much Does Country Matter in Emerging Economies? Evidence from Latin America." *International Journal of Emerging Markets*, 7(3): 263–288.

6

ENVIRONMENTAL SENSIBILITY AND FIRM STRATEGIC ACTIONS

How to become sustainable while avoiding greenwashing

Mike Rosenberg, Pascual Berrone and Horacio Rousseau

A little more than fifty years since the publication of Rachel Carson's *Silent Spring* (1962), concern for our natural environment has become a widespread and fundamental concern for civil society. Carson's book is commonly regarded as a milestone in environmentalism since it openly challenged the consequences of industrialization and increased public concern and awareness on a subject that had until that time been of little interest. Since the book's publication, environmental issues have been written into government regulation and become standard business practice in North America, Europe, Japan, Latin America and even less developed countries.

This increase in legal regulation coincided with a general agreement regarding the sizable impact that human beings have on the planet. Environmental science shows that during the past century alone, the world extracted thirty-four times more natural resources than in previous times and that the use of fossil fuels went up by a factor of twelve. In other words, if societies continue deploying resources at the current rate, by the year 2050, we will need two planets to sustain us (EC, 2014). For these reasons, preoccupation with sustainability has reached new heightened levels in institutions, organizations and civil society.

Sustainability, however, has also entered into the political debate in many countries and while on the one hand international institutions such as the Intergovernmental Panel on Climate Change (IPCC) are warning that the world has only a short window available to avoid catastrophic impacts (IPCC, 2018), a number of elected officials continue to reject climate science and vow to protect the fossil fuel industry. This chapter takes a decidedly apolitical approach to the issue and will focus instead on the present state of play in the world of business and the strategic choices facing firms in the years ahead.

Given the social importance placed on environmental issues, it is unsurprising to witness the growing preeminence of firm sustainability within the top management's agenda. While scholars recognize that corporate responses to environmental challenges were slow and reactive during the first waves of environmentalism in the 1960s and 1970s (Berrone, 2016), current corporate initiatives aimed at promoting responsible and sustainable business approaches are numerous and frequently challenge the dominant market logic of free trade and profit maximization (Berrone, Fosfuri, & Gelabert, 2017; Waddock, 2008). These initiatives reflect the critical role played by society in exerting pressures on companies by increasing the expectations on firms' environmental performance and the level of transparency in their operations and reporting.

While some studies argue that this upsurge of interest on environmental matters is attributable to the role of values and moral motivations (Bansal, 2003), most of the literature suggests that firms embrace sustainable practices mainly as a way to gain social legitimacy (Berrone, Gelabert & Fosfuri, 2009; Hoffman, 2001). Legitimacy is a "generalized perception or assumption that the actions of an entity are desirable, proper, or appropriate within some socially constructed system of norms, values, beliefs, and definitions" (Suchman, 1995, p. 574). Legitimacy is strategically important for organizations since it grants them a social license to operate (Oliver, 1991), which is a particularly critical resource in environmentally sensitive industries. As shown by Bansal (2005) in her longitudinal study of Canadian oil and gas, forestry, and mining firms, corporate sustainable development is largely driven by social legitimacy concerns. Additionally, her study found that organizational capabilities such as international experience and organizational size were important drivers of corporate sustainable development, therefore showing how internal organizational features also determined how firms responded to institutional pressures.

Increased expectations for firm sustainability also stem from sources other than social pressures, including both market and non-market actors. Non-market actors, such as national and supra-national regulatory agencies, NGOs and even religious authorities are now making their presence felt in the corporate landscape. The importance of non-market actors lies in their relentless efforts to monitor firms' environmental behaviors based on strong beliefs and values regarding the environment. These motivations are particularly strong in environmental organizations, therefore compelling firms to learn how to deal with activists' claims and pressures in a reasonable way.

In the West, firms now take for granted landmark legislation enacted largely in the 1960s and 1970s which protects air and water quality and regulates several aspects of how businesses interact with the natural environment. Legislation has become even stricter in recent decades, with legal sanctions that can eventually lead to penal prosecutions for managers (Gray & Shimshack, 2011). Regarding the actions of environmental NGOs, the increasing popularity of green campaigns is undeniable, leading to substantive changes in polluting sectors (Hoffman, 1999) by successfully increasing public awareness and prompting most businesses and industries to claim to be on board with the green phenomenon. In this regard, the business sector can no longer ignore the part it plays. With or without its consent, the push for environmental sustainability has ultimately transformed into the push for corporate sustainability.

Market actors also represent a major force behind the adoption of sustainable practices. An growing segment of consumers thinks about the environmental impact of what they do. They routinely recycle glass, plastics and paper and pay attention to the environmental reputation of the companies with whom they do business. Increasing environmental awareness has become evident in the role played by shareholders. Forty-six years ago, Friedman (1970) famously noted that the social responsibility of firms was to increase their profits; nowadays it is responsible investors themselves who are using their equity stake in corporations to put public pressure on its management. This form of shareholder activism has gained popularity in publicly traded companies during recent years and shifted the focus from standard corporate governance issues (such as management pay) to environmental and social-related aspects (i.e., reporting environmental impacts).

Research in this area has shown that shareholder proposals presented at shareholder meetings act not only as a reflection of minority shareholders discontent (Martin, Gomez-Mejia & Makri, 2016; Martin, Gómez–Mejía, Berrone, & Makri, 2017). But also as an effective mechanism for responsible investors to spark a dialogue with senior executives and board members about firms' social and environmental behaviors (Rousseau, Berrone & Walls, 2014). Furthermore, researchers have found that companies financially reward CEOs who lead firms with better environmental performance, especially when using long-term proactive strategies such as pollution prevention (Berrone & Gomez-Mejia, 2009).

Historically, the aforementioned pressures to increase firm sustainability were mostly a concern for firms operating in North America and Europe. In recent years, however, firms in Latin America have also started including sustainable matters as a core part of their strategic agenda. A significant driver behind this change lies in a shift in attitudes, values and preferences regarding environmental matters among the Latin American population. A recent study of over one thousand people from Argentina, Peru, Chile, Mexico and Colombia, led by the trend observatory Trendsity (Mociulsky & Alarcón, 2016), provides evidence of a new generation of "sustainable natives" in the region.

Sustainable natives grew up with high levels of environmental awareness and consider themselves to be the first generation that is truly committed to safeguarding the environment. Trendsity's study suggests that the increased environmental concern from younger generations will have broad strategic implications for firms in the region. Almost 80 percent of the respondents consider that firms are responsible (and liable) for environmental degradation, and almost 60 percent are willing to pay a price premium for greener products. Hence, Latin American firms willing to maintain their social license to operate and cater their products to these generations will need to develop a strategy that prioritizes environmental goals.

Other evidence, echoing Trendsity's report, suggests that the need to strategically respond to various demands for corporate sustainability will not fade in the short term and that demands made by market and non-market actors will only increase. In fact, environmental requirements continue to be legitimized, not only by the civil society itself but also by authoritative figures, including political leaders such as Al Gore and public figures such as the award-winning actor Leonardo DiCaprio. Even religious leaders such as Pope Francis have provided strong support for the environmental movement by releasing an encyclical letter highlighting the moral aspects embedded in environmental destruction. The letter calls for renewed environmental awareness, especially among business leaders (Pope Francis, 2015), and presents sustainability as a moral imperative.

In spite of these important endorsements and a growing environmental awareness, not all firms embrace the challenge to improve their environmental behavior. Firms who are unwilling or even incapable of consistently reducing their environmental impact tend to resort to "symbolic" actions (as opposed to substantive actions). These symbolic actions are aimed at influencing public perception without altering core practices. In the next section, we explore this issue in greater depth.

Symbolic responses to the growing demands for sustainability: the rise of greenwashing

Despite executive interest in sustainability, practice has taught us that profiting from environmental initiatives is a long and winding road. Most companies have a difficult time when it comes to bridging the gap between green concerns and green consumerism, manufacturing green products without sacrificing quality and understanding what it means to be a green business in the first place. For the most part, becoming a green company takes a sizable amount of resources, time and risks (Bansal & DesJardine, 2014), frequently demanding not only the adoption of long-term strategies but also the redesign of current routines and processes. Such difficulties have driven many opportunistic companies to try to reap the benefits and value derived from "greening" the company on the outside without making the necessary investments on the inside; scholars have labeled this a symbolic response to institutional pressures (Short & Toffel, 2010).

Dominant among such responses is the practice of greenwashing. Greenwashing is defined as "marketing or PR intended to deceive consumers into believing that a company is practicing environmentally friendly policies and procedures" (Lane, 2013). Companies that engage in greenwashing aim to improve the firm's legitimacy, reputation and market capitalization without investing the necessary resources to substantively improve their environmental performance. Greenwashing is not new. In 1972, Jerry Mander, a former advertising executive, observed that contaminating sectors such as the oil and gas, automobile, and chemical industries were spending an average of US$1 billion a year on green advertising, with visual images that included animals like dolphins and seals, while investing next to nothing in pollution control (Mander, 1972). This situation worsened over time. Industrial accidents in the 1970s and 1980s increased pressure on corporations, and by 1990, around 25 percent of all household products introduced into the US market were advertised with at least one identifiable green attribute (CorpWatch, 2001). However, with firms making all sorts of environmental claims, the public became skeptical and started to question the real motives behind these branding efforts.

Such actions ultimately backfired as skepticism among consumers, and NGOs spread rapidly, shattering business credibility along with it.

The decrease in business credibility led to an increase in firm monitoring and in a greater social demand for transparency and accountability. Primary and secondary stakeholders have taken a proactive stance on contrasting firms' environmental claims with their actual behaviors. These critical stakeholders do not hesitate to penalize firms through a wide range of different means when they suspect that greenwashing is going on. These penalties are not only reputational but also financial. Empirical studies have shown that financial penalties include negative reactions from stock analysts, higher financial volatility and lower survival rates (Bansal & Clelland, 2004; Ortiz-de-Mandojana & Bansal, 2015).

While there are substantial dangers for firms that engage in greenwashing, the risks are even greater for firms operating in strong polluting industries (Berrone & Gomez-Mejia, 2009). One clear example is the recent Volkswagen scandal, which presented itself as a company that was actively committed to environmental stewardship. However, the company was caught rigging diesel engine emissions tests in North America and Europe by installing software devices in engines that could detect when they were being tested, enabling them to change their performance and improve results. Such cheating didn't go unpunished. A few days after the scandal broke, company shares plunged 30 percent as investors realized the costs associated not only with a damaged brand and low customer trust but also with potential litigation. The US Environmental Protection Agency (EPA) alone sought to fine Volkswagen up to US$18 billion (Berrone, 2016). Analysts estimate that several years will pass before Volkswagen can regain consumer and public trust (Medland, 2016).

Despite these negative consequences and the existence of many other high-profile cases in which corporate value was destroyed by greenwashing, many companies still fail to perceive the real dangers of deceptive symbolic actions. Such dangers have reached new levels due to the lower costs of monitoring and the greater availability of information. More intense monitoring means greater difficulty in faking and getting away with unrealistic environmental claims, especially when the company belongs to an environmentally sensitive industry. Moreover, there is a competitive dimension to greenwashing. Symbolic actions are easily imitated by rival firms, having become so much the norm as to be virtually meaningless. Consequently, companies stand little chance of differentiating themselves from their rivals based on environmental marketing or PR alone. In fact, firms that merely adopt environmental behavior in a symbolic manner without pursuing substantive actions may be perceived as deceitful and suffer reputational harm that could seriously undermine corporate performance.

In sum, the message is clear: although firms might be tempted to greenwash, the results are generally disastrous since the truth eventually comes out. On the one hand, pressures on businesses to be sustainable will grow because society and firms' stakeholders, in particular, are increasingly unwilling to accept a poor corporate environmental track record. The focus that powerful stakeholders now have on environmental issues requires that top managers start thinking strategically about firm sustainability. On the other hand, increased monitoring and greater transparency has eliminated greenwashing as an option. Faced with this dead-end situation, what can CEOs do to start creating a path toward sustainability in a way that is aligned with their firm's situation? In the next section, we offer a framework for the development of a substantive, firm-specific sustainability strategy.

A framework for the development of firm sustainability

Since the chances of becoming sustainable effortlessly and overnight are slim and the temptation to engage in symbolic actions such as greenwashing is high, CEOs need to know the first steps to take to move their firms in the desired direction. With this purpose in mind, we offer a framework (based on the work by Rosenberg, 2015) that provides an approach for understanding a firm's starting point with respect to the issue of environmental sustainability. Our framework acknowledges that the development of firm sustainability cannot be based on a one-size-fits-all approach. To be effective, it needs to consider the businesses that the firm is in; the markets it serves; and the characteristics of its shareholders, board and management team.

The overall framework helps identify two aspects of a firm's situation. The first is the firm's *environmental sensibility*, which refers to the relationship that the people involved with the firm have with the natural environment. Several factors lead to environmental sensibility, and the purpose here is not to say that a greater or lower intensity of these factors is better or worse but to provide a factual checklist to determine what it is. Among these factors, we include the following:

- The nature of the business itself, since some industries – such as energy, mining and certain heavy industries – face much greater scrutiny than other sectors so, such as most service industries.
- The level of commitment from shareholders, who may have a deep interest in environmental causes and potentially trade financial returns for ecological value added.
- The intensity of outside pressures, which can lead to an increase in environmental sensibility since the attention of special interests and the news media will force managers and employees to pay more attention to the environmental impact of the company.
- The interest of employees and customers in environmental issues, because a company will do more in this direction to maintain its customer base or to ensure that it remains an employer of choice.

The second aspect of the framework is the *level of compliance* that a company chooses to have with the myriad rules and regulations which affect its operations. While the option of noncompliance is not seriously considered, a firm can take a minimalist approach and simply set out to fulfill all the legal requirements in each territory in which it operates. Such a situation is legal and may represent the lowest cost alternative for some companies. Most firms, however, will frequently find enough reasons for taking actions that go *beyond compliance*. Reinhardt (1999) argues cogently that good reasons to go beyond compliance have to do with competitive strategy, increasing differentiation, cost reduction, redefining markets and hedging against risks in case the regulatory or market environment changes in the future. Gray and Shimshack (2011) argue that another reason to go beyond compliance could be to attempt to mollify public opinion and thus forestall the development of more stringent environmental regulations. These reasons, as well as ethical conviction, may lead executives to become highly interested in strategies that allow their firms to surpass the minimal requirements.

Figure 6.1 plots environmental sensibility against the level of compliance and shows six strategic options that fall along the diagonal. For example, a firm that has a minimal level of compliance and low sensibility may choose to follow the strategy referred to as *take the low road*. The *wait-and-see* option implies a slightly higher level of both compliance and sensibility, and even greater sensibility is required to fully implement a *show-and-tell* strategy. Both *think-ahead* and *pay-for-principle* options are about adopting leading positions in compliance but perhaps different levels of sensibility.

Interestingly, choosing to *break the law* requires a higher level of environmental sensibility than simply complying with it, since some level of risk analysis and cost-benefit analysis should be conducted before pursuing such a choice. Except for *break the law*, there is nothing right or wrong about adopting any one of the other five options presented. What makes sense for one firm will be different than

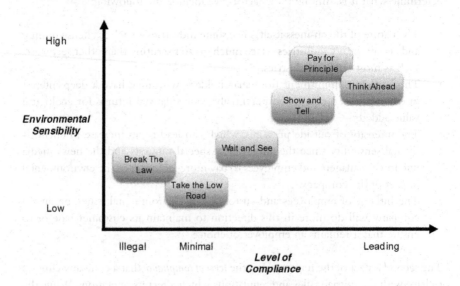

FIGURE 6.1 Strategic Options

Source: From Michael Rosenberg, Strategy and Sustainability, 2015, Palgrave Macmillan, p. 91.

what makes sense for another. While the scale for both sensibility and compliance shown on Figure 6.1 is only illustrative, each of the six strategic options is explored in sequence because the capabilities or functions that need to be developed are essentially cumulative in nature. Thus, a firm can move from one option to another by adding additional capabilities. Each strategic option will be discussed in more detail the next section.

Strategic options

Take the low road

The first strategic option shown in Figure 6.1 is referred to as *take the low road*. While taking the low road doesn't sound particularly appealing, it may be the most rational approach given a company's circumstances. The basic idea is to minimize the cost of compliance due to the CEO and the board understanding that environmental issues are of little strategic importance to the firm. This strategic option is based on the notion that not all firms share the same responsibility regarding their impact on the environment. While all firms (and people) have a certain environmental impact, the fact is that some firms have a much greater impact than others. Those who have a minor impact can therefore do their fair share by just complying with regulations and making sure they don't break any laws.

In many retail businesses, for example, the key issues are to get prime locations in strip malls and shopping centers, train employees and keep the cost of goods sold as low as possible and sales high by appealing to the mass market. One example is the owner of a small food franchise with just over a hundred outlets, which has adopted a positioning based on what sells in the food court – taste, value and fun. In this case, the senior management team, the franchise owner and the employees don't have any specific identification with environmental issues, nor do the customers. Thus, the approach is to comply with state health and safety laws, such as disposing of used cooking oil in a responsible way, and leave it at that. Energy and climate control are often provided by the shopping center and specific stores have little say in decisions about the energy mix, level of air conditioning and lighting. The chain chooses not to operate in California due to the state's strict environmental regulations.

If the chain were, however, one of the nation's largest, then the situation would be different. Consider the case of McDonald's and the issue of packaging. In November 1990, faced with a rising number of cities banning polystyrene plastic and rising pressure from its customers, McDonald's worked with the Environmental Defense Fund and abandoned its traditional "clamshell" box for hamburgers and replaced it with paper and cardboard. The new packaging had 90 percent less bulk and represented total cost savings for the company. But according to McDonald's officials at the time, the driver of this change was public perception and pressure. In such a case, the difference between McDonald's and the much smaller chain of restaurants mentioned above is its public profile, which intensifies its environmental sensibility.

In businesses with low environmental impact and little or no legislation affecting its operations, the environmental sensibility of senior management, employees and even customers may be relatively low. In such cases, *take the low road* may represent a realistic and appropriate strategic option, as many companies in the financial sector have realized. The Spanish bank BBVA, for instance, recognized that given its industry characteristics, it decided to adopt responsible banking rather than talk about corporate sustainability. While becoming a sustainable bank does not make much sense in the financial services industry, becoming a responsible bank does (Berrone, 2016).

Banco Santander Rio (Argentina) also takes a similar stand. For Santander Rio, being a responsible bank entails engaging in actions such as providing their customers with clear information to understand the consequences of different financial choices and providing training and education to vulnerable youth in small communities where the bank operates. By understanding how the specifics of their industry shape what it means to be sustainable for the firm, top management of both BBVA and Banco Santander Rio get the message across the firm in a way that appeals more directly to executives given the connection between responsible banking and the tasks that employees perform on a day-to-day basis.

From an implementation standpoint, it is important to make the choice explicit and work through the strategic implications, such as ensuring that neither the legal nor social license to operate are put at risk due to environmental issues, that there are no imminent catastrophic risks, that there is no disruptive technology on the horizon and that the basic assumptions concerning regulations, competitors and customers apply across all of the regions and countries in which the company operates, including its extended supply chain. In short, if CEOs choose to *take the low road*, they must make that choice explicit and carefully communicate it to the unit managers around the company who could misinterpret *take the low road* for implicit permission to cut corners and take risks with respect to compliance.

Break the law

Although we cannot recommend this strategy, we recognize the temptation for firms to do less than the law demands when the cost of compliance is high and no downside is perceived with noncompliance. The perception that there is no downside may result from a lack of economic penalties associated with the discovery of environmental wrongdoing, the low probability of being discovered or both. The strategy of breaking the law should not be confused with a firm which opts to *take the low road* and unwittingly goes over the line. In this case, senior management will take steps to correct a problem as soon as it is detected. With the *break-the-law* option, senior management try to either avoid specific rules or regulations or set up internal processes so that such infractions occur with statistically low frequency. The legal risks associated with this choice are significant, as governments in many countries are increasingly attempting to prosecute deliberate or even unintentional damage to the environment in criminal courts.

There are also strategic risks inherent in following this strategy that may outweigh legal issues. Firms face the possibility of being found out, not by the government but by motivated interest groups who might jump on the issue of noncompliance to attack the company and put its social license to operate at risk. There is also a deeper dimension associated that should be taken into account which has to do with the impact that such practice can have on the overall culture of the company. When senior management either directs its employees to disregard rules and regulations or sets up a managerial system in which they are encouraged to do so, it is requiring its own people to behave in an unethical manner. Doing so has both direct and indirect consequences.

A direct consequence is the degradation of the ethical climate: the "shared perceptions of prevailing organizational norms for addressing issues within a moral component" (Cohen, 1995: 51). A degraded ethical climate can reinforce the negative behaviors that led to wrongdoing in the first place, therefore severely affecting the firm's ability to comply with legal standards. It also diminishes individual job satisfaction and well-being and reduces organizational commitment (Martin & Cullen, 2006). An indirect effect of a degraded ethical climate is that it drives managerial attention to cheat instead of finding solutions, ultimately reducing the motivation to look for novel (and legal) ways to deal with environmental problems by developing enhanced internal capabilities (Rousseau, 2017). Hence, the question is that if managers encouraged or allowed to infringe certain rules, then what is to stop them from breaking others?

A final aspect of the *break-the-law* option, as shown visually in Figure 6.1, is that it requires higher environmental sensibility than the *take-the-low-road* option. The idea here may appear counterintuitive at first. To deliberately avoid compliance, one must first understand the cost of that compliance and then perform some sort of cost-benefit analysis to determine that it is better to not comply. This requires an accurate estimation of the financial implications of both sides of the equation. In contrast, a company that chooses to *take the low road* doesn't need to actually know the cost of compliance as a separate line item in its profit-and-loss accounts.

Wait and see

Moving up the diagonal of Figure 6.1, the next strategic option is to do more than the minimum in compliance and take a much more proactive stance in monitoring environmental issues in all five of the strategic issues we raised. The strategic logic of the *wait-and-see* option is to be ready to adjust the firms' practices, portfolio of products and services and communication policies if and when it is determined that it makes sense to do so.

There are four key functions for making this approach work. The first is to develop a process to assess the legal requirements for each operating unit and track its compliance with hard data. This represents a continuous process given the changing nature of environmental regulation. The second is to understand and track the firm's portfolio of products and services in terms of its environmental footprint, both in production and usage. The idea here is to leverage information systems (either new ones or modifying existing IT platforms) to gain accurate data on this subject.

With these two elements in place, the third key function is to actively monitor medium- and long-term trends in legislation, consumer response and the activities of environmental interest groups and social media to spot emerging trends that could have a wide strategic impact on the firm's competitive advantage or even in its daily operations. The fourth (and last) is to prepare different levels of management in advance of the possibility of a reaction in the future. This is because changing a firm's managerial culture is a complicated process and can take years to accomplish.

An interesting example of a *wait-and-see* approach is the PSA group, the company resulting from the merger of Peugeot and Citroën. While the firm was certainly not a first mover in the sustainability arena (it introduced its first electric car in 2010), it nonetheless actively monitored environmental trends that would influence the business, especially customer preferences. By doing so, it recognized the importance of achieving cutting-edge efficiency in car fuel consumption, a particularly important issue for European customers. While PSA initially waited to see how the sustainability trend would affect its industry and prepared itself by heavily investing in research-and-development activities, it is now a leader in environmental performance. Because of this position, in 2016 the company was able to join the Dow Jones Sustainability Index, the longest-running global sustainability benchmark and a key reference point for investors.

An implicit assumption with this option is that environmental issues will increase in importance over time. Therefore, CEOs need to develop internal capabilities by continuously diagnosing their firm's current situation and by integrating such knowledge into their management information systems. We expect that when a firm chooses to *wait and see*, environmental sensibility will increase over time, since collecting the technical data will begin to raise the awareness of environmental issues among those responsible for operations and management control. Sensibility will also increase in the marketing team, because it will be increasingly asked for data on environmental footprint of their products and services. Finally, an uptick will also occur among legal and corporate affairs professionals, who will be more frequently asked to track environmental legislation and interest groups. In fact, all this information could later be used to develop key performance indicators, at the individual and business unit levels.

The Argentinean dairy company Mastellone Hermanos SA provides a useful illustration of the value of the *wait-and-see* strategy. A family firm established in 1929, Mastellone embraces a strategy that allows them to be fully compliant with current regulations without losing flexibility to prepare for new challenges. For instance, the company recognizes that water is central for most of its industrial processes. While pressures on water usage are not currently strong in Argentina, the company perceives that regulation (and societal attitudes toward water use) could change rapidly in the future. To be ready for changes in water-related policies,

Mastellone is developing novel technologies that allow it to accurately track water use by process and product line and to measure the degree of toxicity of the effluents flowing into public waters. The firm is also engaging in a dialogue with different actors in their supply chain to increase their awareness regarding any possible shifts in environmental standards.

A final important consideration for a firm that follows the *wait-and-see* option is communication. Companies should be mindful of their communications to external stakeholders since the main objective of this strategy is to minimize the cost of compliance and avoid taking action until alignment is shown with the medium- and long-term interests of the firm. While this basic idea can be compelling for CEOs, it might be perceived as cynical by outside interests and even regulators. This can open the company up to criticism if not managed well.

Show and tell

Although many companies publish annual sustainability reports and may have dedicated teams working on the issue, what distinguishes the *show-and-tell* approach is the incorporation of a firm's performance in its internal and external communications such that it becomes part of the culture and brand identity.

In compliance, choosing this option requires a firm to apply relatively high standards in all countries and territories where it operates. This caution is necessary since the firm has a high public profile and is therefore subject to greater scrutiny of interest groups and regulators. In fact, activists tend to target high-status firms, knowing that doing so can increase the visibility of their actions (Briscoe & Safford, 2008). Thus, such firms may choose to adopt the environmental standards they have in their home markets as their own internal code of conduct.

The rationale for choosing *show and tell* stems from a conviction that the firm's customers, employees and other critical stakeholders value a commitment to environmental sustainability principles. The consumer goods company Unilever has become a pioneer in applying this strategy. It has come to terms with the need to go beyond a *wait-and-see* strategy to adopt a view that places good environmental behavior on par with company growth. To adopt the longer-term view that this requires, Unilever did away with quarterly profit reports in 2009. This allowed the company to develop a sustainable business model that was not continuously compromised by short-term stock market pressures. Interestingly, this shift has actually rewarded shareholders, as Unilever has increased profits at a steady pace over the last few years. By reducing short-term pressures, the company has also attracted long-term investments, which has allowed the firm to successfully develop new products that are both embedded with purpose and capable of reducing the company's reputational risk. All of this has translated into lower capital costs and higher shareholder returns.

Companies in Ibero-America might find the *show-and-tell* strategy attractive given the importance of gaining the trust of powerful actors such as local activists and unions in this region. For instance, Acindar, Argentina's largest steel producer, has adopted Global Reporting Initiative (GRI) guidelines to produce an award-winning sustainability report in which it highlights several actions, such as investing US$30 million to improve the quality of air released from their plants and setting a goal of reducing 98 percent of water use in the production of steel wire.[1]

These actions allow the firm to accomplish several goals simultaneously: mitigate the environmental impact in their local communities, improve workers' health, reduce overall costs and shield themselves from future legal liabilities by anticipating changing regulations in the Argentinian steel industry. As Acindar's managers recognize, accomplishing such goals requires substantial changes in internal processes – frequently across functional silos – to yield results that are worth communicating to external audiences.

The company also recognizes indirect positive spillovers from adopting *show and tell*. The process of adopting sustainable practices triggers a slow cultural change in the company that allows the firm to be more responsive to novel customer needs, such as the increasing demand for high-performance products in construction companies aiming for the Leadership in Energy and Environmental Design (LEED) certification. Such cultural change also allows the firm to attract and retain employees from younger generations.

The danger with *show and tell* is that if serious problems are uncovered or if unfounded accusations are made, the entire effort can be written off as greenwashing by activists, and thus, potential damage can be done to the firm's reputation and financial value. Evidence of a double standard between developed and developing countries can be used by activists to challenge a firm's social license to operate, while catastrophic incidents like Bhopal or *Deepwater Horizon* can open the firm up to tremendous criticism.

To avoid such problems, there are five important capabilities for a firm to effectively pursue a *show-and-tell* strategy: (1) compiling accurate and real-time data concerning its environmental performance, (2) internal controls, procedures and culture that assure compliance, (3) strong communications competencies carried out by an experienced team, (4) robust and precise financial models in place, so that the cost of compliance and going beyond this in certain areas is well-known and (5) senior management's fluency in environmental sustainability concepts, so that senior executives can not only consider issues and choices at the highest level but also communicate them easily and in a compelling way to the press, shareholders, community groups and government representatives.

Choosing *show and tell* – as compared to *take the low road* and *wait and see* – will add significant costs to the business. The main source of added costs will be the development of the functional capabilities which will, most likely, require dedicated people and resources to support their efforts. These costs need to be balanced against a clear understanding of the benefits of improving a firm's environmental performance. These benefits may include an increase in sales or margins, depending on consumer behavior; a positive impact on the firm's share price; the ability to attract and retain talent; a reduction in energy costs; or an improvement in community or government relations (Aguilera et al., 2007). As in the case of Acindar, executives should pay attention to both the costs and benefits of sustainable actions in order to focus on those initiatives that will generate the greatest value to its most important stakeholders.

Finally, if the business case for *show and tell* is not clear, top managers should carefully weigh this option. Once a firm begins to proactively and systematically share its environmental performance, it will be difficult, if not impossible, to stop at some later date from a PR and regulatory point of view. Hence, this strategy requires a high level of managerial commitment and the bottom–up participation of employees.

Pay for principle

When the business case is not compelling and a specific group of shareholders decides to go down the path of *show and tell* (or even further), *pay for principle* is a strategic option. Over the last ten to twenty years, a number of entrepreneurs, venture capitalists and public officials have found themselves in agreement with the goals of the environmental movement. Due to their convictions, they have chosen to lead their companies in taking proactive roles to minimize their environmental impact or offset their impact with other activities. The rationale here is a deep belief that reducing air and water pollution, protecting the natural landscape or taking active steps to mitigate climate change are crucial tasks and should form part of the CEO's agenda even though there is no apparent business case to support these measures. With *pay for principle*, the strategy must be made explicit so that other shareholders are able to freely choose to be a part of the effort or sell their holdings.

What adds some confusion to the issue is that the entrepreneurs involved in such projects often hold a different rationale for their choices and put forth their own ideas about how business and environmental sustainability can be done hand in hand without trade-offs or a cost-benefit analysis. In some cases, such as Patagonia and Whole Foods Market, companies have actually latched onto a market segment which strongly identifies with environmental sustainability. Such identification prompts some customers to give their business to the firm because of its positioning. This can generate substantial firm value, since they are often willing to pay higher prices.

Ibero–American customers also seem to be willing to support firms that engage in a *pay-for-principle* strategy. According to Nielsen (2015), Latin American customers are willing to pay a price premium, between 23 and 29 percent more, for greener products. This premium goes up for the millennial generation (the cohort born between 1981 and 1996).

An interesting example of a firm that has adopted *pay for principle* is the Brazilian cosmetics company Natura. The company earned US$2.4 billion in revenues in 2015, becoming one of the largest B Corporations in the world. As a signal of its commitment to sustainability, Natura has a rule of investing 3 percent of its revenues in innovation, which has led to initiatives such as the creation of a natural park and innovation hub in Pará, Brazil. Natura also invests heavily in the communities where the company operates, providing education and technology that enables small local firms to ultimately become suppliers for the firm.

However, as with other firms who adopt the *pay-for-principle* strategy, Natura is willing to pay the price of high environmental sensibility. Business media has pointed out how Avon, Natura's main competitor, generates almost five times more revenue than Natura, with only twice as many sales representatives (Mendoza Escamilla, 2016). This suggests that its stringent environmental commitment could ultimately be hurting firm growth. Nevertheless, Natura stands by its principles. In its 2015 sustainability report, the firm stated that its goal was not merely mitigating impact or complying with regulations but having a positive and lasting impact in the environment, regardless of short-term costs.[2]

The airline industry also provides an interesting setting for analysis. By investing in highly efficient aircraft and implementing slightly slower flight plans, airlines can reduce their carbon footprint. By taking these measures, Richard Branson's company, Virgin Atlantic, plans to reduce its carbon emissions per mile by 30 percent between 2007 and 2020. The question is, to what extent is this policy, driven by the opportunity to reduce fuel prices, a perception at Virgin that its customers value the company's commitment in this area or the passion that Branson brings to the issue? Like many of the issues connected with environmental sustainability, answering such questions requires sound technical data, deep consumer insight and complex mathematical models to tease out the different aspects of the question.

The key for effectively implementing *pay for principle* is clarity of thinking on the part of the CEO and the board. Such clarity entails constantly revising the assumptions on which the firm is based and explicitly separating out those aspects of the strategy that already make sense according to clear business criteria and which are a function of conviction and principle.

With *pay for principle*, communication with the public, shareholders and regulators will be even more critical as sustainability becomes a central part of the firm's positioning and message. If, for example, the rational for adopting *pay for principle* comes from the ethical or religious conviction of the firm's founders or major shareholders, then the option of making those convictions a transparent and integral part of the firm's internal and external communication should be explored.

Think ahead

In the case of Virgin, we could ask, what type of fleet will regulators and the traveling public, taking into account future jet fuel costs, require in 2020? Changing a fleet of airplanes takes time. Thus, Branson and his team may be predicting that successful airlines in the future will be more efficient and have a lower carbon footprint (in terms of tons of CO_2 per mile or kilometer) than the industry average today, so the company should act now. This strategy is referred to as *think ahead*.

There is evidence that public concern and regulations will be higher in the future than at present. This could lead the CEO to consider the strategic option of *think ahead*. The argument for *think ahead* is that if society's attitude toward certain industrial practices shifts and requires a more environmentally friendly approach, such a shift may come about suddenly. This could catch reactive business leaders off guard, immediately positioning their firms as environmental laggards. As with most sustainability initiatives, the question is a matter of time: will firms be able to react quickly enough to respond to changing circumstances, or should they take steps years in advance to prepare?

From a risk management point of view, the central issue is to avoid putting a firm's legal or social license to operate in doubt if its current practices fall afoul of changing norms. In terms of market positioning, it takes years for a firm to develop a trusted position. If society is suddenly willing to pay more for a perceived environmental benefit or unwilling to work with firms that do not have some minimal baseline, then a firm can miss a lucrative opportunity, or worse, it can lose business to a competitor perceived to perform in a more sustainable manner.

This is a particularly important consideration for small and medium enterprises (SMEs) in Latin America, such as those in the agricultural and food industries. Large multinational companies like Carrefour and Walmart are prioritizing sustainable suppliers, thus creating fast advantages for local SMEs that thought ahead and developed high environmental standards. Simultaneously, environmental regulation is catching up in Latin America. Companies that apply *think ahead*, such as Acindar, are investing in what will later become a first-mover advantage. This advantage can have even greater weight in environmentally sensitive industries.

One of the key requirements for *think ahead* is the ability to reflect on trends while imagining the future. This can be done by taking advantage of tools such as scenario planning (Wack, 1985). Another key capability for the *think-ahead* option is a well-developed change-management process that makes it possible to predict how long it will take to increase the firm's environmental sensibility and compliance level if senior management decides to do so. If, for example, it is thought that five years is required to change the culture of a firm so that it will support the *show-and-tell* strategy, then the firm should embark on implementing such a culture at least five years before it is required by competitive and market dynamics. Additionally, senior managers should consider that fixed assets, such as fleets of ships and airplanes, manufacturing plants, pipelines and mines, require many years to develop and become productive enough to generate positive financial returns. Changing the structure of such assets requires time, and thus, in some industries, it might turn out to be strategically critical to adopt *think ahead*.

While the development of scenarios and the technical work involved can be delegated to specialists, only senior management can drive such an effort. If the management team makes the wrong bet on the future, CEOs must be deeply involved in the process so that they can take full responsibility, whatever the result.

The stakes can be quite high when choosing a *think-ahead* strategy, depending on the size of the investments made relative to the size and financial strength of the company. On the downside, there is a risk of doing too much too soon and finding oneself having higher investment levels or higher operating costs relative to competitors who did not make similar investments or changed their processes. At the same time, there may be sudden shifts in the way the general public, consumers, regulators and other interested parties – such as investors and financial institutions – see specific issues, making it difficult to evaluate how much time firms will need to react. These shifts have often been triggered by highly visible environmental disasters such as oil spills or toxic chemical releases that could not be foreseen by managers in different industries. Scholars have called this capacity organizational resilience "the ability of organizations to anticipate, avoid, and adjust to shocks in their environment" (Ortiz-de-Mandojana & Bansal, 2015, p. 1,615). In these cases, being resilient and thinking ahead can help the firm be in the right place at the right time, generating a significant competitive advantage.

Conclusion

In this chapter, we have explored the growing importance of environmental matters in the corporate agenda and the different paths that organizations can take to develop strategies with greater ecological awareness. The chapter also sums up the historical relationship between businesses and the natural environment and how this has changed from being a fringe issue to becoming a core concern in a firm's strategy. Since it is unlikely that concerns about issues such as industrial contamination and climate change will fade away in the foreseeable future, symbolic actions alone will not enable firms to retain their licenses to operate or generate significant financial and reputational benefits. On the contrary, symbolic actions can lead to significant penalties for firms, especially those operating in environmentally sensitive industries.

We recognize that despite the growing importance of corporate sustainability, some businesses are still struggling to find a way to increase their environmental performance without entirely jeopardizing short-term financial performance. Given the complexity of this challenge, many companies resort to symbolic actions such as greenwashing to deal with increasing institutional and market pressures to become sustainable. A framework has been offered here to avoid this pitfall and to understand a firm's initial position and the required capabilities needed to become more sustainable in a way that is organically aligned with the firm's strategic goals.

The framework features six different strategic responses or options for firms to follow, depending on two core dimensions: the firm's environmental sensibility and the planned level of legal compliance. Assessing the firm's environmental sensibility allows CEOs to understand the fundamental nature of the firm's relationship with the natural environment. This allows the company to choose a strategic option that is consistent both with the firm's goals and with the environment in which it operates. These options range from *take the low road* – minimal compliance when environmental matters have low strategic importance – to *thinking ahead* – becoming an environmental steward that can adapt in a changing landscape when environmental concerns are a major strategic factor.

Going from *take the low road* to *thinking ahead* requires developing complex and specific business functions that result in enhanced organizational capabilities. To develop these, firms need to commit to substantial investments and remain patient in the absence of short-term results. Although the Ibero-American context poses several strategic challenges for companies, developing a long-term environmental commitment is not impossible. Throughout this chapter, we have provided examples of Ibero-American companies investing in capability development to sustain strategies when there is high environmental sensibility. The cases of BBVA, Banco Santander Rio, Natura, Mastellone and Acindar show how it is possible to develop and maintain sustainable strategies even when they operate within different contexts.

A central aspect of our framework is that it does not establish a priori which strategic option should be adopted. As explained, firms operate in industries and settings with different environmental footprints and with stakeholders who have varying levels of interest in environmental issues. In addition, CEOs should consider the appropriateness of a strategic choice, depending on their firm's profile and status, board and management capacities and overall strategy, among other factors. Such characteristics differ significantly for a small fast-food chain as compared to a large franchise such as McDonald's.

The existence of trade-offs is an implicit assumption embedded in the most evolved strategic options. Firms aiming for a *show-and-tell*, *pay-for-principle* or *think-ahead* strategy need to understand that green investments require a long-term vision and uninterrupted commitment since the benefits of investing in social and environmental activities take a long time to accrue. Certain organizations, such as family-owned firms, seem to be particularly good at dealing with this trade-off, since family executives naturally develop an emotional attachment to their firms that motivates them to safeguard their reputation (and that of their families) by investing in better environmental performance (Berrone et al., 2010). In any case, the key is to ensure a long-term commitment from senior management that will lead efforts in the same direction throughout the organization. Such commitment manifests itself in the choices made by leaders in the trade-off between short-term economic results, the larger question of a firm's role in civil society and even the ethical viewpoint of key stakeholders.

In conclusion, the adoption of sustainable practices is increasingly becoming a social, institutional and market demand for firms. Firms who break the law, greenwash or cause socially unacceptable levels of environmental degradation may suffer large reputational and financial penalties that threaten their survival in the long term. While academic research suggests that firms profit from adopting a green stance, it is also true that not all firms will profit equally. Furthermore, not all firms have the resources required to become environmental stewards. Our framework offers guidance on the choice of a strategic approach to sustainability that recognizes different organizational realities and visions for corporate sustainability. Thus, it offers a concrete way to bring environmental issues into the boardroom without promoting an unrealistic view of strategic possibilities, a view that often ends in skepticism and symbolic action.

Notes

1 www.acindar.com.ar/es/sustentabilidad/reportes-de-sustentabilidad
2 http://natura.infoinvest.com.br/enu/s-15-enu.html

References

Aguilera, R. V., Rupp, D. E., Williams, C. A. and Ganapathi, J. (2007). "Putting the S Back in Corporate Social Responsibility: A Multilevel Theory of Social Change in Organizations." *Academy of Management Review*, 32(3): 836–863.

Bansal, P. (2003). "From Issues to Actions: The Importance of Individual Concerns and Organizational Values in Responding to Natural Environmental Issues." *Organization Science*, 14(5): 510–527.

Bansal, P. (2005). "Evolving Sustainably: A Longitudinal Study of Corporate Sustainable Development." *Strategic Management Journal*, 26(3): 197–218.

Bansal, P. and Clelland, I. (2004). "Talking Trash: Legitimacy, Impression Management, and Unsystematic Risk in the Context of the Natural Environment." *Academy of Management Journal*, 47(1): 93–103.

Bansal, P. and DesJardine, M. (2014). "Business Sustainability: It Is About Time." *Strategic Organization*, 12(1): 70–78.

Berrone, P. (2016). *Green Lies: How Greenwashing Can Destroy a Company (and How to Go Green Without the Wash)*. Createspace Independent Publishing Platform.

Berrone, P., Cruz, C., Gomez-Mejia, L. R. and Larraza-Kintana, M. (2010). "Socioemotional Wealth and Corporate Responses to Institutional Pressures: Do Family-Controlled Firms Pollute Less?" *Administrative Science Quarterly*, 55(1): 82–113.

Berrone, P., Fosfuri, A., & Gelabert, L. (2017). Does greenwashing pay off? Understanding the relationship between environmental actions and environmental legitimacy. *Journal of Business Ethics*, 144(2): 363–379.

Berrone, P., Gelabert, L. and Fosfuri, A. (2009). "The Impact of Symbolic and Substantive Actions on Environmental Legitimacy." *IESE Working Paper* (Vol. 3).

Berrone, P. and Gomez-Mejia, L. R. (2009). "Environmental Performance and Executive Compensation: An Integrated Agency-Institutional Perspective." *Academy of Management Journal*, 52(1): 103–126.

Briscoe, F. and Safford, S. (2008). "The Nixon-in-China Effect: Activism, Imitation, and the Institutionalization of Contentious Practices." *Administrative Science Quarterly*, 53(3): 460–491.

Cohen, D. (1995). "Creating Ethical Work Climates: A Socioeconomic Perspective." *The Journal of Socio-Economics*, 24(2): 317–343.

CorpWatch. (2001). Greenwash Fact Sheet. www.corpwatch.org/article.%0Dphp?id=242

European Commission. (2014). "A Healthy and Sustainable Environment for Present and Future Generations." The European Union Explained.

Friedman, M. (1970). "The Social Responsibility of Business Is to Increase Its Profits." *The New York Times Magazine*, 32–33.

Gray, W. B. and Shimshack, J. P. (2011). "The Effectiveness of Environmental Monitoring and Enforcement: A Review of the Empirical Evidence." *Review of Environmental Economics and Policy*, 5: 3–24.

Hoffman, A. J. (1999). "Institutional Evolution and Change: Environmentalism and the U.S. Chemical Industry." *Academy of Management Journal*, 42(4): 351–371.

Hoffman, A. J. (2001). "Linking Organizational and Field-Level Analyses: The Diffusion of Corporate Environmental Practice." *Organization & Environment*, 14(2): 133–156.

Inter-governmental Panel on Climate Change. (2018). The Special Report on Global Warming of 1.5° C (SR15).

Lane, E. (2013). "Green Marketing Goes Negative: The Advent of Reverse Greenwashing." *Intellectual Property & Technology Law Journal*, 25(1): 20.

Mander, J. (1972). "Ecopornography: One Year and Nearly a Billion Dollars Later, Advertising Owns Ecology." *Communication and Arts Magazine*, 2: 45–56.

Martin, G., Gomez-Mejia, L. and Makri, M. (2016). "Conflict Between Controlling Family Owners and Minority Shareholders: Much Ado About Nothing." *Theory & Practice* (In Press).

Martin, G., Gómez–Mejía, L. R., Berrone, P., & Makri, M. (2017). Conflict between controlling family owners and minority shareholders: much ado about nothing?. *Entrepreneurship Theory and Practice*, 41(6): 999–1027.

Martin, K. and Cullen, J. (2006). "Continuities and Extensions of Ethical Climate Theory: A Meta-Analytic Review." *Journal of Business Ethics*, 69(2): 175–194.

Medland, D. (2016). "Volkswagen: When 'Hubris' Leads to A Corporate Governance Disaster – and Shareholder Pain." *Forbes*. https://www.forbes.com/sites/dinamedland/2016/03/12/volkswagen-when-hubris-leads-to-a-corporate-governance-disaster-and-shareholder-pain/#7758c27d31e1

Mendoza Escamilla, V. (March 2016). "La Empresa que Sí Quiere Pagar el Precio de Ser Sustentable." *Forbes*. https://www.forbes.com.mx/natura-la-empresa-que-si-quiere-pagar-el-precio-de-ser-sustentable/

Mociulsky, M. and Alarcón, X. D. (2016). "Valores Sustentables de las Nuevas Generaciones." *Revista Mercado*, 32–34.

Nielsen. (2015). Consumer-goods' Brands That Demonstrate Commitment to Sustainability Outperform Those That Don't. www.nielsen.com/us/en/press-room/2015/consumer-goods-brands-that-demonstrate-commitment-to-sustainability-outperform.html (19 January 2017).

Oliver, C. (1991). "Strategic Responses to Institutional Processes." *Academy of Management Review*, 16(1): 145–179.

Ortiz-de-Mandojana, N. and Bansal, P. (2015). "The Long-Term Benefits of Organizational Resilience Through Sustainable Business Practices." *Strategic Management Journal*, 37(8): 1615–1631.

Pope Francis. (2015). Laudato Si': On Care for Our Common Home. http://w2.vatican.va/content/dam/francesco/pdf/encyclicals/documents/papa-francesco_20150524_enciclica-laudato-si_en.pdf.

Reinhardt, F. (1999). "Market Failure and the Environmental Policies of Firms: Economic Rationales for 'Beyond Compliance' Behavior." *Journal of Industrial Ecology*, 3(1): 9–21.

Rosenberg, M. (2015). *Strategy and Sustainability: A Hardnosed and Clear-Eyed Approach to Environmental Sustainability for Business*. London: Palgrave Macmillan.

Rousseau, H. E. (2017). "Corporate Sustainability: Toward a Theoretical Integration of Catholic Social Teaching and the Natural-Resource-Based View of the Firm." *Journal of Business Ethics*, 145(4): 725–737.

Rousseau, H. E., Berrone, P. and Walls, J. L. (2014). "Let's Talk: Studying Dialogue Among Firms and Outside Actors on Social and Environmental Issues." *Academy of Management Best Papers Proceedings*, 2014(1).

Short, J. and Toffel, M. (2010). "Making Self-Regulation More Than Merely Symbolic: The Critical Role of the Legal Environment." *Administrative Science Quarterly*, 55(3): 361–396.

Suchman, M. C. (1995). "Managing Legitimacy: Strategic and Institutional Approaches." *Academy of Management Review*, 20(3): 571–610.

Wack, P. (1985). "Scenarios: Uncharted Waters Ahead." *Harvard Business Review*, 63(6): 139–150.

Waddock, S. (2008). "Building a New Institutional Infrastructure for Corporate Responsibility." *The Academy of Management Perspectives*, 22(3): 87–108.

7

ENTREPRENEURSHIP IN THE DIGITAL ECONOMY

Latin American "unicorns"

Enrique Chamas and Adrián A. Caldart

The high growth potential of emerging economies makes them attractive markets for both national firms and those from developed economies. Nonetheless, firms from developed markets often face a series of challenges when establishing operations that require them to innovate and adapt their business models to new social, economic and cultural environments, as well as to unstable institutional frameworks.

This chapter examines the adaptation challenges that companies face – and their critical drivers of success – when establishing operations in the online space in Latin America. Through a multiple case study research design, we documented the core strategies and abilities that proved instrumental in shaping, adapting and renovating internet-based business models in the region. Our sample comprises highly successful Latin American e-commerce firms, an interesting business ecosystem that has thus far remained under-researched.

By and large, these firms have designed their business models by drawing on the experiences of peers in developed markets, most notably the United States, while adapting core elements that have enabled them to obtain remarkable results in Latin American markets. These firms constitute a mix of four world-class Latin American IT businesses that have effectively "tropicalized" their value propositions and earned the status of unicorns, defined as technology companies that achieved a market capitalization of US$1 billion in under ten years after their creation. All four companies are traded on the stock market, and three are listed on the NASDAQ exchange (see the Appendix).

There is a limited body of management research on emerging markets regarding the main drivers of corporate performance and strategy implementation (Nicholls-Nixon et al., 2011; Xu & Meyer, 2013). Much has been written on context conditions in emerging markets, their differences with developed markets (Frazier, Gill & Kale, 1989; Khanna & Palepu, 2006; Xu & Meyer, 2013, Liu et al., 2013; and Marquis & Raynard, 2015) and their impact on corporate strategy and performance

(Terpstra & Sarathy, 1994; Wright et al., 2005; Khanna, Palepu & Sinha, 2005; and Hoskisson et al., 2013). Yet little is known about the reality of the Latin American unicorns that emerged during the first decade of the new millennium.

This in-depth examination aims to help CEOs reflect more systematically on the strategic aspects of business model adaptation, implementation and change by using internet technologies in emerging markets.

General strategic principles of e-business models in emerging markets

Among the most salient characteristics of operating in the digital economy is the online transfer of information regardless of physical location and the widespread availability of basic hardware and software at relatively low prices. These conditions open up numerous opportunities for globally minded entrepreneurs with an interest in emerging markets. Consequently, cost-related obstacles and challenges linked to bridging physical expanses either disappear or fade to the background. Yet other aspects, like administrative and legal issues, become much more significant for online businesses when it comes to organizing their payment methods, building their logistics infrastructure, contracting suppliers and obtaining the necessary government approvals.

In Latin America, the internet is allowing manufacturers and intermediaries to access markets that previously were either difficult or impossible to serve, at least directly and massively, because of institutional voids (Khanna & Palepu, 2010). The impact of digital networks has caused business models to multiply and expand from brick-and-mortar models like Tiendas Falabella – South America's largest department store chain, with operations in Chile, Argentina, Peru and Colombia and with more than 65,000 employees – to online marketplaces like Mercado Libre and OLX, two of the firms examined in our research.

Similarly, the development of the Argentine technological giant Globant would be exceedingly difficult outside the digital realm. This company develops complex equipment across twelve facilities and numerous Latin American cities, a task that would be unfathomable without internet technology. The same can be said of Mercado Libre, the most important retailer in Latin America and worth US$15 billion by mid 2018; OLX, a digital platform for buying and selling pre-owned goods with 330 million users in ninety-four countries; and the online tourism company Despegar.com.

Our study focused on a sample of four internet firms established in Argentina that, as previously mentioned, achieved the noteworthy status of becoming both "unicorns" and publicly traded companies. This study commenced with the analysis of publicly available information taken from their corporate websites, annual reports, press releases and academic case studies. After this initial analysis, primary data was collected in each firm through in-depth, semi-structured interviews of twenty-one senior executives from the firms under study and sixteen additional interviews with academic and corporate experts. We then developed a cross-analysis of the cases, which led to the identification of four commonalities in the online strategies of the sample firms. We characterized these factors as follows: (1) converting institutional voids into sources of opportunities; (2) adaptability and complementarity; (3) governance; and (4) local management.

Converting institutional voids into sources of opportunities

The Latin American unicorns all managed to combine the best of both worlds. On one hand, their mastery of world-class technology and marketing allowed them to offer outstanding user experiences. On the other hand, they turned potential obstacles into opportunities by successfully adapting their business models to fill institutional voids.

Khanna and Palepu (2010) were among the first to point out the potential of converting institutional voids in emerging markets into investment opportunities. Mercado Libre launched their own financing companies – Mercado Pago – as a means to facilitate online purchases by offering credit, foster loyalty around their core activity and expand their client base. Mercado Libre also created internet advertising companies, delivery services and e-commerce services within its ecosystem.

These activities function as independent business units yet operate within the Mercado Libre marketplace platform. The company also recently began to offer credit to marketplace sellers in countries where it operates. Their experience is an example of how companies can exploit opportunities in emerging markets by innovating their business models and offering additional services that can, at the very least, build brand loyalty and potentially justify higher prices (Chakravarthy & Coughlan, 2011; Khanna, Palepu & Sinha, 2005; Eyring, Johnson & Nair, 2011).

Adaptability and complementarity (adapting to national markets)

The first finding of our research relates to the core drivers that enabled these firms to build and sustain a competitive advantage in their respective market segments. Leveraging technology, they knew how to adapt the business model to the peculiarities of their markets by spearheading operations that complement their core business, allowing them to in turn overcome the institutional voids inherent in Latin American economies.

Authors including Dawar and Frost (1999), Khanna and Palepu (2006) and Shankar et al. (2008) have highlighted the availability of country-specific strategic assets – contacts with local governments, in-depth knowledge of the local market and distinctive products based on specific emerging-market consumer tastes – as sources of competitive advantage for national enterprises over foreign firms.

While these factors are all undoubtedly relevant, our findings underscore business model adaptation and innovation as a driving force behind the success of the firms included in our sample. In addition, rather than designing a comprehensive strategy for Latin America as a whole, the companies that we analyzed all adopted country-specific strategies – or, at most, strategies oriented toward a small group of countries – and went to great lengths to optimize user experience by overcoming institutional voids inherent in each.

Many of the capabilities required by local companies and individuals to compete in emerging economies are context-specific, so this know-how may represent barriers to entry for foreign companies (Meyer & Tran, 2006). Mercado Libre, for instance, keeps its platform open but doesn't charge a premium for each transaction as it does in other countries, because the e-commerce market is far less developed in Central America. It mainly seeks to boost traffic and build customer relationships until the market is ripe enough to implement its standard marketplace model. To this same end, the company also implemented initiatives in countries with limited access to banking services, including prepaid cards for online purchases in Brazil, Colombia, Mexico and Venezuela and microcredits for salespeople in Argentina and Brazil.

Emerging markets also employ sales systems that differ from those in developed markets. In some countries, clients have the option of financing purchases in installments or using the company's proprietary financing systems. Mercado Libre and Sodimac, the most important construction material and home improvement retailer in Latin America, are examples of firms that offer these services.

Other differences in emerging markets include country-specific tax breaks, the use of cash as a method of payment – an issue that should also be considered in monetization systems – and alternative sales channels like a telephone service, since Latin Americans frequently prefer to deal with a person as opposed to a machine. Similarly, issues like theft and fraud have a direct impact on delivery and logistics systems, making issues such as in-store deliveries far more difficult in some Latin American cities. Motorcycles are also more widely used as a courier channel rather than national postal services.

E-commerce web pages must also be adapted to the region. Mercado Libre, OLX and Despegar.com all offer websites that can be accessed using less sophisticated phones. Monetization systems must be modified as well, with vendors accepting cash payments if buyers don't own a credit card or if they have insufficient credit at the moment of purchase. Mercado Libre, for instance, has sixty-four payment alternatives, and Despegar.com offers more than thirty-five.

The failure to adapt to market peculiarities explains the disastrous results of several multinational firms in Latin America. Examples include Amazon's incursion into Brazil in 2012. The sheer size of Brazil – its 120 million internet users equal the population of Mexico – make it a gigantic market for e-commerce players. Nonetheless, the country has major barriers in place when it comes to selling imported products, which comprise the bulk of Amazon's offerings.

Like Amazon, Brazilian e-commerce sites incorporate one-click shopping and other features that make them quite competitive in their user experience and their treatment of big data. Moreover, after observing Amazon's successful entry into other countries, Brazilian firms dug in their heels and devised schemes to thwart their efforts.

The sales strategy of the Swiss company Le Shop offers another cautionary tale. Among the top European online players, Le Shop launched the first totally online supermarket in Argentina in 2000. Eleven years later, however, it was forced to close operations after failing to achieve the necessary sales volume to compete in purchasing power with local brick-and-mortar competitors like Carrefour, Walmart and Jumbo.

Governance: developing an ecosystem around the main business

In line with research by Khanna and Palepu (2006), our findings underscore the importance of outstanding performance and solid governance in emerging markets. Based on the Casadesus-Masanell and Ricart (2010) conceptualization of a business model as the particular set of choices that an organization makes about policies, assets and governance, as well as their associated consequences (Casadesus-Masanell & Ricart, 2010), we can conclude that governance plays a pivotal role, since resource providers can't rely on the enforcement of contracts in emerging markets.

Good governance – understood as organizational mechanisms that ensure a company honors its commitments to investors, customers, employees and business partners – also enables firms to affirm a solid reputation, an invaluable asset when dealing with stakeholders. In short, firms must consider other aspects, like delivery systems and purchase- and sales-financing mechanisms, that strategically complement their core business.

The most solid models have their own business ecosystem and offer services that complement their main business activity (delivery, financing, consulting, insurance, etc.) as part of their value proposition. Although these services may operate independently, the main business either owns them or exercises significant influence over their governance and management. In this way, intercompany synergies emerge within the *business ecosystem*, defined as a collection of (many) companies engaged in joint production, whose choices and actions are interdependent (Boudreau & Hagiu, 2008).

An ecosystem strategy can be considered as one that takes a partner company's business model to be as critical as the focal firm's (Adner, 2017). In this regard, business ecosystems are contexts within which the success of a value proposition depends on fostering the alignment of partners that work together to transform a winning idea into positive market results (Priem, Butler & Li 2013; Adner, 2017).

Emerging markets have transactional arenas in which buyers and sellers are not easily or efficiently able to come together (Khanna & Palepu, 2010). Within this context, the challenge for managers is to design business models that facilitate the purchasing process for clients as much as possible, which is why strong alliances or ownership accords among the intervening parties are so crucial. Business models will also be more successful if they effectively address activities that are determining factors in the region: solid data protection systems, brand reliability, secure delivery and financing systems. Mercado Libre, for instance, exploits this need for safety by waiting to pay sellers until buyers have acknowledged receipt of the merchandise. Buyers and sellers are also given a platform to rate each other, information that is included in their purchasing history for future transactions.

From a client standpoint, commercial transactions have three fundamental moments: assortment (being able to find what we are looking for), payment and delivery. The more these processes can be optimized, the better the user experience. Based on our research on the online companies included in the sample, we conclude that the logistics (including product delivery to the customer) and the management of payments pose challenges. In this regard, an effective and flexible payment service (including financing) and solid delivery logistics systems represent important differentiation factors for firms operating in Latin America.

As mentioned earlier, Mercado Libre offers its own financing service (Mercado Pago) and a delivery service (Mercado Envíos). Within its platforms, sellers can contract advertising services within or outside the marketplace (Mercado Publicidad), take out loans to use as working capital of their business (Mercado Crédito) and leverage services to set up their own e-commerce within or outside the Mercado Libre marketplace (Mercado Shops). These activities all form part of the same ecosystem, giving the marketplace tremendous capacity to generate and retain value within its diverse subgroups. Thus, through its five proprietary marketplace business units, Mercado Libre is capable of offering clients high-quality services thanks to a solid ecosystem.

In these cases, we observed one important difference compared to similar business models of peers in developed countries: in emerging countries, companies tend to form an ecosystem of fully controlled companies. Then they seek to improve the purchasing experience, which may be weakened by institutional gaps, and use those same companies to maximize the performance of the entire business model.

This is an important difference with counterparts in developed markets like Amazon and eBay. The success of these firms doesn't require them to control their ecosystems through ownership, because they can rely on the quality of other institutions. For instance, the reliability of the Royal Mail enables ebay.co.uk and amazon.co.uk to rely on it to deliver products, with no need for a formal agreement.

Local management: building trust

Local management teams with stellar skills and a global vision were a common feature among the companies that we researched. These qualities enabled them to effectively "tropicalize" business models that had proven successful in developed markets and adapt them to the Latin American business landscape. Thanks to exceptional execution, they are able to compete side by side against world-class companies from developed countries.

This finding is consistent with the idea proposed by Bhattacharya and Michael (2008) of developing business models to overcome obstacles. The specific capacity or talent of the local management teams we studied is closely related to the notion of strategic flexibility (Garud & Kotha, 1994; Sanchez, 1995; Rindova & Kotha,

2001), defined as the ability to precipitate intentional changes and adapt to environmental shifts through the continuous rethinking of current strategies, asset deployment and investment strategies Evans, 1991; Bahrami 1992; Sanchez, 1995) or with the firm's ability to reallocate and reconfigure their organizational resources, processes and strategies to deal with environmental changes (Zhou & Wu, 2010).

Strategic flexibility is within the boundaries of the firm. Its intangible nature suggests that it is dynamic and firm-specific, since managerial and problem-solving skills are intrinsic to firms and emerge within them (Chen et al., 2017). Strategic flexibility is an important dynamic capability that enables firms to achieve a competitive advantage in turbulent markets (Teece, Pisano & Shuen, 1997; Zhou & Wu, 2010; Liu et al., 2013).

Smart local companies have harnessed the benefits of globalization to bridge existing gaps in technology, capital and talent with their rivals from the developed world. Moreover, contrary to popular belief, local winners in emerging markets frequently exploit the latest technologies (Bhattacharya & Michael, 2008), as evidenced by Globant, Mercado Libre, Despegar.com and OLX.

Despite limited talent resources in emerging markets (Khanna & Palepu, 2006), the local management teams in the companies researched are all highly professional and experienced. Many of the CEOs and top-level managers we interviewed had left senior positions in multinational firms or international jobs to join local leaders. They are familiar with the local terrain and know how to work around institutional voids, which in turn allows them to better identify and meet customers' needs.

Conclusions

This chapter explored the use of online strategies to address contextual issues in emerging markets and their impact on business model configuration. Although many studies have been conducted on growth opportunities in emerging economies and the necessity to adapt business models, we are not aware of research focused on the identification of approaches and success factors related to online strategies in these markets (even less so in Latin America) nor on research that explores innovation in business model design based on successful companies born in emerging markets and developed later in other countries.

One of the conclusions of our study is that the internet opened up tremendous opportunities for the implementation of online business models in Latin America and will likely continue to do so in the future. On one hand, online business models can overcome institutional voids that might hinder brick-and-mortar models. On the other hand, they can take advantage of significant internet penetration to reach underserved markets – for instance, those far from urban areas that often suffer from a lack of infrastructure and access to financing. For this reason, pure-play business models like Netflix can operate from the northern hemisphere and serve clients in Latin American cities, circumventing the inherent roadblocks in developing and monetizing business models in these countries.

Yet beyond these purely digital models, the institutional voids intrinsic to emerging markets – those that impact the availability of financing or the efficiency of delivery logistics, for instance – require a more nuanced approach. In this regard, managers must be cognizant of the main drivers of internet-based business models' success.

According to our findings, successful e-business models in Latin America are grounded mainly on four core principles: first, if they discover institutional voids that hinder their specific business, they overcome them and also find associated business opportunities; second, they consider each national market as unique and try to adapt the business model to that specific market; third, they develop an ecosystem around the main business, with complementary client services, maintaining control but not necessarily ownership; and finally, they contract local management to rapidly gain the confidence and trust of clients.

A second conclusion is that ecosystemic thinking has become quite widespread and strategically effective as a result of globalization, digitalization and shifting industry boundaries, as suggested by Velu et al. (2013). What appears to create value in the firms we researched is a high level of integration, infusing the business model with services capable of bridging institutional voids in the locations or regions where it operates.

As mentioned earlier, success in these markets entails continuous brand-building efforts since e-commerce culture tends to be low, as well as the implementation of business model strategies over time to ensure delivery to the client. It also requires a platform that acts as an own ecosystem integrator for services complementary to the core business and a range of payment options that consider the broad variety of client profiles in Latin America, where, in many countries, half of the workforce falls outside the formal employment system and/or has limited access to banking services.

These important considerations also positively impact sales generated from core business. Other important factors include adeptly managing local talent to adapt the business model to fast-changing circumstances, which are common in emerging markets (strategic flexibility), as well as the ability to internationalize the business to gain market volume.

Finally, CEOs considering the possibility of developing online businesses in emerging markets should note three revolutions currently underway in the manufacturing, logistics operations and retail spheres. Manufacturers must decide whether they will continue to offer retailers a portion of their margins or implement their own e-commerce channel; retailers must define what to do with their coverage and pick-up points and whether to join the region's main marketplaces; and logistics operators must prepare themselves to handle both large and small volumes, since they at present almost exclusively handle large-volume transactions. At this point in time, it is still unclear who will survive the battle.

APPENDIX
Overview of sample firms

Mercado Libre

Mercado Libre (www.mercadolibre.com) was established in 1999. Over the years, it has grown into one of the most important online business platforms in Latin America, with operations in nineteen countries in the region and in Portugal. From the outset, its founders were cognizant of the significant advantages of e-commerce platforms in terms of volume, availability of information and accessibility, and they thus viewed Mercado Libre as a unified technology platform that was big enough to manage the needs of all the region's markets.

The company went public in 2007 and, until 2016, experienced biannual growth at an astounding rate of 35 percent. By December 2017, Mercado Libre had more than 8,200 employees and operations in Argentina, Peru, Brazil, Colombia, Chile, Mexico, Uruguay, the United States and Venezuela. Mercado Libre, Inc. is the eighth most-visited online retail site in the world, offering e-commerce and related services. Its platforms offer users a comprehensive service portfolio that streamlines e-commerce transactions while adapting to the diverse cultural and geographical challenges across Latin America.

Its e-commerce platform offers sellers and buyers a solid online business environment, fostering a burgeoning e-commerce community in Latin America, a region with more than 605 million people and one with the fastest-growing rates of internet penetration in the world. Its proprietary ecosystem comprises six related e-commerce services: classified services (*Mercado Libre Clasificados*), a payment solution (*Mercado Pago*), an advertising platform (*Mercado Libre Publicidad*), online shops (*Mercado Shops*), a shipment service (*Mercado Envíos*) and credit for working capital (*Mercado Crédito*).

In terms of web traffic, Mercado Libre leads the market in unique visitors and page views in Argentina, Brazil, Chile, Colombia, Costa Rica, Ecuador, Mexico,

Peru, Uruguay, Bolivia and Venezuela. It also operates online trade platforms in the Dominican Republic, Panama and Portugal.

OLX

OLX – short for online exchange – was created in Argentina in 2006 by internet entrepreneurs Fabrice Grinda and Alec Oxenford and initially funded by US venture capital firms, including Bessemer Ventures and General Catalyst Partners. By 2017, OLX was among the world's most important free platforms for online classified ads.

To date, OLX has 4,000 global employees and operates in fifty languages and forty-five countries, including Argentina, Bangladesh, Brazil, India, Indonesia, Portugal and Poland. Every day, millions of users around the world purchase or sell goods, search for jobs or look for rental properties using the OLX platform, which has become a household name in emerging markets.

In August 2010, Naspers acquired a 67.8 percent stake in OLX, Inc., which it later increased to 95 percent. In 2014, the company reached a milestone when it joined an elite club of internet giants including Instagram, Facebook, Messenger and Snapchat by reaching 200 million active monthly users.

Despegar.com

Created in 1999, Despegar.com now has 4,500 employees and more than US$4 billion in annual sales through its commercial offices in twelve countries and operations in twenty-one. In 2016, Despegar.com was the fourth-largest tourism company in the world in terms of sales, with Brazil accounting for 50 percent of its total sales volume. Through its website, the company offers a broad suite of travel products in the region, including airfare, hotel bookings, travel packages and other travel products. Over a twelve-month period, ending in June 2017, the platform attracted 140 million unique visitors. From January to June 2017, 65 percent of transactions were made by repeat customers.

When the platform launched in 1999, it was focused solely on the sale of airline tickets. As of June 2017, it had expanded to offer products from more than 250 airlines, 300,000 hotels, 900 car rental agencies and 250 destination-service providers throughout Latin America. At the same time, its award-winning mobile app had 33 million downloads, making it the most downloaded online travel app in the region. Mobile traffic and transactions represent a significant portion of web traffic: mobile web accounts for roughly 55 percent of total visits and 27 percent of total transactions, whereas mobile apps reflect 50 percent of total visits and 23 percent of transactions.

The company began trading on the NASDAQ exchange in September 2017.

Globant

Established in 2003, Globant is a leading global corporate software development company whose products combine creativity, innovation, design and technology. As of 2017, it had 6,000 employees, annual revenues of US$432 million and fourteen global offices in several Argentinian cities, as well as in Colombia, Mexico, Uruguay, the United Kingdom and the United States. The company was listed on the NASDAQ exchange in 2014.

Since it was first launched, Globant has sought to go global. The company started by setting up offices in Uruguay, Colombia and Mexico, followed by an acquisition of a Brazilian company. Most recently, they established operations in Chile and India. Argentina-based employees comprise 60 percent of Globant's total global workforce. In the United States, the firm has more than three hundred employees.

Upon the recent acquisition of a company in India, they began to harness Indian talent to serve developed markets. This global approach makes Globant highly competitive, yet cost arbitration is not their objective (their products aren't less expensive than their competitors in developed markets). In fact, Globant tends to be far more expensive. In terms of revenue per employee, they come in second on the top tier of the most important global companies as clients are willing to pay a premium for the firm's innovative products. Globant also has a competitive service offer.

Over the past fifteen years, Globant has evolved from a Latin American company specialized in offshore services to a global leader in software creation and emerging technologies. Recent technological advances such as big data, mobile, cloud, gamification, customer-friendly designs and design interfaces have transformed the way companies relate to their internal and external clients. By identifying this shift early on, Globant was able to build partnerships with major players like Google and LinkedIn.

Moving forward, they aim to continue to create digital journeys that constantly challenge the status quo through a unique combination of engineering, innovation and design.

References

Adner, R. (2017). "Ecosystem as Structure: An Actionable Construct for Strategy." *Journal of Management*, 43(1): 39–58.

Bahrami, H. (1992). "The Emerging Flexible Organization: Perspectives from Silicon Valley." *California Management Review*, 34(4): 33–52.

Bhattacharya, A. K. and Michael, D. C. (2008). "How Local Companies Keep Multinationals at Bay." *Harvard Business Review*, 86(3): 84–95.

Boudreau, K. and Hagiu, A. (2008). "Platform Rules: Multi-Sided Platforms as Regulators." HBS Working Paper Number 09–061.

Casadesus-Masanell, R. and Ricart, J. E. (2010). "From Strategy to Business Models and Onto Tactics." *Long-Range Planning*, 43(2–3): 195–215.

Chakravarthy, B. and Coughlan, S. (2011). "Emerging Market Strategy: Innovating Both Products and Delivery Systems." *Strategy & Leadership*, 40(1): 27–32.

Chen, Y., Wang, Y., Nevo, S., Benitez, J. and Kou, G. (2017). "Improving Strategic Flexibility with Information Technologies: Insights for Firm Performance in an Emerging Economy." *Journal of Information Technology*, 32(1): 10–25.

Dawar, N. and Frost, T. (1999). "Competing with Giants: Survival Strategies for Local Companies in Emerging Markets." *Harvard Business Review*, March–April, 119–129.

Evans, J. S. (1991). "Strategic Flexibility for High-Technology Maneuvers: A Conceptual Framework. *Journal of Management Studies*, 28(1): 69–89.

Eyring, M. J., Johnson, M. W. and Nair, H. (2011). "New Business Models in Emerging Markets." *Harvard Business Review*, 89(1–2): 88–95.

Frazier, G. L., Gill, J. D. and Kale, S. H. (1989). "Dealer Dependence Levels and Reciprocal Actions in a Channel of Distribution in a Developing Country." *The Journal of Marketing*, 50–69.

Garud, R. and Kotha, S. (1994). "Using the Brain as a Metaphor to Model Flexible Production Systems." *Academy of Management Review*, 19(4): 671–698. http://dx.doi.org/10.5465/AMR.1994.9412190215

Hoskisson, R. E., Wright, M., Filatotchev, I. and Peng, M. W. (2013). "Emerging Multinationals from Mid-Range Economies: The Influence of Institutions and Factor Markets." *Journal of Management Studies*, 50(7): 1295–1321.

Khanna, T. and Palepu, K. G. (2006). "Emerging Giants: Building World-Class Companies in Developing Countries." *Harvard Business Review*, 84(10).

Khanna, T. and Palepu, K. G. (2010). *Winning in Emerging Markets: A Road Map for Strategy and Execution*. Brighton, MA: Harvard Business School Press.

Khanna, T., Palepu, K. G. and Sinha, J. (2005). "Strategies That Fit Emerging Markets." *Harvard Business Review*, 83(6): 63–76.

Liu, H., Jiang, X., Zhang, J. and Zhao, X. (2013). "Strategic Flexibility and International Venturing by Emerging Market Firms: The Moderating Effects of Institutional and Relational Factors." *Journal of International Marketing*, 21(2): 79–98.

Marquis, C. and Raynard, M. (2015). "Institutional Strategies in Emerging Markets." *Academy of Management Annals,* 9(1): 291–335.

Meyer, K. E. and Tran, Y. T. T. (2006). "Market Penetration and Acquisition Strategies for Emerging Economies." *Long-Range Planning*, 39(2): 177–197.

Nicholls-Nixon, C. L., Davila Castilla, J. A., Sanchez Garcia, J. and Rivera Pesquera, M. (2011). "Latin America Management Research: Review, Synthesis, and Extension." *Journal of Management*, 37(4): 1178–1227.

Priem, R. L., Butler, J. E. and Li, S. (2013). "Toward Reimagining Strategy Research: Retrospection and Prospection on the 2011 AMR Decade Award Article." *Academy of Management Review*, 38(4): 471–489.

Rindova, V. P. and Kotha, S. (2001). "Continuous Morphing: Competing Through Dynamic Capabilities, Form and Function." *Academy of Management Journal*, 44: 1263–1280.

Sanchez, R. (1995). "Strategic Flexibility in Product Competition." *Strategic Management Journal*, 16: 135–159.

Shankar, S., Ormiston, C., Bloch, N., Schaus, R. and Vishwanath, V. (2008). "How to Win in Emerging Markets." *MIT Sloan Management Review*, 49(3): 18–24.

Teece, D. J., Pisano, G. and Shuen, A. (1997). "Dynamic Capabilities and Strategic Management." *Strategic Management Journal*, 509–533.

Terpstra, V. and Sarathy, R. (1994). *International Marketing*, 6th ed. Oak Brook, IL: Dryden Press.

Velu, C., Barrett, M., Kohli, R. and Salge, T. (2013). *Thriving in Open Innovation Ecosystems: Toward a Collaborative Market Orientation*. Cambridge, England: University of Cambridge Press.

Wright, M., Filatotchev, I., Hoskisson, R. E. and Peng, M. W. (2005). "Strategy Research in Emerging Economies: Challenging the Conventional Wisdom." *Journal of Management Studies*, 42(1): 1–33.

Xu, D. and Meyer, K. E. (2013). "Linking Theory and Context: 'Strategy Research in Emerging Economies' after Wright et al." *Journal of Management Studies*, 50(7): 1322–1346.

Zhou, K. S. and Wu, F. (2010). "Technological Capability, Strategic Flexibility, and Product Innovation." *Strategic Management Journal*, 31: 547–561.

8

MANAGING STRATEGIC ALLIANCES

*Africa Ariño**

Strategic alliances (SAs) are increasingly necessary to compete in today's business environment. However, alliances are not an easy undertaking, and their failure rate is high. At least two companies, with different agendas, are involved in an alliance, and this presents a high likelihood for conflict. This chapter discusses some factors that CEOs need to take into account when creating and managing alliances. These factors relate to partner search and selection, governance and management bodies, alliance negotiation, contracts and partner-relationship dynamics. Finally, this chapter presents factors to take into consideration when bringing an alliance to an end.

In an environment dominated by the growing internationalization of industries, rapid technological change and an escalation of market uncertainty, companies that do not reach a certain size face serious difficulties in their continued survival. To address those environmental changes, companies need to use their resources and capabilities more efficiently, or they may even need to gain access to critical resources that they lack. Furthermore, technological change or market uncertainty may generate doubt about what resources will be needed to compete in the future. SAs are a powerful way for companies to use their resources and capabilities more efficiently and to access new ones.

The importance of alliances is underscored by the number of companies using them as a building block for the future. A global CEO survey conducted by PwC (2016) confirmed that many CEOs pursue alliances to boost corporate growth. Another survey by BPI Network (2014) of global senior-level executives indicates that a large majority deem alliances vital for growth.

In this chapter, I use the term strategic alliance in a broad sense: a formal agreement between two or more companies to achieve certain goals – both common and private – by sharing resources in a context of uncertainty about the results. Firms can achieve many types of goals through alliances, such as reducing costs and obtaining economies of scale, gaining access to new markets and to new technologies, locking out competition, developing new capabilities, reducing risks or complying with official requirements to enter a new country.

Types of alliances

Alliances can by classified into types by looking at various dimensions. One useful classification is the nature of the resources that the partner companies contribute. On one hand, *critical mass alliances* are those in which partner companies contribute resources of a similar nature. These alliances enable partners to reach a sufficient level of scale for certain activities to be profitable. Alliances in the airline industry, in which partners share flights, fleets and crews, are one example of critical mass alliances. On the other hand, *complementary alliances* are those in which partner companies contribute resources of a different nature. These alliances enable partners to access resources that they lack and thus undertake new activities. An example of a complementary alliance would be a biotech company with strong innovation capabilities that partners with a large pharmaceutical lab with significant marketing capabilities.

The generic advantage of any alliance is that it provides access to resources that the firm lacks which would be costly or time-consuming to obtain in any other way – no matter if these resources are similar or different in nature to those that the company has. Despite the advantages, alliances present difficulties that arise from the necessary cooperation of two (or more) companies that are different and that remain autonomous while interdependent.

In alliances, interdependence and the potential for conflict coexist. In addition to its common goals, each firm may have its own explicit objectives with respect to the alliance. The potential for conflict depends on the combination of private and common goals – that is, the extent to which the various goals overlap – and on the importance attached to those goals. The potential for conflict is more salient in complementary alliances than in critical mass alliances. As each partner contributes different resources and capabilities to the alliance, they may learn from one another and internalize the partner's contributions. Thus, they may embark on a so-called learning race, in which whoever learns faster will no longer need the other partner (Ariño, 2006).

Partner search and selection

Getting the right partner is of particular importance to SA success. Who the partner is shapes the combination of resources and capabilities available to carry out the joint project. It may also reduce uncertainty in the alliance operation. Assessing fit is an ongoing process of exploration and discovery that takes place while searching for and selecting a partner, and it continues through alliance negotiations. The earlier a fit, or perhaps misfit, is identified, the better for all involved (Reuer et al., 2010). Fit must be assessed according to various dimensions:

• Strategic fit: to what extent are each partner's goals for the alliance compatible, and to what extent is the resulting combination of resources appropriate to carry out the alliance project?

- Organizational fit: will the companies be able to work well together?
- Operational fit: is it feasible to efficiently combine the resources that each company contributes to the alliance?
- Human fit: do the executives and other employees involved in the alliance feel comfortable working together?
- Values fit: do the companies share similar sets of values?

Typically, an assessment of fit will start from visible partner traits. As search, selection and negotiation unfold, assessment will move to features that are less obvious to outsiders. This is why strategic and organizational fit may be considered during partner search and selection, while operational, human and values fit are assessed during negotiations. However, if the company has solid knowledge of the potential partner from past relationships, the process is greatly simplified. Box 8.1 provides two opposite examples of partner compatibility in two international alliances in the automotive sector.

BOX 8.1   PARTNERS' STRATEGIC COMPATIBILITY: A MUST FOR ALLIANCE SUCCESS

When searching for the right partner, managers should look for companies whose interests are aligned with those of their own company: their common goals must be clear. Two alliances in the automotive industry illustrate the need for partners' strategic compatibility: the Grupo Salinas and First Automobile Works (FAW) alliance, one in which the partners' strategic incompatibility led to failure, and the alliance between Marcopolo and Tata Motors, in which strategic compatibility was clear and the partnership was successful.

Grupo Salinas and First Automobile Works

Grupo Salinas, one of the largest business groups in Mexico, wanted to grow its market base in the country's base of the pyramid. It created an alliance with FAW, one of China's top-five car manufacturers, which was seeking to expand its market presence in the United States through Mexico. A divergence in the companies' goals became evident during the 2008 global crisis, signaling that the commitment of the parties was weak. Initially constant communication and interaction between businesses began to decline. Neither party had the ability to grow their mutual business. How did the story unfold?

In 2007, Grupo Salinas decided to search for a partner with world-class technology that could produce low-priced cars to sell to the underserved low-income market. Managers from Grupo Salinas had talks with more than ten Chinese automobile manufacturers before finally partnering with FAW. Founded in 1953, FAW was a major Chinese car manufacturer. In 1991, FAW joined Volkswagen in the production of automobiles. In the following decade, they created joint ventures with other foreign firms, including Toyota, Mazda and Audi. By 2006, FAW was one the largest vehicle manufacturers in China, with 1.4 million cars produced and 140,000 employees. FAW exported cars to seventy countries.

Grupo Salinas and FAW signed a memorandum of understanding in 2007 to start marketing automobiles in Mexico by the first quarter of 2008. They had a long-term project and plans to introduce a new line of cars in Mexico for low-income consumers – a new, underserved market segment. The vehicles would initially be imported from China, and after three years, they would be produced in a jointly developed plant in Mexico's Michoacán State. This would enable Grupo Salinas to avoid the 50 percent import duties applicable to imported Chinese cars, which would render them uncompetitive and unprofitable.

However, the alliance collapsed before the plant was built. When the 2008 global recession hit, the incompatibility of their interests became apparent. At the same time, Michoacán suffered from violence related to the government's war against drug trafficking and organized crime. Lastly, the cars did not comply with US safety and environmental standards, eliminating the possibility of exporting them to the United States, which was FAW's primary goal.

Marcopolo and Tata Motors

Marcopolo, a leading Brazilian global company specializing in body building for buses and coaches, and Tata Motors, an Indian multinational automotive manufacturing company, had a clear goal for their alliance. Marcopolo saw an opportunity where others saw a threat. The company wanted to enter the Indian market despite the high level of deterioration of bus fleets and low bus penetration figures. Because of its experience in Brazil, the firm had developed unique capabilities to build bus bodies capable of withstanding bad road conditions. However, because they had a limited knowledge of the Indian market and lacked connections there, Marcopolo actively searched for a local partner.

It found a potential partner in Tata Motors, a member of the mighty Tata Group. Negotiations with the Tata Group were initiated. The deal seemed interesting to both parties, since Tata Motors manufactured only chassis, which eliminated a source of potential conflict of interests. The alliance became profitable in late 2009, less than three years after having signed the agreement. Both parties deem the alliance as a huge success.

Executives need to keep in mind that partner companies need not be identical to form effective alliances: it is enough for them to be compatible and aware of the sources of any differences. This requires an attitude of understanding toward differences and a willingness to engage in open discussions if conflict arises.

The main challenge in finding the right partner stems from the fact that partners in an alliance remain independent organizations. To the extent that there is a good partner fit and that they are compatible, the challenge will be lessened. However, as already mentioned, the final decision on selecting the partner is made during alliance negotiations.

Negotiating alliances (Reuer et. al., 2010)

Negotiations provide an opportunity to confirm the company's initial assessments of partner fit achieved while searching for and selecting the preferred partner. A thorough preparation is critical for a successful negotiation. In preparing negotiations, executives need to keep in mind three general considerations:

- The purpose of an alliance is to cocreate value with the partner. Unless value is in fact created, the eventual partners may have nothing to share. Thus, negotiations should focus on value creation as much as on value sharing.
- The analysis to prepare alliance negotiations should be based on a deep understanding not only of the company's needs, but also of those of the preferred partner. Putting oneself in the partners' shoes entails acknowledging the mutual interdependence that will result from the alliance and understanding the potential partner's needs.
- The initial assessment of the suitability of the counterpart as the preferred partner is still to be confirmed throughout the negotiations.

Preparing well for negotiating requires addressing the following issues:

- Who will participate on the negotiation team?

  In addition to advisors – such as strategy consultants, investment bankers, accountants, legal advisors and so on – executives from both corporate and business levels should participate on the negotiation team since they bring complementary perspectives and interests. Executives at the corporate level have a broader perspective of the alliance. They want to get the deal done quickly so that they can move on to their next assignment. Executives at the business level, however, understand well the difficulties that the alliance will pose. They are in the best position to ask tough questions early on and demand solutions to key operational issues. They bring a down-to-earth perspective that ensures alliance feasibility even though it may slow down the process. Those in corporate positions will keep negotiations moving on a timely basis.

- What issues should be brought to the table?

  Executives must make a thorough two-sided analysis of each party's interests. They need to understand the real interests at stake in the negotiation and not just those stated explicitly. Executives must be aware of the alternatives and possible outcomes if they do not reach an agreement. Establishing the best alternative to a negotiated agreement – or BATNA, as termed by Roger Fisher and William Ury – for each party provides a comparison level that serves as a "baseline" for the negotiation: surpassing that limit would mean that no agreement would be possible.

• How should negotiations be approached?

Executives from the initiating company need to ensure that their preferred partner will choose their company, as well. This takes persuading the partner-to-be that the initiating company can help satisfy their strategic needs It is crucial to make a good case for how a proposed alliance will benefit the potential partner. But in so doing, executives confront the danger of disclosing too much information. In some cases, once the potential partner has that information, it might go ahead with the business opportunity and leave the company aside. Knowledge-based businesses – such as science-based or information technology–based businesses – are particularly prone to this problem.

There are two general approaches to the actual negotiation process: a narrowband approach or a broadband approach. Executives who take a narrowband approach focus mostly on the details of who will carry out which tasks and who will contribute which resources to the alliance. In contrast, those who take a broadband approach arrive at this only after engaging in discussions to explore jointly the alliance's potential value. These discussions provide an opportunity to confirm their expectations about the counterpart and make final assessments of fit. In the process, they create an atmosphere of openness and start building a trust-based relationship. Alternatively, those discussions may lead partners to conclude that it is better not to initiate the alliance – a much better outcome than creating an alliance that is doomed to failure. Box 8.2 provides an example of this situation.

BOX 8.2 NOT CREATING AN ALLIANCE MAY BE A GOOD NEGOTIATION OUTCOME

Grupo Palomar (GP) and Laboratorios Australes (LA)[1] initiated negotiations to create an alliance in the medical equipment industry. In the end, they decided not to enter into an agreement.

GP was a major Spanish distributor of medical equipment and related consumables for hospitals. The group was active in a number of product segments, generated an annual income of €60 million and employed 270 people. LA was an Argentine company that manufactured and distributed chemical reagents for clinical analysis and distributed related equipment. In an industry

[1] Company names have been changed to protect confidentiality.

dominated by multinational companies, LA's domestic market share reached 60 percent and its overseas sales accounted for about 60 percent of its total sales of €10 million. LA had 140 employees.

The two companies started conversations about creating a joint venture to distribute GP's products in Argentina. In the initial negotiations, GP proposed taking a majority stake with the corresponding decision-making power: "We want to have the majority stake in the international joint venture, not so we can do as we please, but with clauses that protect you and keep us from doing anything that would harm your business. Now there will be losses; we do not think that it is fair that you alone will have to incur them. We propose a stake within the 30 and 49 percent range."

However, LA representatives were not keen on this idea. "There are aspects about the knowledge of the business that are yours. But a simpler version would be 50/50, to avoid confusion regarding minority protection. The discussion should center on the political power, not the economics." GP showed concern about possible deadlocks that a 50/50 governance structure might lead to.

As the negotiations evolved, GP sent a first letter of intent insisting in awarding themselves the majority of board representation. LA interpreted this as disrespectful. Moreover, they believed that GP's suggestion neither protected the interests of the minority, as promised earlier, nor adequately valued LA's logistical support.

In turn, LA's later counterproposal was viewed as unfair by GP. LA proposed that GP disburse the first US$2 million; only then would LA start disbursing their corresponding US$1 million. Nonetheless, they wanted to have a 50 percent representation on the board and some stringent voting requirements, such as unanimous approval of certain board-level decisions.

GP persisted in its efforts to produce a proposal that LA would deem fair. Putting an effort to accommodate LA's requests regarding capital disbursement, GP proposed offering US$1 million at a time. For each US$1 million, GP would first disburse its 66.6 percent, and then LA would complete the remaining 33.3 percent. They also tried to accommodate LA's desire that sensitive decisions be made with 100 percent of ownership being present but lowered the condition of favorable vote to their initially proposed 70 percent. Regarding decision-making at the board, GP went back to their initial proposal of requiring only a majority of votes from those members present at a meeting. The board structure was again proposed to be made up of five members, but they conceded that two of the members be from each partner and that the fifth one would be an independent party known and respected by both companies. They did not agree to LA's proposal that new companies created under the alliance's umbrella would be controlled by LA and proposed that the controller would have both executive and auditing powers.

LA again perceived a lack of respect from GP when GP's vice president informed LA that he intended to visit a distributor of cardiology equipment in

Buenos Aires. Apparently, this company was interested in doing business with the GP-LA alliance. LA did not welcome this news, as the various drafts of the letter of intent had clearly stipulated that the parties would refrain from nego-tiating with other parties while they were in negotiations with each other. LA asked for an LA representative to be included in that meeting, a request that GP opposed. LA's CEO worried that he had been left out of those negotiations and that GP had behaved against the agreed-on rules. From GP's perspective, how-ever, they were not breaking any rules. They were simply exploring options to be jointly exploited by GP and LA via the joint venture once it became operational.

GP decided to end negotiations. They recognized they had overestimated LA's capacity to support the alliance's local operations. In addition, LA's proposal that GP disburse their share of investment before LA started disbursing theirs did not come across as sensible. Under such conditions, the alliance would not benefit GP, and moving forward, it would likely generate important costs for the partners.

Even if an alliance is built on trust, good contracts are necessary to prevent pos-sible abuses. At the same time, an excessive focus on legal issues may lead to distrust among parties. In the next section, we discuss the role of contracts in alliances.

Alliance contracts (Campbell & Reuer, 2001; Ariño & Reuer, 2004)

Drafting a contract consumes resources – both cash and time. Paying lawyers and other professionals involved is expensive. Executives' time is a hidden cost: every hour dedicated to designing a contract means less time for other projects. The more detailed a contract, the more resources will be consumed while drafting it. However, the more detailed a contract, the less room for opportunistic behavior in case of unforeseen events. Consequently, executives need to think carefully about whether the benefits from a detailed contract outweigh the costs of drafting it. In making a decision, executives need to consider the following issues:

- Can the alliance assets be used for other purposes?

  If the answer is no, then it may be worthy having a detailed contract. Assets that are specific to the alliance activity require safeguards that protect the invest-ments made. If not, the partner may threaten to terminate the alliance to cap-ture more value.

- Have the partners worked together in past alliances?

  If the answer is no, a detailed contract may pay off. Lacking past alliances and mutual experience, partners face uncertainty about how the counterpart will behave. Even if they trust each other, they still need to develop a good understanding of each other's procedures, management styles, cultures and so on. In the absence of this understanding, they may be better off protecting their interests with detailed contracts.

• Does the alliance have a pre-established termination date?

If the answer is yes, a detailed contract may be of value. As an alliance's termination date approaches, issues such as ownership of proprietary technology and disclosures of confidential information become prominent if not stipulated in advance. Also, in the absence of later reciprocation opportunities, one partner may take advantage and behave opportunistically. At the same time, when the day on which the alliance ends is known, it is easier to foresee relevant contingencies and arrive at suitable responses, making contract design less costly.

• How strategically importance is the alliance?

If the answer is very, a detailed contract may be called for. Strategically important alliances involve greater risks than more peripheral ones. They require careful deliberation to mitigate the risk of creating a competitor or of having valuable resources fall into the hands of a third party.

In the contract, the partners should also establish a management structure and corporate governance rights. In the next section, we explain how governance and management bodies affect the future success of the SA.

Decision-making bodies

Decision-making bodies include those that make governance decisions – the board of directors in a joint venture or the steering committee in a purely contractual alliance, for instance – and those that make management decisions. An important trade-off when designing these bodies involves protecting the partners' interests versus granting enough autonomy to the management team. Steps should be taken to prevent the alliance from constricting the management team's initiative or from taking on a life of its own that is at odds with the partners' interests. The following considerations may help achieve the necessary balance:

• The more vital the alliance's activity is for the partners, the more necessary control becomes.
• The more complex and volatile the environment is, the greater the need for independence for the management team to speed up decision-making.

In any case, the relationship between governance and management bodies must be clearly defined. This includes considering what decisions belong to management bodies, which ones to governance bodies and which ones must be taken by the partner firms. Defining what the reporting lines will be and what information must be provided to whom and when are also important. Even if the same people are making both governance and management decisions, it should be clear to everybody what "hat" they are wearing at all times: that of overseeing the alliance or that of managing its daily operations. The following design principles provide guidance in this regard.

Principles for designing governance bodies (Bamford & Ernst, 2005)

- It is necessary to determine whether a governance body will play an active role in the alliance's management (greater control) or whether it is essentially a supervisory body (greater independence).
- Members of governance bodies from the different partners must have a comparable rank in their respective companies. If not, their different decision-making capacity will be a source of conflicts. Particularly in the case of a board of directors, all directors must work for the good of the alliance and not for that of the party that appointed them.
- Decision-making rules need to be established, bearing in mind two situations that may arise. First, if decisions are based on consensus, this may give rise to deadlocks. Second, if one of the parties has a controlling vote, this partner will usually want to control decision-making. One way to protect the minority partner is to provide this company with veto rights when deciding on particularly important issues.
- It is crucial to determine how confidential information can be used. If executives need to be free to share information with other people in their companies, this must be clearly acknowledged in the legal documents.

Principles for designing management bodies

- The distribution of management responsibilities does not necessarily have to be equal; one of the parties can even take full responsibility for day-to-day business through a management contract with the alliance. The guiding principle should be to assign responsibilities according to what will lead to excellence in all areas.
- When a partner's contributions come from its people, they must be included in the SA. This is often the case when partners' contributions entail implicit knowledge, which is difficult to articulate and convey and which is held (either individually or collectively) by the people who work in that company. Otherwise, outsiders may be hired to occupy positions of responsibility.
- An alliance is a learning opportunity, both for executives as professionals and for partner companies as organizations. The more people are involved with the SA, the greater the learning opportunity will be. However, turnover of personnel assigned to the SA has to be kept under control. If the change rate is too high, it may be necessary to rebuild the relationship practically from square one.

Having governance and management structures that suit the partners' preferences and goals will help ensure the satisfactory operation of the alliance. However, these elements are not enough, since the relationship with the partner needs to be nurtured as the alliance is forged.

Managing the relationship with the partner (Ariño et al., 2001)

A strong and positive relationship with the partner is a key element in an alliance's successful development. To the extent that partners feel comfortable with each other and trust each other, solving inevitable eventual conflicts will be easier. Initially, the quality of the relationship depends on the quality of the interactions during negotiations – and during previous alliances, if the partners had any.

Once the alliance becomes operational, partners continue to evaluate their ongoing interactions. These evaluations either improve or worsen the relationship. For instance, if the counterpart holds to its commitments, even in circumstances which make it difficult to do so, relational quality improves. Partners develop trust and become more tolerant of minor deviations from what was planned. On the contrary, if the counterpart acts only in accordance with its own interests when faced with difficulties, relational quality worsens. The company that observes such a behavior may decide to protect its own interests, fueling mistrust. Partners enter either a virtuous cycle that will help them achieve their goals or a vicious cycle that will end up destroying the alliance. In addition, the reputation for ethical behavior travels beyond the borders of the alliance and will leave a company and its executives in a better (or worse) position as trustworthy counterparts.

The conflicts that partners will sooner or later face relate to the various aspects of fit or misfit:

* Strategic conflicts depend on the mix of partners' individual and common goals – that is, on how compatible the various goals are and on the importance that each partner places on each set of goals. An alliance in which compatible common and individual goals prevail will operate more smoothly than one in which incompatible private goals are stronger for one or both partners. In the worst scenario, the alliance may contribute to creating a competitor.
* Organizational conflicts arise from differences in managerial practices, which relate to differences in partners' organizational structure and size and their corporate and national cultures. Cultural intelligence helps resolve organizational conflicts. Partners' conscious efforts to understand the motives and thoughts underlying their counterparts' actions and intents help develop cultural intelligence. Proactively engaging in new interactions in the face of apparent misunderstandings, as well as showing appreciation for the counterpart's practices, can serve to diminish conflict.
* Operational conflicts may develop as partners realize that the efficient combination of their resources is not as easy as it might have appeared at the outset.

These conflicts relate to the compatibility of committed resources, such as information technology systems, manufacturing facilities, distribution systems or any other type of resource committed to the alliance.

- Human conflicts may appear when people involved in the alliance feel uncomfortable working together. Alliances may require the exchange of confidential information, but this is unlikely to take place unless everyone is comfortable with each another. Also, executives are used to making decisions, so it may be hard for them to share decision-making power. At the end of the day, egos should not be discounted as a likely source of human conflicts.
- Value conflicts emerge over the course of decision-making. It is one thing to be vocal about values and quite another to live by them. The actual values of a company show in the weight assigned to the various criteria used in decision-making.

If partners face major conflicts, then disputes and misunderstandings may trigger a deadlock. Some mechanisms to resolve a deadlock are fast and inexpensive and have the benefit of flexibility – such as a casting vote from the president or a swing vote from a third party. If the deadlock results from a prolonged and fundamental dispute, the time may have come to bring the alliance to an end. Alliances may terminate even if they are successful. In the next section, we discuss the decision to terminate the SA, either because it failed or because it accomplished its main purpose.

Bringing alliances to an end (Inkpen & Ross, 2001)

Eventually, all alliances come to an end. But termination is not synonymous with failure. Alliance termination may have been planned from the beginning. Also, the partners may decide to exit an alliance once the intended goals have been achieved. In such cases, bringing the alliance to an end is a sign of success. Still, there are occasions when the partners recognize that the costs of keeping the alliance operational outweigh its benefits.

- Regarding when to end an alliance, it makes sense to bring an alliance to an end when the costs it generates are greater than the benefits it brings. This may be the consequence of partners' conflicts or of changes external to the alliance:
  - As the alliance unfolds underlying partners' conflicts of the types outlined earlier may surface, such as incompatible goals, different decision-making styles and power asymmetries. Coordination and management costs may increase to such an extent that it is simply not profitable to keep the alliance alive. As noted previously, this is less likely to happen when, during negotiations, partners have been careful in assessing their mutual fit.
  - Changes external to the alliance may affect the value that partners derive from it. Partners may shift their strategic priorities such that the resources

contributed by the partners are not as valuable as they were when the alliance was created. Also, changes at the industry level (e.g., strong consolidation, growth slowdown, etc.) or in the macro-environment (technological, political, or economic shifts) may significantly affect the value derived from the alliance.

The decision to bring the alliance to an end requires reflection. An alternative to termination could be alliance restructuring, but this also involves important costs.

- How to end the alliance
  It may not be easy for partners to agree about when and how to bring an alliance to an end. Including exit mechanisms in the alliance contract may avoid problems at the final stage and reduce the costs of termination. Contractual provisions regulating termination should include the following:

  - Termination scenarios for the expiry of a pre-specified time lapse; the termination for cause either related to performance – such as failure to meet a pre-specified target – or unrelated to performance – including regulatory changes; the insolvency of a partner; the change of control of a partner; a material breach; a breach of law; or a prolonged deadlock out of a fundamental dispute.
  - Termination procedures, methods to govern the termination of an alliance, can be relatively simple and easy to apply – for example, automatic renewal clauses or termination for convenience. Others are not only complex but also risky to apply – for example, "Texas shoot-out" or "Russian roulette."[2] The risk that some of these complex procedures involve is illustrated in Box 8.3.

BOX 8.3   ILLUSTRATION OF THE RISKS INVOLVED IN THE "RUSSIAN ROULETTE" TERMINATION PROCEDURE

A Spanish family shared ownership of a joint venture with a foreign partner. At a certain point, the Spaniards wanted to acquire the partners' shares. To this end, they initiated a "Russian roulette," a mechanism included in their contract. Since they were willing to acquire shares, they offered a price that – in their opinion – the partner could not resist selling at. It turned out that the partner decided to acquire rather than sell. All of a sudden, the family found themselves out of business with a substantial amount of cash. Since they had not planned on starting any new ventures, they could not immediately invest the cash in a new company, much to the delight of the Internal Revenue Service.

- Termination consequences: the partners may obtain significant benefits from planning the aftermath. Important issues need to be clear, such as the disposition of assets and liabilities, protection of proprietary information and property, distributorship arrangements, rights over sales territories and obligations to customers, personnel reallocation and the transfer of contractual obligations taken on by the alliance.

Conclusions

Alliances are becoming increasingly important to the CEO agenda – a trend that will continue given the demands from the current business environment.[3] Cross-industry alliances have frequently become necessary for companies to remain competitive in a changing landscape. Forging a successful alliance requires recombining strategic assets in new ways. Access to, rather than ownership of, those assets is of utmost importance.

SAs open up valuable opportunities but can present difficulties. Beyond their strategic capabilities, CEOs need to apply their leadership and political skills. Moreover, CEOs need to face alliance interactions with integrity and in a way that is consistent with the values of the managers and organizations involved. Alliances are built on relationships, and these need to be based on trust. Efforts to leave positive impressions on the managers involved is imperative (see Chapter 2.6). By paying attention to the issues identified in this chapter, CEOs can boost the chances of success for the alliances they pursue.

Notes

* The author gratefully acknowledges the support of the Joaquim Molins Figueras, chair of Strategic Alliances.
1 Company names have been changed to protect confidentiality.
2 Additional information about these procedures may be found in Ariño, Reuer and Valverde (2005).
3 For further information on the management and governance of strategic alliances, please see Das and Teng (1999), Doz and Hamel (1998), Dyer et al. (2001), Hoang and Rothaermel (2016), Hughes and Weiss (2007), Kumar (2014) and Wassmer et al. (2010).

References

Ariño, A. (2006). "Strategic Alliances, an Option to Enable Corporate Growth." DGN-648-E, IESE Business School.
Ariño, A., de la Torre, J. and Ring, P. S. (2001). "Relational Quality: Managing Trust in Corporate Alliances." *California Management Review*, 44(1): 109–131.
Ariño, A. and Reuer, J. J. (2004). "Designing and Renegotiating Strategic Alliance Contracts." *Academy of Management Executive*, 18(3): 37–48.
Ariño, A., Reuer, J. J. and Valverde, A. (2005). "The Perfect 'Pre-nup' to Strategic Alliances: A Guide to Contracts," *CriticalEYE Review*, June, 52–57.
Bamford, J. and Ernst, D. (2005). "Governing Joint Ventures." *The McKinsey Quarterly*, Special edition, 63–69.

BPI Network. (2014). "Grow from the Right. A Report on the Strategic Value of Business Alliances and Compatible Partner Matching." www.bpinetwork.org/thought-leadership/studies/51#flashMessage

Campbell, E. and Reuer, J. J. (2001). "International Alliance Negotiations: Legal Issues for General Managers." *Business Horizons*, 44: 19–26.

Das, T. K. and Teng, B-S. (1999). "Managing Risks in Strategic Alliances." *Academy of Management Executive*, 13(4): 50–62.

Doz, Y. L. and Hamel, G. (1998). *Alliance Advantage*. Boston, MA: Harvard Business School Press.

Dyer, J. H., Kale, P. and Singh, H. (2001). "How to Make Strategic Alliances Work." *Sloan Management Review*, Summer, 37–43.

Hoang, H. and Rothaermel, F. T. (2016). "How to Manage Alliances Strategically." *MIT Sloan Management Review*, 58(1): 68–76.

Hughes, J. and Weiss, J. (2007). "Simple Rules for Making Alliances Work." *Harvard Business Review*, November, 122–131.

Inkpen, A. and Roos, J. (2001). "Why Do Some Strategic Alliances Persist Beyond their Useful Life?" *California Management Review*, 132–148.

Kumar, R. (2014). "Managing Ambiguity in Strategic Alliances." *California Management Review*, 56(4): 82–102.

PwC. (2016). "Joint Ventures and Strategic Alliances. Examining the Keys to Success." www.pwc.com/us/en/deals/publications/joint-ventures-strategic-alliances.html

Reuer, J. J., Ariño, A. and Olk, P. (2010). *Entrepreneurial Alliances*. Boston, MA: Pearson Prentice Hall.

Wassmer, U., Dussauge, P. and Planellas, M. (2010). "How to Manage Alliances Better than One at a Time." *MIT Sloan Management Review*, 51(3): 77–84.

9

SPONTANEOUS LEARNING IN THE FIRM

The concept of footprints

Rafael Andreu

In this chapter, we explore a concept that explicitly considers learning in the strategy execution process, taking into account associated knowledge and experience accumulation dynamics. In particular, we turn our focus on *spontaneous learning*, which arises from human interactions whether participants like it or not and often goes unnoticed. This peculiar unconscious trait confers the phenomenon a few salient characteristics, some of which are relevant to improving the understanding of management and its practice.

The fact that spontaneous learning occurs naturally and affects the quality of future interactions means that firms, as long as they require people to execute plans and strategies, cannot define their outcomes based solely on economic performance. Thus, management should take spontaneous learning into account and promote positive learning to ensure that future interaction-based executions improve over time and enhance the firm's *overall* performance. This sort of learning-based reflection helps produce explicit relevant consequences on human interactions in the firm which otherwise tend to be neglected.

From this perspective, spontaneous learning becomes a significant phenomenon that complements the customary understanding of general management roles and responsibilities. In particular, it helps to conceptualize the functions of *strategizing*, *organizing* and *renewal*, in which dynamics learning and specifically spontaneous learning processes are highly relevant. As we will observe, adopting a viewpoint based on this type of learning has a number of implications for the development of the firm's internal and external missions and for its business model.

As an interesting consequence, the approach proposed suggests understanding the management profession as one that naturally and essentially includes ethics as a core ingredient. In this sense, managers who are unethical cannot be considered as true managers. Moreover, it understands corporate social responsibility (CSR) as intricately intertwined with management, to the extent that its usual conception may seem contrived.

As we will see, this complementary perspective of management, management roles and, in particular, the main areas of responsibility of CEOs points to a humanistic approach consistent with the tradition of IESE Business School and other institutions akin in outlook. Before developing this concept further, let us review some of its characteristics and highlight some key management implications.

Value creation (and destruction) inevitably encompasses spontaneous learning and leaves footprints

When we refer to the value created or destroyed by a firm, its market capitalization and so on, we measure it in economic terms as if there were no other way to assess the firm's worth. However, firms spontaneously create and destroy other kinds of value, whether they realize it or not, due to the simple fact that their operations require people to interact both within and outside the organization: with customers, other firms and society in general.

All organizational interactions – between vendors and customers, CFOs and bankers, buyers and suppliers, managers and their team members – produce more than a profit margin, a loan agreement, a purchase commitment or an economic and financial plan, since participants always unintentionally learn (or unlearn) something and take that result away with them. Consequently, future interactions, even with the same people and the same objectives, will most likely not render the same result. These learning experiences leave footprints that condition future interactions and, in turn, generate new footprints on participants and those around them.

Footprints, permanently and spontaneously updated, are assets that can influence the firm's future operations and overall performance

Footprints, whether positive or negative, leave their traces on people, firms and organizations and inevitably impact their future, much in the same way as accumulated economic resources. In this sense, firms possess a dynamic depository of footprints in the form of individual and collective knowledge, which is acquired during interactions as learning takeaways. In other words, in the process of creating (positive or negative) economic value, firms inevitably and spontaneously leave positive or negative footprints on people, both inside and outside the firm. From this standpoint, *the output of firms cannot be narrowed down to purely economic results, because their activities also produce footprints.* For this reason, footprints should be taken into account as a "component of corporate performance" that could potentially have a major impact on its future.

Considering footprints as consequences of management actions – in strategy implementation, for example – helps senior managers adopt a broader and more realistic perspective of their role. What footprints will likely be left – and on whom – when they execute their firm's mission or business plan? Since footprints are inescapable, how can senior managers ensure that they are positive and enhance future performance, understood as economic and as consequential from other footprints? To consider this challenge with rigor, let's start by defining the main characteristics of footprints.

Defining footprints

Footprints are the product of spontaneous learning in individuals and groups when they interact to execute a firm's operations. Specifically, footprints are

- *Inevitable*, since people learn through the interaction whether they want to or not.
- Often *naturally linked to the emotions of the people experiencing them*, thus making the process of retaining them a personal experience.
- *Personal and nontransferable*, since they result from the learning process of each particular individual. Only the specific individual or group that holds a footprint can enact it.
- *Ubiquitous*, because they appear inside and outside the firm through interactions with stakeholders (customers, suppliers, employees, etc.).
- *Likely to affect everyone involved in an interaction*, from its initiator to those who implement it. From a management perspective, footprints of particular interest are those experienced by managers in interactions that they initiate as part of their professional responsibility.
- *Difficult to erase*, as doing so requires unlearning, which is never easy.
- *Almost impossible to compensate for*, whether by layering it with other footprints in the same person or others or with money.
- Largely *difficult to foresee* because people's reactions (including one's own) are impossible to totally predict.
- *Potentially far-reaching in scope, depending on where, when, how and in whom they are produced*: an elderly woman deceived by a salesperson who convinces her to purchase preferred stock (a perpetuity!) is affected differently than a passerby on a city street who gets cheated in an illegal card game.
- *Potentially capable of affecting society in general* through interactions among people in the firm's sphere and in their social environment.
- Either *individual or collective*, where collective footprints refer to spontaneous learning that affects the coordination of a group when performing a collective task and thus may potentially affect the performance of concrete group undertakings.
- *Cumulative, path-dependent* knowledge.

Footprints can also be *caused* by someone with good or bad intentions – for example, to reinforce a training program or to deceive someone. But this chapter won't consider these types of footprints, since they aren't spontaneous. Nonetheless, footprints should not be ignored, because if so, they tend to develop negatively, particularly when they stem from reckless management.

Footprints can have positive or negative consequences

We would intuitively agree that the footprints on the aforementioned senior citizen are negative. Both the elderly woman and the passerby are worse off *with* their footprints than without them, as well as those who inflicted them since they learned something too − their own footprints. Not all footprints are negative, of course; they can also be positive. For example, consumers may come away satisfied after a successful shopping experience, and sales representatives may derive a sense of pride if they believe they have genuinely solved a problem for a customer. In these cases, both sides are better off after the interaction.

What criteria can we use to distinguish between positive and negative footprints and avoid relying on intuition? One possibility is to ask the recipient if a footprint leaves them better or worse prepared for future interactions along two main dimensions:

1   What the individual seeks from the interactions
2   The degree of respect for personal dignity, which should be maintained at all
    costs

The first dimension is obvious, since it gauges the operational capabilities of whoever gets the footprint to enhance their future performance. Thus, it is measured in an economic-like manner. However, limiting the assessment to a sole criterion would mean leaving the bar too low; footprints must also respect people's dignity, although they may do this to differing degrees.

The second dimension is relevant because the determining factor of a negative footprint is that it results in the degradation of the recipient − that is, treatment that violates the basic characteristics of human beings, such as deception, deprivation of liberty, lack of personal or professional development, fraud or denying the recipient's capacity to evaluate and make decisions.

We can therefore propose to classify a footprint as *negative* if it results in a degrading treatment of its recipient, regardless of how well it scores in the operational dimension. On the other hand, we can say that a footprint is *potentially positive* on the whole if it doesn't violate the recipient's fundamental rights while reinforcing some of them and truly respects the individual and ideally allows them to grow as a person. It would be *wholly positive* if, in addition, it makes the recipient better from the operational standpoint.

Crucially, people may also leave positive or negative footprints on themselves as a result of interactions with others, on whom they also leave footprints. The good sales representative who is proud of their work is an example; another is the person who deceitfully "sells" preferred stock to an elderly person. The first can potentially improve as a sales representative and become a better person; the second has perhaps learned how to cajole rather than sell and, as a result, risks becoming more dishonest – which would make them less of a good person.

In summary, we can conclude that a positive footprint leaves its holder better off, whereas a negative footprint leaves them worse off when it comes to effectively pursuing future interactions. Also, as one may deduce, the quality of interactions left by footprints can potentially play a direct role in future economic performance. Moreover, since footprints permeate society at all levels, we can expect positive footprints from firms to make a positive impact and promote growth in human development.

A footprints-based taxonomy of corporate missions

To illustrate this footprint-based analysis, let's perform a prediction exercise that attempts to forecast the quality of the footprints resulting from a firm's external and internal mission for its various stakeholders. We start with a brief definition of what we mean by a corporate mission: a concise and clear expression of its raison d'être, or reason for being.

Distinguishing between internal and external missions is less straightforward and common. The definitions proposed Pérez López,[1] which inspired those of Rosanas,[2] are representative and also pioneering to an extent:

> The external mission represents the real needs that an organization seeks to satisfy through the products or services it offers.[3] In short, the external mission includes fulfilling the needs of individual customers.
>
> The internal mission consists of the *actual* needs of the stakeholders that an organization seeks to satisfy (such as employees), insofar as it determines the quality of the products or services necessary to fulfill the organization's aims.

Note that these definitions emphasize something that the general definition of "mission" addresses only implicitly: they focus on *people's* needs. Regarding the company's raison d'être, they respond more to the question of "for whom" rather than "why."

Moreover, a company's internal and external missions are interdependent by nature. Customer needs are met through operations undertaken within the company, which in turn address the personal and professional needs of those who carry them out, either adequately or not (and, as discussed, footprints appear as a consequence). Thus, the internal mission is both an end in itself and a means of fulfilling the external mission.

For this reason, the external and internal missions must act in harmony with each other. For example, if an engineering firm aims for maximum efficiency, it won't be able to provide excellent services if it disregards the technical training of its employees or neglects their professional development. The personal and professional growth of employees would also be undermined if they were continuously given dull assignments or if policies in place to promote respect and consideration for their contributions were disregarded at the first setback. In the same vein, it's hard to imagine a team of heartless mercenaries capable of providing excellent service.

As we'll see in the next section, the external missions of some companies imply business models that in effect require abusing or degrading their employees to achieve corporate objectives. In other words, their external missions necessitate an internal counterpart whose implementation leaves negative footprints on employees and stakeholders. Thus, consistency between internal and external missions is desirable and in fact necessary.

Real-life examples will help facilitate understanding mission statements within this context. The Appendix reproduces actual mission statements taken from corporate websites during the second quarter of 2013. Take some time to read them and note your immediate reactions. What responses do they elicit as you read them?

A few conclusions can be drawn from this selection of mission statements:

1   Corporate missions vary dramatically even among firms operating in the same industry.
2   Most mission statements refer explicitly to economic performance and/or value, and some refer only to shareholders in this respect.
3   They generally describe *what* they want to do and focus much less on *why* and *for whom*.
4   Some are quite extensive. Does this suggest a lack of clarity? In your view, are all points equally relevant?
5   Some mission statements mention issues that sound purely politically correct (mentions of environmental protection, CSR, etc.), whereas others go as far as recognizing their shortcomings in specific areas to underscore their commitment.
6   Some are unique, like La Fageda's.[4] If we form an opinion of La Fageda solely on its mission statement, what do you think differentiates it from others?

Based on these observations, we can discern three general features that characterize most of these mission statements:

- Nearly all refer to an external mission and are far less concrete in their internal mission. La Fageda, whose mission statement is essentially internal, is the exception.
- Beyond terms like "customers" and "shareholders," few refer to people or groups of people, either internal or external, except in general terms, with allusions to "stakeholders" or "talent."
- Consequently, there are few references to the creation of footprints – for instance, the impact of training and development or the need to uphold universal respect and human decency. Some even suggest the generation of negative footprints, by which they implicitly consider employees as mere pawns

who are compensated to fulfill a mission of which they do not seem to be part. These firms seem to lack an internal mission.

Of course, there are exceptions, such as the mission statements of Southwest Airlines, La Fageda and Johnson & Johnson, although the last one contains no reference to footprints.

Therefore, we define a "complete" mission statement as one that includes both internal and external components and the most important footprints that it aims to generate in both components. Complete mission statements add more meaning to the firm's raison d'être and serve as guides for decision-making and managerial action.

Figure 9.1 serves a useful guide to consider a firm's complete mission. It accounts for both the internal and the external components and appraises the footprints created in the firm's different domains. Note that footprints may appear in any of the four cells; that certain aspects of the *external* mission can cause *internal* footprints, whether positive or negative; and that certain aspects of the *internal* mission can cause *external* footprints, whether positive or negative.

The mission of the "ideal" firm generates only positive footprints, both externally and internally. The annotation (++) indicates its ambition to achieve solid economic results. In contrast, criminal organizations such as mafias strive for excellent economic performance yet generate negative footprints in all domains. NGOs emphasize their external mission and aim to create as many positive footprints as possible in this domain, without stating an explicit economic objective. Moreover, many expect their external mission to generate positive footprints internally as mere by-products. The mission of firms in the "many" category doesn't neglect economic performance and emphasizes the external context to varying degrees,

	Internal Mission	External Mission
Positive Footprints	Positive footprints arising from the Internal Mission	Positive footprints arising from the External Mission
Negative Footprints	Negative footprints arising from the Internal Mission	Negative footprints arising from the External Mission

FIGURE 9.1 Missions and Footprints

Source: Author.

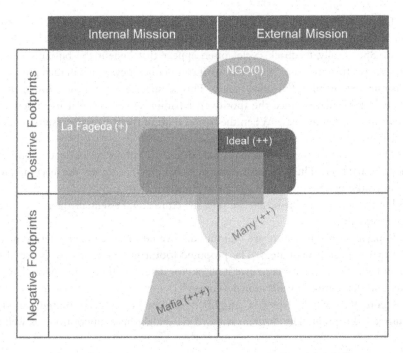

FIGURE 9.2   Map of Typical Corporate Missions versus La Fageda's Mission

Source: Elaborated by the author

which are not distinguished in the figure. Therefore, positive and negative foot-prints can be expected in both domains.

Lastly, Figure 9.2 specifically highlights La Fageda and the predominance of its internal mission and corresponding footprints, with an inevitable (though minimal) occurrence of negative footprints but without overlooking economic performance to achieve its internal mission.

Plot your organization in the diagram and reflect on the result. It is common to expect higher quality in external footprints (on customers, shareholders, etc.) than in internal footprints (on employees, managers, etc.). As noted earlier, when foot-prints are neglected – for instance, when firms don't specifically manage them but make a concerted effort to ensure that they are positive – they are likely to eventu-ally become negative and trigger a dysfunctional imbalance.

A brief footprints-based perspective of business models

A similar analysis can be conducted on a business model level. As mentioned in Chapter 2.4, a business model, as defined by Ramon Casadesus-Masanell and Joan Enric Ricart,[5] is a framework that represents how a firm's most important deci-sions (or "choices," as they say) are made to implement the strategy implied by its mission. Using this concept, desired outcomes are attained that in turn facilitate or condition other decisions and desired outcomes.

The resulting framework of decisions and consequences leads to a scheme that can be represented graphically to analyze the dynamics of decision-making processes. Specifically, feedback cycles often appear that benefit the business model, because as a firm increases its operations, it gains coherency, which in turn promotes dynamic sustainability (virtuous cycles). This is especially true if the consequences involved have inertia since the (positive) dynamic remains even if its underlying causes intermittently cease. When the first condition is not met, the resulting circle is vicious, so a negative dynamic emerges.

The types of footprints that may materialize in virtuous cycles depend on how they are managed. This requires examining with greater scrutiny the learning processes of the people involved in order to discern whether cycles deemed virtuous within the context of the business model structure could essentially generate negative footprints.

Imbalances of this nature are typically discovered in the implementation phase of a firm's mission or strategy. The proposed footprints-based analysis is useful to circumvent these imbalances, since it allows for detecting them early on and, most likely, implementing organizational solutions.[6]

Figure 9.3, which depicts a simplified version of Ryanair's business model, illustrates this point. The diagram is based on widely held suppositions, as well as

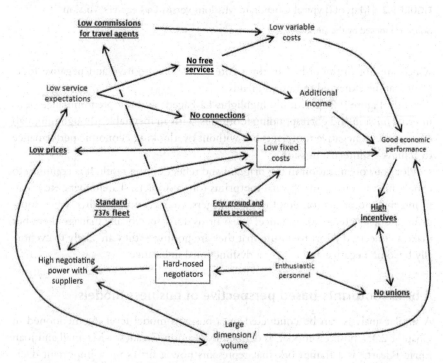

FIGURE 9.3 A Simplified Business Model for Ryanair

Source: Elaborated by the author from an original business model representation by Prof. Ramon Cadasadesus-Masanell.

assumptions behind the different arrows that are not explicit. In this regard, the figure assumes that "Low commissions to travel agencies" was a corporate decision made by Ryanair to implement its strategy and support its mission. Other decisions should be clear.

Next, view the dynamics of Ryanair's business, focusing on virtuous cycles and their sustainability. Figure 9.4 depicts four such cycles overlaid on the business model diagram.

The consequences stemming from the implementation of decisions that configure a business model can turn out to be negative from a footprints standpoint. In other words, there can be adverse business models that facilitate the appearance of harmful footprints. As we will see, a footprints-based analysis of the business model can help identify potentially counterproductive models in this sense.

The idea is to pinpoint footprints that may emerge as a result of implementing specific decisions and gauge their quality. In the case of Ryanair, one can conceivably identify areas where footprints may emerge, bearing in mind that footprints may have also appeared in the analysis of the firm's mission and strategy, as mentioned earlier. The next step is to validate these footprints, making sure that they continue to make sense within the context of the business model, and if not, adjust the different business perspectives to achieve a coherent whole.

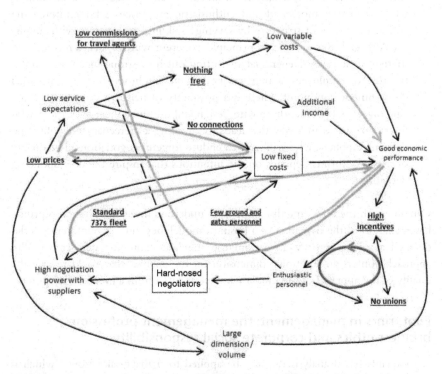

FIGURE 9.4 An Example of Virtuous Cycles in Ryanair's Business Model

Source: Elaborated by the author from an original business model representation by Prof. Ramon Cadasadesus-Masanell.

The next step entails a thorough footprints-based analysis. In Figures 9.3 and 9.4, for example, we could analyze the following aspects:

1   The consequence "Low service expectations" can be understood as an "antici-pated" footprint in potential customers, which they could find demeaning even if their expectations are extremely low. The Ryanair manager responsible for this area should take this into consideration.

2   A standardized fleet allows for specialized maintenance operations, regardless of whether Ryanair operates proprietary or leased aircraft. This affords them high negotiation power with suppliers and ultimately translates into lower fixed costs, enabling the corresponding virtuous cycle in Figure 9.4. Making this a reality, though, requires outstanding efficiency and quality control which leads to learning that may in turn cause footprints.

    These reflections highlight the need for a solid fit between the organization and its management systems, to ensure that they reinforce the firm's respon-sibility structure and facilitate an integrated environment where people can develop their potential and pursue their learning interests. A footprints-based approach can be beneficial when devising business models because considera-tions of this nature are not common in standard analysis.

3   Another cycle regards decisions on incentives and strategies to avoid unions while attracting motivated and enthusiastic employees who reinforce the company's low-cost structure by serving as skillful negotiators with suppli-ers. Although this cycle is, in principle, coherent with Ryanair's mission and strategy, it deserves deeper analysis to find out how strong incentives impact the role of employees as negotiators and the implications from a personal development standpoint. There is a possibility of negative footprints occur-ring on several people: those who design and use these incentives, those who internalize them in a way that leads to adopting a mercenary mentality and Ryanair suppliers, who will have to endure forceful negotiations. The quality of these footprints depends on the intentions that inspire the corresponding decisions.

Our aim with the foregoing discussion is to underline the benefits of a footprints-based analysis of the dynamics of a business model, beyond self-reinforcing cycles deemed as virtuous or vicious from the standard economic perspective. This approach confers an additional dimension on the analysis that could reverse the quality of the appraisal of the model when performed from a broader viewpoint.

Footprints in management: the management profession, business ethics and corporate social responsibility

A footprints-based analysis can also be applied to managerial actions,[7] which is especially useful for essential aspects of management practice. This analysis raises questions regarding how and on whom negative footprints can appear as a result of such actions. This could have strong implications for the management profession, including the need for business ethics and a clear stance on CSR.

The management profession

Since footprints are spontaneous, trying to avoid them is futile. They can, of course, be ignored, but sooner or later they will surface either directly or through unintended and perhaps unpleasant consequences. By then, however, it will be too late: facing them head-on will only make them even "more inevitable."

Consequently, CEOs who ignore footprints (especially negative ones) by using the excuse that they are too busy attending to other (i.e., economic) matters are not among the best professionals. Ignoring negative footprints or fostering them, even unintentionally, amounts to a disregard for one basic responsibility of the managerial profession. It shows a lack of respect for human dignity and an improper lack of interest in how to avoid disrespecting the dignity of others in the future.[8] CEOs are similarly irresponsible when they fail to promote positive footprints, because this leads to missed opportunities for human and economic development.

Hence, CEOs must learn to identify footprints and not overlook them as a result of a lack of insight or vision. And this is only the first step. One can identify, understand and classify footprints and simply record them "for future reference," which usually means, even with good intentions, "identifying and compensating the victims," often economically. Things are not so simple, however. Many footprints can't be covered up or compensated for that way. Of course, people appreciate financial compensation and go home a bit less annoyed, but they do so with negative footprints still etched on their minds. Moreover, people may consider compensation an insult, which implies adding yet another negative footprint.

In short, as footprints tend to persist in each person, they should be properly managed. Some managers, however, think that the task of managing footprints is too demanding. Ignoring them would obviously be an easier course of action, but people are going to learn and acquire footprints regardless, and they deserve respect (at least as much respect as managers would ask for themselves).

This is nonnegotiable in the same way as the law of gravity is for physicists. The challenge is precisely *managing footprints and economic performance simultaneously* on a day-to-day basis, as part of every managerial action. In this sense, these two dimensions – economic performance and footprints – should be considered in such a way that even a solid performance in one doesn't automatically "compensate for" a poor one in the other. Ideally, good management actions will score positively in both dimensions.[9]

This requires a conception of the management profession that differs from the usual by framing managerial responsibility from a *complete value* (economic plus footprints) perspective. Proper management entails creating sufficient economic value and positive footprints simultaneously; trying to offset one for another disfigures the problem. A competent CEO will recognize footprints and make managerial decisions that promote the positive while avoiding the potentially negative ones. This is far more effective than simply masking negative footprints after the fact with, say, a coating of money.

In summary, managers have the following obligations:

1   To help generate positive footprints by inspiring people to learn – themselves included – in a way that, at very least, does not degrade them.
2   To prevent negative footprints by getting to their root causes and not simply addressing their symptoms.[10]
3   To respect the above constraints while generating the best possible (positive) economic performance.[11]

Managers who fail to fulfill these obligations are derelict in their duties, which is something that society should not accept. Is management really such a demanding profession? Undoubtedly, yes. It is sometimes said that management is somewhat of an art. In a sense, this may be true, except that artists enjoy far more freedom than managers, who must inherently abide by nonnegotiable and fundamental require- ments. A good manager is much less of an artist than appearances would suggest; management is by nature a *normative* endeavor.

Management ethics

Earlier we defined negative footprints as those that denote a lack of respect for human dignity and leave the person worse off in a fundamental way. In other words, executing a management decision can produce a deterioration of certain traits of the people involved (the decision maker and whoever executes the decision).

This automatically puts ethics on the table since it refers to individuals doing something that denigrates themselves or others *as human beings*. In this sense, gener- ating positive footprints in people becomes a genuine *ethical* obligation.

Managing is not about being a good professional in the economic domain and superficially addressing ethical concerns as an optional extra. Ethical duties are an intrinsic part of the managerial profession. To sum this up, "Good managers are ethical – or they aren't in fact managers." No exceptions. Executives who don't feel capable of managing this way should look for another profession.

Corporate social responsibility

As a follow-up to the preceding discussion, the managerial profession doesn't require conventional CSR measures, frequently deployed to cover up negative footprints on a particular group of stakeholders by trying to leave positive footprints on other groups, even those with no direct contact with the company. This approach is both insincere and ineffective, as negative footprints will likely remain despite these CSR efforts. It is much simpler than that if we approach it from a footprints perspective. Let's illustrate how that could be done: firms, during their normal course of opera- tions, focus (exclusively) on economic performance. As the closing of a reporting period draws near, they allocate a portion of their cash flow to social aims that are usually unrelated to the negative footprints generated by these "normal" business operations. But in general, this doesn't make the negative footprints go away.

The same argument might be used the other way around to justify a purely economic objective: "If we don't make money, we can't engage in social action" – without recognizing that *the company, whether it likes it or not, inevitably engages in social action each and every day through its footprints, simply because its operations involve people.* In other words, if a firm is forced to generate negative footprints in order to make money and corporate revenues don't suffice to render the social action positive, it actually ends up with negative social actions and a deficient economic performance – an unacceptable situation by all accounts.

If we turn the situation around, the absurdity becomes more apparent. Imagine that we ignore the footprints left by the firm's daily operations (as is typical) and that it reports negative economic results for the next period. Would we then expect the firm to carry out a few negative yet lucrative social actions to render the overall economic result positive?

In short, just as an ethical outlook is an indisputable attribute of a good manager, so too is the avoidance of negative footprints the foundation of CSR efforts. Managers must aspire to reach this minimum threshold; anything beyond this point is welcome, albeit optional.

Some implications for management training, education and development

Given the importance of spontaneous learning for the management profession, it is worth briefly exploring its implications for management training and education. More often than not, footprints are overlooked in this endeavor, because emphasis is placed on the explicit, model-based, formal management disciplines – operations, finance, accounting and so on – despite the fact that these areas also contain relevant person-related facets.

From a footprints-based perspective, several implications emerge. First, since footprints directly impact the firm's future performance, there is a normative issue to consider: the evaluation of management actions can't be reduced solely to economic results while leaving everything else to the discretion of the manager; there are good and bad management acts beyond economic consequences. Management is not an art, and managing is not like directing an orchestra: there is no orchestra score to follow and an exact rehearsal isn't an option. The direct inference is that *good, complete management education should be normative, taking footprints into account.*

Second, since the learning behind footprints can't be foreseen and is often linked to emotions, good management implies a proactive approach to knowing the people involved in decisions and their implementation as well as possible. Not knowing them well enough is likely to result in *negative learning.* Of course, the opposite also applies: you must let your colleagues and teammates *easily know you* to achieve effective collaboration. From a management education standpoint, methods that foster mutual knowledge in settings that mirror real-life scenarios can help.

Third, some footprints with particular characteristics need to be effectively recognized in training efforts. Managing *collective footprints* is one example. In situations that require teamwork with people from different organizations, backgrounds and areas of expertise, managing footprints is more complicated than managing individual ones. Teaching people in this situation is more demanding.

To leverage these insights, learning initiatives should put students/trainees in the role of decision makers and aim to replicate their organizational contexts so that relevant footprints can be realistically anticipated and addressed using well-designed management acts. This in turn calls for appropriate teaching materials and environments and for professors who thoroughly understand the normative dimension of management. Their role will resemble that of an experienced coach rather than a knowledgeable theorist, although a mix of both would be ideal.

Accordingly, management education institutions such as business schools need to design external missions (for students) and internal ones (for faculty) consistent with the considerations discussed in this chapter, and they need to view the management profession through a footprints-based lens. Similarly, if business schools accept the premise that spontaneous learning leads to footprints, they should make every effort to ensure that the models and theories underlying their teaching and research align with this view.

Also, the development of teaching materials that adequately reflect the complexity of real-life business scenarios and facilitate a deep understanding of complete management acts (decision plus implementation) and the persons involved is a practical issue that must also be resolved. Faculty development and training are key to reinforcing the professor's role as coach rather than offering hard-and-fast rules when faced with explicit management challenges.

Finally, new technologies as applied to management teaching and education are especially useful when conceived primarily as facilitators to teach and use explicit model-based disciplines. Using them to help professors in their coaching role is much more difficult and involved; counterproductive simplifications of real-life situations and their dynamics are to be avoided. For these purposes, blended approaches that combine technology (mainly information and telecommunications) and more traditional teaching methods tend to the most effective.

Certain exaggerations in the use of "row" technology are grossly inappropriate because they often lose the essence of the real-life situations that make management such a demanding profession. Good, well-balanced and effective technology-based solutions are still hard to come by, although in general, they are (slowly) improving. Thus, a word of caution is in order, along with a hopeful desire for good research and developments in this area. That said, there is still a lot of hard work to be done.

Conclusions

As a social discipline, management inescapably involves people, who learn both purposefully and spontaneously. A sole focus on the first type of learning leads to incomplete outcomes and inadequate management practices. For this reason, organizations must consider footprints as an additional dimension during *strategizing*, *organizing* and *renewal* processes.

This new dimension uncovers often-overlooked aspects of core management tasks and fosters positive learning in individuals beyond mere operative learning. Management acts must consequently be evaluated along *all* dimensions, which makes management a challenging profession. The footprints-based perspective also provides a framework to better understand how business ethics and basic CSR are naturally integrated into basic management responsibilities.

APPENDIX

Examples of mission statements, 2013

Gas Natural Fenosa

"Gas Natural Fenosa's mission is to meet the energy requirements of society, providing its clients with quality products and services that are respectful to the environment, offering shareholders growing and sustainable performance and employees the possibility to develop their professional competencies."[12]

KPMG

"We provide value based on the knowledge and experience of our professionals, in the interests of our clients, our people, and our community."[13]

Dover Corporation

"Our goal is to be the leader in every market we serve, to the benefit of our customers and our shareholders."[14]

Citigroup

"Our goal for Citigroup is to be the most respected global financial services company. Like any other public company, we're obligated to deliver profits and growth to our shareholders. Of equal importance is to deliver those profits and generate growth responsibly."[15]

Microsoft

"At Microsoft, we work to help people and businesses throughout the world realize their full potential. This is our mission. Everything we do reflects this mission and the values that make it possible."[16]

Google

"Google's mission is to organize the world's information and make it universally accessible and useful."[17]

Johnson & Johnson

"We believe our first responsibility is to the doctors, nurses and patients, to mothers and fathers and all others who use our products and services. Research must be carried on, innovative programs developed and mistakes paid for. We are responsible to the communities in which we live and work and to the world community as well."[18]

Southwest Airlines

"Dedication to the highest quality of customer service delivered with a sense of warmth, friendliness, individual pride, and company spirit.

To our employees:

> We are committed to providing our employees a stable work environment with equal opportunity for learning and personal growth. Creativity and innovation are encouraged for improving the effectiveness of Southwest Airlines. Above all, employees will be provided the same concern, respect, and caring attitude within the organization that they are expected to share externally with every Southwest customer."[19]

Mercadona

"To meet the needs of all its stakeholders, mainly its customers, as well as workers, suppliers, society and investors, and to achieve the maximum profitability through differentiation in price and quality, specializing in hygiene and food products under its own brand."[20]

Nestlé

"As the No. 1 food products company and world leader in nutrition, Nestlé's mission is to provide greater well-being than any other company to more people around the world through its wide variety of pleasant and innovative foods and drinks of excellent quality, taste and added value, and obtaining good returns to ensure the growth of the company."[21]

La Fageda

"To provide work on market terms to people with intellectual disabilities and severe mental illnesses in the region, who are able to perform work, as well as to provide occupational therapy services, lodging and leisure to such people. The cooperative La Fageda is not for profit, in that the net income of its commercial operations is reinvested into further job creation in the company and increased resources for therapeutic care and the services for workers and people taken care of by the organization."[22]

BBVA

"BBVA is a global financial services group committed to providing the best solutions to its customers, profitable growth to its shareholders and progress in the societies where it operates. This is the organization's mission, which gives life to the organization and justifies the business project that the company represents."[23]

ACS

"Pursuing global leadership:

- Positioning itself as one of the main players in all those sectors in which it takes part as a means of boosting its competitiveness, maximizing value creation in relation to its clients and continuing to attract talent to the organization.
- Meeting the needs of our clients by offering a diversified portfolio of products, innovating daily and selectively investing to increase the range of services and activities offered.
- Continuously improving quality, safety and reliability standards in the services offered.
- Expanding the group's current client base through a permanent commercial effort in new markets.

Optimizing the profitability of the resources managed:

- Increasing operating and financial efficiency and offering attractive profitability to the group's shareholders.
- Applying strict investment criteria in line with the company's strategy of expansion and growth.
- Maintaining a solid financial structure which facilitates the raising of resources and the maintenance of a low cost thereof.

Promoting sustainable growth:

- Improving the society in which we live by helping to grow the economy, generating wealth through the ACS Group's own activities, thereby guaranteeing the well-being of citizens.
- Respecting the economic, social and environmental backdrop, innovating in the establishment of company procedures and respecting in each of its activities, the recommendations of the main domestic and international institutions.

- Helping the economy to grow by creating stable, respectable and fairly remunerated employment."[24]

Bodegas Torres

"Our mission is to maintain our 100-year-old tradition as a self-financed and independent family company with an international projection. To pursue the goal of turning every customer into a friend. To be a leader in the premium wine and brandy industry, offering better and more differentiated products. To be leaders too in design and in communicating the culture of wine. Contributing to the well-being of our staff, the efficient advancement of society and environmental protection."[25]

Zara – Inditex

"To develop fashion garments of average quality to meet customer expectations at a great price for the young and adults."[26]

DKV Medical Insurance

"As health experts (DKV Medical Insurance and its health, income and accident departments and DKV Services) and a preferred partner in other categories (ERGO Life, Home and Funeral), through differentiation based on the value proposition 'Truly interested in you' with a service that exceeds customer expectations. Also as the best company for those who feel co-responsible for their health within the framework of a company that is responsible, innovative, open, and with an exemplary organization supported by a comprehensive management model to promote the development and commitment of our people and a new relationship model with stakeholders promoting the incorporation of new technologies and building partnerships."[27]

Telefónica

"Telefónica's purpose is to be recognized as an integrated group that provides integrated solutions to each customer segment, whether in mobile or landline communications, voice, data, and services, which is committed to its stakeholders through its ability to meet its commitments to all: the customers, employees, shareholders and society of the countries in which it operates.

The company's aim is to attain customer satisfaction as the only possible path for growth and value creation for all stakeholders. Telefónica seeks to achieve its vision on the one hand through anticipation and commitment and on the other through closer and more intimate relationships, understanding the expectations and needs of its stakeholders.

The Telefónica Group's main objective is to understand and meet the needs of the people with whom it relates, transforming technological innovations into communications solutions to facilitate and improve the lives of customers and contribute to the development of society. In this way, Telefónica can build lasting relationships based on trust."[28]

Hewlett-Packard

"To provide products, services and solutions of the highest quality and deliver more value to our customers that earns their respect and loyalty."[29]

Procter & Gamble

"We will provide branded products and services of superior quality and value that improve the lives of the world's consumers. As a result, consumers will reward us with leadership sales, profit and value creation, allowing our people, our shareholders and the communities in which we live and work to prosper."[30]

Notes

1 J. A. Pérez López, *Fundamentos de la dirección de empresas*, 2nd edition. Madrid: Rialp, 1994.
2 Rosanas, J. M. Més enllà de l'eficàcia: un punt de vista humanista i realista de la presa de decisions, les organitzacions i les persones. Andorra la Vella: Crèdit Andorrà, 2010.
3 According to Pérez López, a "consumer's real need" is understood to mean a need whose satisfaction is not an obstacle for addressing more complex needs of the consumer as a person.
4 See J. A. Segarra (second quarter of 2011), "La Fageda: otra empresa responsable . . .," in *Universia Business Review*, and "Cristóbal Colón: psicólogo y empresario" in *AgendaViva*, Fall 2012.
5 "How to Design a Winning Business Model." *Harvard Business Review*, January–February 2011.
6 The doctoral thesis written by Pilar Ramírez, *Integración de la consideración de las personas y su dirección en el diseño y análisis de modelos de negocio* (March 2014) contains a number of illustrative examples on the footprints-based approach examined in this chapter.
7 By managerial actions, we mean not only the decision-making process but also the subsequent implementation endeavor. See R. Andreu and J. M. Rosanas (May 2008) *Toma de decisiones y actos directivos*, mimeo, IESE.
8 In this regard, I recall how a human resources vice president of a large multinational responded to a department head who expressed concern about the heavy workloads of certain employees and the impact it was having on their private lives: "The solution is divorce," he said. That manager was not only ignoring the negative footprints his policies were leaving on employees but also suggesting to aggravate them for the sake of economic performance. Two adjectives come to mind to describe him: heartless and incompetent.
9 Otherwise, one could "compensate for" murder with a Pulitzer Prize–winning piece or slavery if it leads to a lucrative business model. We would all agree that these situations are unacceptable, right?
10 A tragic example: a Chinese company tried to erase the negative footprints caused by several employees who had died by suicide by installing nets on the windows from which they had jumped.
11 If the best possible outcome is not positive under these conditions, the corresponding "business" does not deserve to be called as such.

12 www.gasnaturalfenosa.com/en/the+company/1285338472733/about+us.html, trans-
    lated from Spanish.
13 www.kpmg.com/uy/es/acerca/nuestramision/paginas/default.aspx, translated from Spanish.
14 www.dovercorporation.com/in/gn/dover-india/overview.
15 www.citi.com/jordan/homepage/ww_us.htm.
16 www.microsoft.com/enable/microsoft/mission.aspx.
17 www.google.com/about/company/, translated from Spanish.
18 www.jnjcanada.com/explore-our-company
19 www.southwest.com/html/about-southwest
20 www.mercadona.es/corp/esp-html/memoria2013.html#menuB, translated from Spanish.
21 www.empresa.nestle.es/es/sobre-nestle/mision-vision-valores, translated from Spanish.
22 www.fageda.com/es/quienes-somos, translated from Spanish.
23 http://accionistaseinversores.bbva.com/TLBB/micros/bbva2012/en/Executivesum
    mary/Visionandmission.html, translated from Spanish.
24 www.grupoacs.com/index.php/en/c/aboutacs_corporatestrategy_mission, translated
    from Spanish.
25 www.torres.es/wps/portal/web/inicio/sobreNosotros/nuestraVision/!ut/p/c4/04_
    SB8K8xLLM9MSSzPy8xBz9CP0os3gTlyBfJydDRwOLADdDA08T1yBvT_cQA4
    NgA_3g1GL9gmxHRQAO4UNF/?WCM_GLOBAL_CONTEXT=, translated from
    Spanish.
26 www.zara.com/, translated from Spanish.
27 http://dkvseguros.com/empresa-responsable/mision-vision/, translated from Spanish.
28 www.telefonica.com/en/about_telefonica/html/strategy/mission-values.shtml, trans-
    lated from Spanish.
29 http://www8.hp.com/us/en/hp-information/about-hp/corporate-objectives.html
30 www.pg.com/en_US/company/purpose_people/pvp.shtml

PART 3

The institutional configuration of the firm

10

DESIGNING THE BOARD OF DIRECTORS

A tailor-made suit

Alfredo Enrione

All over the world, boards of directors are under pressure. Markets are demanding greater accountability and dedication from CEOs, as well as responsible risk-taking, tight management control and value creation. More than ever, boards are expected to set the right "tone at the top," promoting healthy organizational culture and values and, overall, assuring the tangible and intangible means for the sustainability of the corporation in the long run. To attain all that, academia should advise boards to exercise best practices, such as diversity in their composition and specific processes or structures, such as audit committees.

However, corporations may radically differ in their life stages, ownership structures and strategic challenges. Beyond common business sense, there is no such thing as an optimal one-size-fits-all board of directors that will maximize the potential value of every company. This chapter presents a practical guide for thinking about the main aspects of board design – that is, size, composition and board structure.

Boards under scrutiny

Corporate governance and boards of directors have increasingly become the focus of global media, academia, regulators and corporations themselves. There are at least five reasons for this trend. First, a number of scandals, malpractices and corporate meltdowns, such as the banking crisis in 2008,[1] have impacted the savings and well-being of millions of citizens. This has translated into political pressures and subsequent regulations, increasing the level of accountability and legal exposure of CEOs and boards of directors. Data from the World Bank database and the European Corporate Governance Institute corresponding to seventy-eight countries shows that the number of new laws and regulations regarding boards of directors is thirty times greater than it was a decade ago.[2]

Second, the lowering of international barriers to trade and globalization has resulted in the progressive integration of financial markets and stock exchanges. For instance, the London Stock Exchange merged in 2007 with the Borsa de Milano. It then merged with the TMX Group of Canada in 2011, and shortly thereafter, the Singapore Exchange was integrated. Finally, in 2016, it announced a merger with Deutsche Börse. This global integration of stock exchanges has encouraged an accelerated convergence of investors' and regulators' expectations. In the past, regulation evolved according to the specific evolution of expectations, realities and scandals of a given country. Today, regulations are adopted at a greater speed and flow freely from one country to another.

Third, global corporate ownership has "democratized." The failure or success of large companies not only affects the sizable fortunes of a few billionaires. On the contrary, the main source of global capital today is the savings of individuals who, at the same time, are represented by institutional investors such as mutual funds, insurance companies, sovereign funds and hedge funds. According to a study carried out by the consultancy firm CityUK, in 2012, institutional investors made up 68 percent of the ownership of companies listed on stock exchanges around the world. To comply with their fiduciary obligations, these companies require positive results, greater transparency and accountability.

Fourth, consumer markets are more competitive than ever, as competitive advantages are rapidly diluted, making it harder for firms to generate high returns over extended periods of time. For example, back in 1965, if a company joined the elite group of Standard & Poor's 500 (S&P 500) stock index, it could expect to remain there for thirty or forty years. By the 1990s, this period was reduced by almost 40 percent. Currently, it is estimated that half of the companies that are now in the S&P 500 will be replaced within the next decade.[3] Thus, the drive to create value for investors puts companies under heavy pressure to raise standards of efficiency and productivity in every domain, including corporate governance practices.

Lastly, the development of information and communication technologies means that companies no longer face masses of consumers but instead well-informed and demanding individuals. Consumers now have the power to express their opinions globally, with the capability of coordinating with others who – if they are equally dissatisfied – demand respect for what they consider to be their rights. Those in corporate governance appear more visible and vulnerable to these hardships, but they are also the ones with the power to revise current business models and make sure that the company satisfies social demands.

The role of the board beyond regulations

Regulation enforces certain structures in the design of corporate boards. For example, in certain countries, the minimum number of members is established by law.[4] In others, the proportions of independent members or a particular gender are stipulated. In some cases, regulators even set guidelines regarding the relationship of the board with other bodies and prescribe other specific internal structures.[5]

However, regulatory frameworks do not offer details on the specific tasks to be performed to fulfill responsibilities. Defining how the board exercises its role is not a trivial matter, because it is vital to determine "the line" between governance roles and those of the management team. Furthermore, this line can vary depending on the circumstances of the company, the characteristics of the CEO and the board and their personal preferences.

In any case, it is possible to establish a set of responsibilities and tasks that are known to affect the value of the company, different from those exercised by the management team, and that, in essence, cannot be delegated by the board (Table 10.1). Central among these are appointing, supervising and rewarding the

TABLE 10.1 Core Responsibilities of the Board

With Regard to CEO	With Regard to the Strategy	With Regard to the Resource Providers and Conflicts of Interest	With Regard to the Core Intangibles
• Appoint the right person, according to the medium-term vision of the company. • Develop short-, medium- and long-term incentive schemes, aligned with the shareholders' interests and that don't promote taking excessive risks. • Evaluate and provide feedback. • Offer advice. • Provide information about the social and business environments. • Expand networks and contacts.	• Make sure that the company has a medium-term strategy to deal with the main opportunities and threats to the creation of value. • Ensure that there are financial and non-financial indicators to monitor strategy. • Control strategy execution and make adjustments. • Monitor the main strategic risks and the risks to value sustainability. • Have direct contact and know opinions of the key members of the management team.	• Protect the interests of all the shareholders equally. • Assure the quality, timeliness, integrity and relevance of the financial accounting information that the company provides to the market. • Foresee and solve, when needed, conflicts of interest between different resource providers. • Ensure that the expectations of key stakeholders are considered in decision-making processes.	• Assure the existence of succession processes for key leadership positions. • Look after the policies, processes and protection mechanisms of the standing and reputation of the corporate brands. • Clarify and assure the existence of protection and control mechanisms for the mission and values of the organization. • Make sure that the organization has mechanisms and complaint channels that allow for detecting threats to reputation and sustainability in a timely manner.

Source: A. Enrione. (2014). A. Enrione "El Directorio y las Tareas de Gobierno," chapter 4 of the book edited by A. Enrione (2014), *Directorio y Gobierno Corporativo: El Desafío de Agregar Valor en Forma sostenida*. ESE Business School Publishing, pp. 63–83.

CEO; approving strategy; and assuring compliance or norms and regulation. Yet if the board truly assumes its responsibility over the long term, it must take charge of protecting key intangible assets such as culture, values and reputation. To provide guidance on these issues, this chapter will provide a summary of the main roles and responsibilities of the board in practice.

The mandate for the board

The structure and composition of boards are, in general, fairly stable over time, and chances to build these from scratch are rare. However, there are circumstances that require complete transformations, or at least very substantial ones. An Initial Public Offering (IPO), the spin-off of a company from its parent company, merger and acquisitions processes and turnarounds after a severe crisis are examples.

The starting point in the design of a board should always emerge from a process of strategic reflection on the medium and long term. This should define the "mandate" for the board and should center on a set of tasks and objectives that, beyond legal requirements, the board should determine its own. What do we want to build over the next five to ten years? What kind of organization do we want to create? What are the key issues? Expansion? Internationalization? IPO? Succession in the family business?

If there is no such mandate, it is virtually impossible to evaluate the quality of a given board: How do we know we have the right personal profiles in terms of industries or experiences? How do we know if board time is allocated in the best way possible? What should be the criteria to design Key Performance Indicators (KPIs) and information dashboards for the board? What committees should the board create? Without this starting point, boards will focus on compliance and following one-size-fits-all structures that may not match the actual needs of the company.

The board mandate emerges from visualizing a future for the organization, a situation that contains a set of aspirations of what it is desired to reach. For example, the idea of expanding to Asian markets or leading the industry in the use of big data. At the same time, this visualization of the future should also incorporate elements that the organization may not control but are highly probable. Examples include likely changes in regulations, demography, politics or the inevitable future succession of the company founder.

The first series of elements of the mandate come from analyzing the wanted and viable evolution of the business. We can start with a SWOT matrix analysis to identify the first evident challenges that the company needs to address, including the possible evolution of the industry in which it operates. What changes are expected regarding actual and potential competitors within the next five years? How could technology evolve within that timeframe? What is the likely evolution of regulation and its impact on the business? How are the expectations of key stakeholders changing?

In view of all these questions, it is possible to identify a series of challenges that need to be addressed. For instance, in the medium term, changing the focus toward new markets, customers or technologies will impact the inner fibers of the organization. The company will need to develop or reinforce a number of capabilities, attract new talent and put into operation new structures and processes. In this regard, the board's mandate should include setting specific objectives and milestones, ensuring the necessary means for achieving these, periodically evaluating the process of execution and making adjustments.

Many times, to achieve the business aspirations, companies undertake changes in their ownership structures. Raising capital, issuing new stock, Mergers &Acquisitions and joint ventures are not only business decisions; they can alter shareholding positions and the functioning of corporate governance. In family-owned companies, for example, changes in ownership occur as a part of their natural succession processes. When shares are passed from parents to children, ownership may evolve from single owner to a group of siblings or from siblings to cousins in the next succession. Under those circumstances, it is natural to expect changes in the composition and functioning of the board. For instance, the first substantial change in the Walmart board occurred in 1970, when the company entered the stock exchange, and the second was after the death of the founder, Sam Walton, when ownership was transferred to his four children.

Therefore, a board should prepare the organization and itself for anticipated changes in ownership. For example, there should be processes and quality standards of information for the stock markets on which they intend to trade their shares. There also should be mechanisms in place for dealing with new board members (e.g., an induction process) or for the resolution of conflicts of interest (for example, when the CEO is also a major shareholder).

Changes in leadership positions can also affect the board. For instance, leadership succession of a controlling family can have a significant impact on its management, composition and functioning. Walmart, for example, has had three board chairs: the founder, Sam Walton; his older son, Samuel Bobson ("Bob"); and, since July of 2015, the son-in-law of the latter, Greg Penner. Likewise, in Santander Bank, the succession of Emilio Botín to his daughter Ana altered the leadership and the board structure.

CEO succession often impacts the board since in many countries, such as the United States and Mexico, the CEO is also often the chair of the board. A change in the top executive may imply a new set of priorities and focal points. In addition, a new leader with distinct experiences, knowledge and social networks may need different complements from board members.

In sum, the board should articulate a mandate that takes into account the business dimension, the ownership dimension and the leadership dimension (see Figure 10.1).

The design of the board

In addition to the provisions established by laws, regulatory authorities and stock exchanges, the design of the board should help achieve the mandate, as defined above.

The design of a team and its processes, particularly in the case of the board, can be quite complex. As Christopher Bartlett and Sumantra Ghoshal have pointed

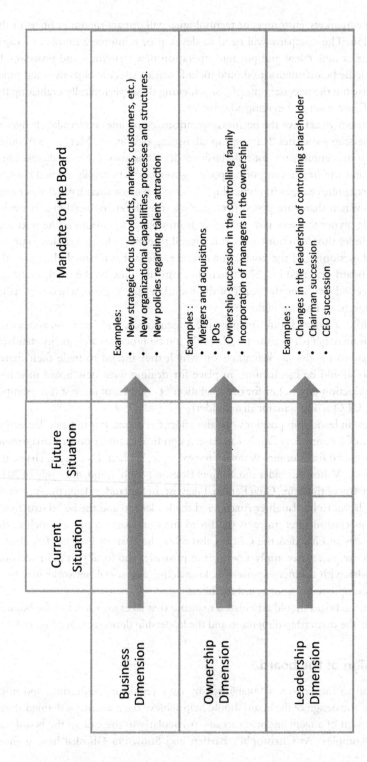

FIGURE 10.1 Defining the Mandate of the Board

Within the figure:

Mandate to the Board

Business Dimension

Examples:
• New strategic focus (products, markets, customers, etc.)
• New organizational capabilities, processes and structures.
• New policies regarding talent attraction

Ownership Dimension

Examples :
• Mergers and acquisitions
• IPOs
• Ownership succession in the controlling family
• Incorporation of managers in the ownership

Leadership Dimension

Examples :
• Changes in the leadership of controlling shareholder
• Chairman succession
• CEO succession

Future Situation

Current Situation

out, human organizations, as "living organisms," should be understood and managed on three different levels:[6] the "anatomy," which refers to all the structures, their parts and pieces; the "physiology," which describes the way that different elements interact with each other, particularly how the information flows inside the organization; and, finally, the "psychology," which involves the shared norms, assumptions and underlying values that guide the members in their actions. As a consequence, a thorough design of the board means addressing multiple elements to respond to the three dimensions (see Table 10.2).

The fifteen elements mentioned in Table 10.2 affect the board's functioning and effectiveness, so they should all be considered when there is an opportunity to partially or totally redesign the board. However, here we will focus on the three most important dimensions of its design: size, composition and committee structures.

The size of the board

On the question of optimal size, the answer most often is "it depends." Keep in mind that a board of directors is no more than a group of people working together with the intention of generating the best possible results in the organization that it is responsible for governing and protecting.

As several research initiatives demonstrate, group size substantially affects the effectiveness in decision-making. So the first criterion when deciding the size should be effectiveness. Hence, and even though there is not unanimity in the

TABLE 10.2 Elements of Design of the Board and Its Main Effects

Affecting the Anatomy of the Board	Affecting the Physiology of the Board	Affecting the Psychology of the Board
• Size of the board • Committees of the board	• Board agenda (how time is managed during the year and in every session) • Structure of managing reports for the board • Structure of the committee's reports for the board • Definitions of attributions for the decision-making between the board and management	• Board leadership • Individual profiles of the board members (age, experience, profession, etc.) • Diversity in the composition of the board • Proportion of independent members • Content of the information for the board • Processes of induction and training of board members • Strategic planning process • CEO evaluation process • Self-evaluation process of the board

Source: Original table by the author for the purposes of this chapter.

research findings, the optimal number should be between five and seven people.[7] Growing beyond that size reduces the effectiveness of decision-making.

The size of the board will also depend on its mandate and on the depth and complexity of the company's challenges. For instance, for a medium-size company with relatively stable products and markets, five board members would probably be sufficient. However, as the company grows in size and complexity, it is likely that the board will have to grow too. Empirical evidence indicates that when companies expand to new market segments or new geographic areas, they typically incorporate new board members who can bring relevant knowledge to help meet new challenges.[8]

Regulation also has an impact on board size. For example, the need for specialized committees (such as in the areas of audit or compensation) will require more members with specific expertise. For instance, following the implementation of the Sarbanes-Oxley Act, the boards of S&P 500 companies grew from nine to eleven members. Regulations may require bringing in certain profiles, such as "independents" or "minorities" (e.g., related to race and gender). In Australia, boards must have a majority of independents, and in Norway, there is a required minimum of 40 percent for each gender. In many countries, the "old boys' club" ended up adding new chairs to the existing board instead of emptying the existing ones, hence increasing the average size of the boards.

Finally, the ownership structure also plays a role in the size of the board. Usually, if there are relevant blocks of shareholders, they would want to have proportional numbers of representatives. For instance, if a controlling family group has major "branches," there would typically be a representative of each one. If, due to regulation or based on common sense, the integration of "independents," minority quotas or specialized profiles is required, the board could easily exceed eight or nine members. Here, the dominant goal is not effectiveness but rather the balance of power in the ownership.

The composition of the board

What "personal profiles" – which may reflect professions, expertise in specific functional areas, markets and business issues – are required of boards? Boards should include a minimum threshold level of knowledge regarding general business issues, the specific industry in which the company operates and the particular challenges relevant to its strategy.

To answer this question, the business challenges emerging from the board mandate should first be considered. Take, for example, a Swiss financial institution. Besides the typical challenges of the industry, such as risk management from credit operations, forex and options, other challenges should also be expected to emerge from the new business models and information technologies that will likely revolutionize the industry in the medium term. In addition, it would be natural to consider the effects of regulatory changes, such as the collapse of Swiss banking secrecy, which took place in 2016 after pressure from the United States.

Thus, a Swiss bank should consider the incorporation of people on its board who have significant experience in the industry and individuals with practical knowledge about the implementation of technologies in innovative business models. It should also consider incorporating members with expanded networks and expertise in international politics and regulations. It should come as no surprise that the large Swiss bank UBS has shifted from a traditional Swiss-only board to better adapt to current business challenges (see Table 10.3).

Similarly, internal challenges such as reorganization processes, expansion, the professionalization of the family company and/or the adaptation of personnel practices within an internationalization process should correlate with the board members' expertise.

Since companies often face numerous business challenges and therefore need a wide range of expertise, boards sometimes grow to sizes that become dysfunctional. That's when they need to prioritize. Three criteria are useful when this occurs. First, remove those "urgencies" that will likely disappear in a few years. Second, reprioritize profiles that may already be present at the senior management level. Finally, move profiles that could more easily be outsourced to advisors and consultants to the bottom of the list; an economist who provides views on growth trends or an attorney who brings insights on a relevant trial are examples of such profiles.

Lastly, once individual profiles have been defined, the overall "balance" of the board should be considered. A reasonable collective balance prevents systematic biases and encourages enriching and comprehensive discussions among board members. For example, it a finance expert would clearly be a great addition to any board. However, a board composed only of financial experts would eliminate the possibility of other perspectives and knowledge, so a diversity of professions and functional experiences should be sought.

Experience in different industries, as long as members have the potential to help meet the company's challenges, is also valuable. For instance, an executive from Federal Express or Disney might offer an interesting vision regarding supply chain issues or customer experience, respectively. Also, demographic diversity should be taken into account. Different genders, nationalities and ages will also help bring different perspectives to the table.

Boards should also consider a balance between insiders and outsiders.[9] In some cases, "outside" directors will help prevent biases and facilitate decision-making in situations where there are potential conflicts of interest. In some cases, "outside" will mean "non-executive" directors; in others, it will mean "independent" or even "non-family."

The proportion of outsiders has special relevance if a transformation process is anticipated in the board's mandate. The need for new perspectives, free from told paradigms, can be valuable. The proportion of insiders and outsiders will affect the willingness and decision-making speed when shifting from the status quo.

Board committees

Although board members typically devote much more time to their work than a decade ago, time will always be a scarce resource. Even two hundred or three hundred hours per year will never seem enough to address in-depth all the key issues

TABLE 10.3 Composition of the UBS Board in February 2017

Name	Age and Nationality	Past Executive Positions	Other Selected Boards	Key Knowledge
Axel A. Weber (chair)	67, Germany	• President of the Bundesbank • IMF • University of Chicago	• Zukunft Finanzplatz • Institute of International Finance	• Banking • Risk • Political institutions • Economic policy • European policy
Michel Demaré	61, Belgium, Switzerland	• CEO and CFO at ABB	• Syngenta • Louis-Dreyfus Commodities Holdings BV • IMD, Lausanne	• Finance • Strategy • Global business
David Sidwell	64, US, UK	• CFO and VP at Morgan Stanley and JP Morgan	• Chubb Limited	• Banking • US policy • Financial markets
Reto Francioni	62, Switzerland	• CEO of Deutsche Börse AG • Corporate finance division of Hoffmann-La Roche	• Board member of MedTech Innovation Partners AG	• Corporate finance • Innovation and technology
Ann F. Godbehere	62, Canada, UK	• CFO and Executive Director Northern Rock, Re Group (insurance)	• Prudential plc • Rio Tinto plc • British American Tobacco plc	• Finance • Risk management • Global business
William G. Parrett	72, US	• CEO Deloitte	• Eastman Kodak Company • Blackstone Group LP • Thermo Fisher Scientific Inc. • Conduent Inc.	• Strategy • Finance • Compliance and risk
Isabelle Romy	52, Switzerland	• Partner at Froriep Legal AG	• Chubb Limited	• Law and regulation • US
Robert W. Scully	67, US	• Managing Director Lehman Brothers, Morgan Stanley, Scully Brothers	• Zoetis Inc. • KKR & Co LP • Dean's Advisors of Harvard Business School	• Commercial and investment banking

Name	Age, Nationality	Positions	Expertise
Beatrice Weder di Mauro	52, Italy, Switzerland	• Professor at Johannes Gutenberg University of Mainz	• Economics • Economic policy
Dieter Wemmer	60, Switzerland, Germany	• CFO Allianz	• Risk • Insurance
		• Robert Bosch GmbH • Bombardier Inc. • TH Zurich Foundation • Economic & Finance Committee of Insurance Europe • Berlin Center of Corporate Governance • Systemic Risk Working Group of ECB and BIS	
Joseph Yam	69, Hong Kong, China	• Executive Vice President of the China Society for Finance and Banking • Advisor to the People's Bank of China	• Banking • China and Asia
		• Johnson Electric Holdings Limited • UnionPay International Co., Ltd. • China Investment Corporation	

Source: Author.

faced by a reasonably complex company. Due to this rising complexity, boards are increasingly structured in committees. Essentially, they fulfill the following five functions:

1   To distribute the workload among board members.
2   To release resources and allow the board to work more efficiently, delegating tasks that could be routine or of a more specialized nature.
3   To ensure that certain important matters receive the necessary time and resources.
4   To make better use of the expertise and specific talents of each board member.
5   To create spaces for individual participation and increase the level of commitment of members.

Typically, there are three types of committees: the executive committee, the stable committees and temporary ad hoc committees. This last group ceases to function when the relevant task or milestone has been completed.

Like the board as a whole, committees also require a clear mandate. This entails an order that clarifies its responsibilities, its deadlines and the limits of its authority. In this regard, and generally within their respective areas, committees have the task of proposing decisions to the board rather than making decisions on their own.

The executive committee

The primary function of this committee is to program the work of the board and provide the agenda and guidelines for its operation. It also acts as the governance body during intersession periods. In some cases, when the board is sizable,[10] this committee would usually assume more extensive functions and take a more active role in making some decisions.

The executive committee is usually composed of the board members with a greater time commitment to the organization and direct influence over management. In most cases, the chair and high-level managers like the CEO or the CFO will take part.[11] On some occasions, this committee will comprise designated board members who lead the other board committees. In other cases, when shareholding ownership is concentrated, a representative of the controlling family or a founder that is still active will typically be represented on the committee.[12]

Stable committees

These committees are typically focused on compliance with law and regulation. For instance, companies that trade shares on US exchanges are required to have three committees: audit, compensation and nominating.

US regulations also affect the size of the board in that they stipulate that there must be a minimum of three independent members on each committee. Members on the first committee cannot be part of the second, and the chair cannot be part of the first committee. So, mathematically, there must be at least seven people on the board. US regulations have impacted boards across the world. Many global corporations have adopted committee structures similar to those required in this country (see Table 10.4).

The auditing committee

In general, this committee has supervisory responsibilities in specific areas: the financial reports that the company provides to the market; the work of external auditors; the internal control systems; risk management; and compliance with internal policies and regulations. Duties may vary depending on the specific laws of each country,[13] and they may also vary if the board decides to delegate some of these duties to other committees, such as those focused on risk, compliance or ethics.

In terms of design, and considering the supervision and guarantor roles, regulators usually require that the committee be made up of predominately independent board members. This means that neither the chair nor individuals holding management positions should serve on this committee. Representatives of the controlling shareholder are also barred from serving on this committee. The law requires having at least one member with significant knowledge and experience in accounting and finance, such as the case of a former partner of an auditing firm, a CEO or a CFO.

Most companies would in fact benefit from an audit committee. The work of this committee should emerge from a strategic reflection process and the board's mandate. What are the key risks associated with achievement of the objectives of the mandate? What control processes should be implemented to the keep track of these matters? What is the quality of the internal processes required to achieve the mandate?

The remuneration committee

Year after year, the specialized press has published the rankings of the highest-paid CEOs. Spectacular numbers – often millions of dollars – make the headlines, generating both admiration and criticism. For example, in 2016 the compensation of Viacom CEO Philippe Dauman increased by 22 percent, exceeding US$54 million. Meanwhile, the value dropped by 42 percent for its shareholders during the same period.[14] So it is not unusual that shareholders allege negligence and sue the boards of publicly traded firms. On top of this, huge financial scandals in recent decades have led regulators to keep a closer eye on CEO compensation. For example, the Securities and Exchange Commission[15] stipulates that compensation committees be made entirely of independent board members.

The specific functions of this committee are more loosely regulated, but they usually include proposals regarding the incentive policies of the board, the CEO and senior executives. They also define goals and specific compensation amounts in the short, medium and long term, including stock options. Finally, this committee usually takes responsibility for the CEO and/or chair succession process.

TABLE 10.4 Committees Operating in the Administration Boards of Global Companies

Company	Alibaba	Apple	BHP	Cemex	Ferrovial	Nestlé	Shell	Sony
Country of Origin	China	USA	Australia	Mexico	Spain	Switzerland	UK	Japan
Industry	Retail	Tech	Mining	Cement	Construction	Food	Oil	Tech
Auditing	Yes	Yes	Yes	Yes	Yes	Yes	Yes	Yes
Remunerations	Yes	Yes	Yes	Yes	Yes	Yes	Yes	Yes
Nominations	Yes	Yes	Yes	Yes	Yes	Yes	Yes	Yes
Other Committees	No	No	1	No	No	No	1	No

Source: Investor relations area of each company.

Even if it is not mandated by law, this committee is usually a good idea. For example, the board is charged with ensuring that the incentives of the management team, especially its leader, are aligned with achievement of the mandate. Retention schemes and succession planning could be particularly relevant if leadership positions are expected to change during the board's mandate.

Nominating committees

This committee focuses on the board itself and its composition, policies and functioning. In companies where the ownership is especially dispersed, this committee has the responsibility of defining and recommending what kind of candidates the board should incorporate. In many cases, the law requires a majority of independent members in its composition.

In cases when this committee is not mandatory, the designation of members is often in the hands of shareholders, and nobody is in place to offer recommendations in this regard. However, if in the board mandate, changes are expected in the ownership structure or leadership positions, having a team assigned to examine the company's needs would be helpful when forming the next board.

Other committees

Beyond regulation, the board has to make sure that all priority matters related to the company's mandate have plans, resources and deadlines for execution. Although the board will be responsible for the achievement of all these objectives, it will not always be possible (because of time, regulation or common sense) to ensure that every subject is analyzed, discussed and decided in the regular sessions. Thus, the board should consider delegating part of its duties (not those that are its responsibility, which cannot be delegated) to a committee. In this respect, the board should also define the time commitment expected of members.

For instance, a corporate governance committee may be created to oversee the performance of the board and its processes, structures and roles. It would take charge of designing and recommending induction processes of new members and the continuous training of its members, and it would recommend the creation of new committees (or the elimination of an existing one).

Lastly, the board should also take into account the need for structuring committees for specific tasks over time, in areas such as strategic planning, the integration process of a merger or management of a crisis.

Conclusion

This chapter has proposed a systematic process for thinking about variables that could affect a board's effectiveness in fulfilling its duties and its capability to add value. A summary of these variables is presented in Figure 10.2.

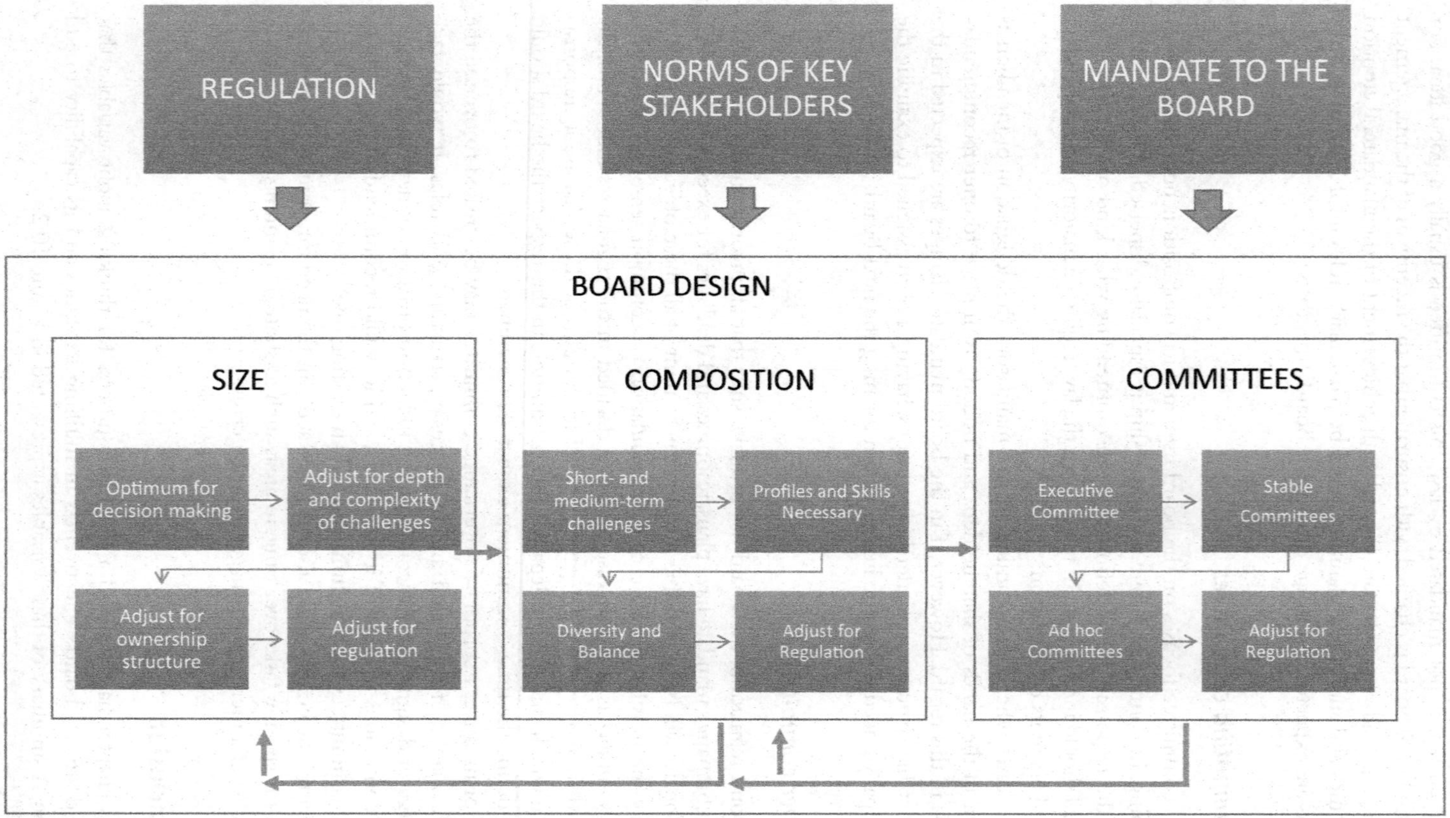
REGULATION
NORMS OF KEY STAKEHOLDERS
MANDATE TO THE BOARD
BOARD DESIGN
SIZE
Optimum for decision making
Adjust for depth and complexity of challenges
Adjust for ownership structure
Adjust for regulation
COMPOSITION
Short- and medium-term challenges
Profiles and Skills Necessary
Diversity and Balance
Adjust for Regulation
COMMITTEES
Executive Committee
Stable Committees
Ad hoc Committees
Adjust for Regulation

FIGURE 10.2 Variables to Consider in the Design of the Board of Directors

As highlighted in the introduction of this chapter, boards of directors are under increasing scrutiny from financial markets and society as a whole. Beyond economic benefits, they are expected to embrace and defend values and standards toward more sustainable environmental and social practices. Thus, boards should strive to implement best practices and seek to meet the company's performance goals. This entails complying with regulations and following the norms of key stakeholders while systematically examining the needs of the companies they manage and protect.

BOX 10.1 LATIN AMERICAN BOARDS IN 2017

Boards of directors in Latin America are facing a number of critical challenges.

Costs and efficiency

The end of the "commodities super cycle" in the 2000s hit Latin American economies hard. Less demand and lower prices for oil, minerals or wood pulp translated into slower economic growth, inflation and currency devaluation. Between 2016 and 2017, local currencies lost 10 to 45 percent of their value against the US dollar.

Cheaper commodities led to public budget deficits. Today, nearly every Latin American government is seeking to increase revenues, ushering in a wave of tax reforms, corporate rate hikes, fewer exemptions and new collecting mechanisms across the region.

Economic pressures are forcing boards and company management to make rapid adjustments. Just a few years ago, billions of US dollars were projected to be invested in greenfield and expansion projects. Now, priorities are much more tactical and short term. Key goals are to cut costs dramatically, improve efficiency, adjust organizations and develop new customers outside of their traditional markets.

Transparency, reputation and compliance

In the age of the internet and social media, business practices are becoming more transparent. Around the world, customers are more informed and more empowered than ever to challenge corporate giants. Latin America is no exception, but the local practices of government or family-controlled corporations are having a hard time adjusting to this paradigm shift. Recent scandals regarding competition and politics demonstrate this.

As state intervention in the economy began to decrease in the 1990s, competition law became more stringent in Latin America. Most governments have strengthened either regulations or supervision and enforcing capabilities. A number of corporations in the paper, poultry and retail sectors have been fined for anti-competitive practices in recent years, for instance, while others have been highly scrutinized. Boards and CEOs are facing economic penalties, severely damaged reputations and drops in market value.

Another area particularly affected area has been the intersection of corporations and politics. In just a few months, a corruption scandal led by Odebrecht, the largest construction company in Latin America, changed the course of political leadership in major countries in the region. The acting president of Perú, Pedro Pablo Kuczinski, was impeached, and the former president of Brazil, Luiz Inácio "Lula" Da Silva, could not run for reelection after being was convicted by the courts. In the meantime, hundreds of thousands protested in the streets asking for new regulations and harsh penalties for the corrupt politicians and bribe givers.

Boards in the region are more committed than ever to proving to regulators, investors and the public that they are committed to transparency, enforcing stricter codes of conduct and making sure that proper compliance processes and structures are in place.

As a result, most boards are now working to strengthen their risk and audit committees. Many are also setting up specialized committees focused on corporate governance or stakeholders/corporate affairs, even when regulations do not force them to do so. At the same time, management structures are being adapted to reinforce ethics, internal audit and compliance functions.

Interestingly, local directors are seeking training and education. Demand in this area has exploded, and in most countries, various executive education programs for CEOs are offered. However, no country is ready yet to discuss a mandatory CEO certification.

Dealing with institutional investors

In Latin America, the most important institutional investors are private pension fund managers (called AFPs).[16] They manage the savings of almost 100 million individuals and account for US$500 billion.

Despite the relative size of the assets under management, these investors have remained passive toward boards and corporate governance. Regulation has restricted their investments in a limited pool of assets: mostly government bonds or local "blue chips" controlled by the either the government or local business groups. Investment strategies dictated by regulation and the lack of deep financial markets left little room for investors to vote with their feet.

However, this is changing. Led originally by Chile and gradually followed by Peru, Colombia and Mexico, regulators now allow pension funds to diversify their investments into other kinds of assets and markets. As a consequence, powers are shifting and local corporations now need to work harder to win the favor of pension funds.

AFPs are also challenging board decisions more often and more vigorously. In one instance, the largest electric holding corporation in the region faced the resistance of AFPs, after eight out of nine board members approved a series of M&A operations. Technically, the company could have moved forward, but the prospect of a long fight in court and in the media convinced them to step back. It took months and US$1 billion more to make the deal happen.

Board members are also increasingly sensitive to these new circumstances. Even those firmly appointed by controlling shareholders now think twice before engaging in a fight with local institutional investors.

Taking diversity more seriously

Recent scandals also raised questions about the quality of board composition. In fact, Latin American boards are extremely homogeneous. For example, in the largest hundred firms in Latin America only 6.4 percent of the seats are held by women in 2015, up from 5.1 percent in 2005. While progress has been made, the region lags far behind others such as Europe (20 percent), the United States (19.2 percent) and Asia-Pacific (9.4 percent).[17]

Nearly half of the largest hundred companies have no female board members. Ambev, Itau Unibanco, América Móvil, Televisa, Cemex, Vale and Banco Chile are among the largest companies with all-male boards. Only eight have two women, and more than one-third of the women on corporate boards are members of the controlling family group. But this homogeneous landscape is being challenged. Several female activist groups are pushing for more female board members, with the help of mass media, think tanks and institutional investors.

In summary, Latin American board seats are not as comfortable as they used to be. Some pressures are context-specific and others are simply the product of global convergence. Yet legal and reputational risks are more real than ever. Although boards are working hard to improve processes and publicize their progress, the jury is still out.

Notes

1 This crisis has been considered by many as the most important financial and economic crisis since the Great Depression.
2 A. Enrione, C. Mazza and F. Zerboni, "Institutionalizing Codes of Governance." Clarke, T., De la Rama, M. (eds). *Fundamentals of Corporate Governance*, 79–90, 2008.
3 See, for example, the study performed by the company Innosight: www.innosight.com/insight/corporate-longevity-turbulence-ahead-for-large-organizations/
4 In Chile, for example, the boards of public companies must have at least five people, and seven if they do not get to choose an independent board member from the controlling shareholder.

5 In several countries, such as Germany, the Netherlands and Finland, company govern-ance is structured on two levels: a supervisory board and a managing board. The first is typically integrated by the board member who are not managers and in the second, the norm is that they are. The chair of the supervisory board is not the CEO.

6 C. Bartlett and S. Ghoshal. "Matrix Management: Not a Structure, A Frame of Mind." *Harvard Business Review,* July–August 1990.

7 See "What Is the Optimal Group Size for Decision Making?" www.shielamargolis. com/2011/01/24 and "How to Design Small Decision Making Groups" www.intuitor. com/statistics/SmallGroups

8 C. G. Raheja. "Determinants of Board Size and Composition: A Theory of Corporate Boards." *Journal of Financial and Quantitative Analysis*, 40(2), 283–306, 2005.

9 According to the Securities and Exchange Commission, for example, members are con-sidered independent if they don't have a labor relationship with the organization and don't receive relevant income from it as consultants, customers or suppliers.

10 As stated above, among companies listed in the S&P 500, the average size of boards was around eleven people, but there are cases with up to nineteen people.

11 Chief financial officer or top executive in financial matters.

12 Walmart, Santander and Google are examples of such cases.

13 In emerging markets, where the shareholding ownership is generally highly concen-trated, the auditing committee serves a protecting role for minority shareholders and a supervisory role over transactions of involved parties when there could be conflicts of interest.

14 www.equilar.com

15 Regulatory authority of public companies in the United States.

16 Administradoras de Fondos de Pensoines (literally Pension Fund Managers).

17 Report by the CWDI: www.globewomen.org/

11

STAKEHOLDER SALIENCE IN LATIN AMERICA

Who really counts?

Adrián A. Caldart, Alejandro A. Carrera and Magdalena Cornejo

The notion of "stakeholder" has become embedded in both management scholarship and management practice. Its origins trace back to the publication of Freeman's *Strategic Management: A Stakeholder Approach* (Freeman, 1984). While the concept quickly gained momentum, there was no immediate consensus regarding the operational question of who or what constitutes the firm's stakeholders. In other words, what individuals and entities do managers consider when making decisions?

An important contribution that addressed this matter was the theory of stakeholder identification and salience (Mitchell, Agle & Wood, 1997). Several studies have provided empirical support for this theory (Agle, Mitchell & Sonnenfeld, 1999; Eesley & Lenox, 2006; Parent & Deephouse, 2007; Magness, 2008; Westremius & Barnes, 2015). This chapter aims to continue on this path to better understand how CEOs operating in Latin America prioritize their stakeholders.

In doing so, we rely on a unique database comprising 538 CEOs based in the region. We also seek to identify to what extent the views of CEOs are affected by contingency factors such as their gender, age, years of experience in their role, the type of firm they lead and their position as professional CEOs or CEO owners.

Who or what really counts in corporate firms: theoretical perspectives

Persons, groups, neighborhoods, organizations, institutions, societies and the natural environment are generally thought to qualify as actual or potential company stakeholders (Mitchell, Agle & Wood, 1997). Yet when it comes to determining "who or what really counts," potential disagreements emerge. In this chapter, we follow Freeman and Reed's (1983) definition of a stakeholder as "an individual or group who can affect the achievement of an organization's objectives or who is affected by the achievement of an organization's objectives" (p. 46).

Despite this clear definition, the question of who or what really matters to managers leads to different perspectives. For further exploration, we focus on three theoretical approaches that generate different conclusions regarding which stakeholders are the most salient in business firms: agency theory, stewardship theory and stakeholder theory.

Agency theory: shareholders as the most salient stakeholder

Berle and Means (1932) posed the classical agency theory problem upon observing that ownership and control in large corporations were often separated. Specifically, agency theory is directed at the ubiquitous agency relationship in which one party (the principal) delegates work to another (the agent) that performs it.

Eisenhardt (1989) explains the issues that agency theory tries to address:

> Agency theory is concerned with resolving two problems that can occur in agency relationships. The first is the agency problem that arises when (a) the desires or goals of the principal and agent conflict and (b) it is difficult or expensive for the principal to verify what the agent is doing. The problem here is that the principal cannot verify that the agent has behaved properly. The second is the problem of risk sharing that arises when the principal and agent have different attitudes towards risk. The problem here is that the principal and the agent may prefer different actions because of different risk preferences.
>
> *(p. 58)*

Agency theory focuses on identifying situations in which the principal and agent are likely to have conflicting goals and then describing the governance mechanisms that limit the agent's self-serving behavior. Researchers concentrated almost exclusively on the special case of the principal-agent relationship between owners and managers of large public corporations (Eisenhardt, 1989).

The theory makes two specific contributions regarding the thinking on relationships between actors in a firm. The first is the treatment of information, which is regarded as a commodity: it has a cost and can be purchased. The implication is that principals (like shareholders) can invest in information systems to control agents' opportunism. One specific information system in our analysis is the board of directors, a stakeholder that is "used" as a monitoring device for shareholder interests.

A second contribution of agency theory is its implications for risk management. Organizations are assumed to have uncertain futures. Under agency theory, uncertainty is viewed in terms of their risk/reward trade-offs, not just in terms of inability to preplan (Eisenhardt, 1989).

The literature identified two broad manifestations of managerial discretion that may incur agency costs. The first regards short-run cost-augmenting activities designed to enhance non-salary income (Jensen & Meckling, 1976). The second manifestation is when managers indulge their need for power, prestige and status by making long-run strategic choices designed to maximize corporate size and growth rather than corporate profits (Baumol, 1959). Jensen (1986) argued that managers have inducements to overly diversify by taking advantage of unrestricted free cash flows, defined in the absence of strong governance (monitoring) or bonding obligations (debt).

Under the agency theory framework, Walsh and Seward (1990) suggest that firm performance "is crucially dependent on the efficient operation of internal and external corporate control mechanisms." Two control cycles are posited. The internal control cycle involves the activities of the board of directors attempting to monitor and control the activities of top managers. The external control cycle constitutes the market for corporate control. The normal conduct of business affairs is based on a continuous cycle of a board's assessment of corporate performance. At this point, the entire cycle repeats itself. If performance is poor, the external control cycle begins to operate through takeover attempts by another firm. As Walsh and Seward stated, "Takeovers represent a perfectly normal and theoretically sound mechanism of ensuring optimal firm performance when a firm's internal control mechanism has been compromised" (Walsh & Seward, 1990).

Agency theory had an enormous impact on how activist shareholders defined their interests and also helped define good corporate governance. In fact, the common call by corporate governance codes and regulations for the appointment of independent directors, the division of roles between the CEO and the chair and the appointment of independent audit committees all reflect the prescriptions of agency theory. Such prescriptions gain added momentum in times of frequent business scandals, provoking calls for stiffer corporate governance regulation in public firms.

Despite the widespread influence on the regulation of corporate governance practices, agency theory raises some questions regarding its assumptions about human motivation. Several academics questioned the power of agency theory to properly explain a full range of management behaviors, particularly when managerial interests do not directly conflict with those of shareholders (Donaldson, 1990). Perrow (1986) states that periods of minimal conflict represent the operational reality for most managers.

Agency theory correctly assumes that personal interests guide the agent. Yet this personal interest should not necessarily be equated with self-interest, as Amartya Sen warns (Sen, 1998). Personal interests may be selfish or altruistic, and although they are always associated with a cost/benefit analysis, they are not necessarily related to monetary goods (Mises, 1980, cited in Benegas Lynch, 1994). However, agency theory tends to link personal interest to a selfish quest to satisfy extrinsic motivations related to salary, career progress, power or similar incentives, discounting the possibility of altruistic behavior.

Sumantra Ghoshal states in his well-known criticism of what Albert Hirschman deemed a "paradigm-based gloomy vision" (Hirschman, 1970, cited by Ghoshal, 2005) that agency theory dangerously paints contemporary managers as "ruthlessly hard-driving, strictly top-down, command-and-control focused, shareholder-value-obsessed." In short, the strict adherence to the agency theory paradigm leads to a perspective that implicitly carries a negative view of human nature.

This bias creates an oversimplified view of human motivation that ignores sources of intrinsic motivation, which are widely acknowledged in sociology, psychology and management literature (Barnard, 1938; Simon, 1946; Selznick, 1957; Ghoshal & Moran, 1996; Ghoshal, 2005). People may act selfishly, and as empirical evidence in agency theory suggests, this behavior may happen quite frequently in organizations. But this fact cannot lead us to affirm that all people act selfishly all the time.

Stakeholder salience within agency theory

According to agency theory, the shareholder is the most salient stakeholder from a normative standpoint. The theory claims that, in practice, such salience is not always evident, due to the failure of shareholders to align managers' behavior with their own interests. In doing so, other stakeholders, such as the board of directors and external investors who take an active role in corporate control, may become relevant.

Stewardship theory: loyalty and alignment as the norm in management behavior

Stewardship theory is another approach rooted in sociology and psychology that acknowledges a set of human values that differ vastly from the assumptions underlying agency theory (Donaldson & Davis, 1991). In the stewardship model, managers are good stewards of their corporations and diligently work to achieve elevated levels of corporate profits and shareholder returns. This theory stresses involvement rather than control, trust rather than monitoring and performance enhancement rather than cost control (Burton, 2000).

The major distinction between agency and stewardship theories is that the former is focused on extrinsic motivation that is tangible, measurable and usually financial, whereas the latter stresses intrinsic motivation derived from opportunities for growth, achievement, affiliation and self-actualization. Managers who are stewards achieve these personal objectives by striving for the success of the organization. In effect, the manager becomes integrated into the organization, therefore aligning the interests of owners and managers without the need for external control mechanisms.

Managers are viewed as interested in achieving high performance and using an elevated level of discretion to act in the benefit of shareholders. Therefore, shareholders can expect to maximize their returns when organizational structures give management the necessary scope to exert effective control (Muth & Donaldson,

1998). The effect of this central proposition of stewardship theory is to predict, in diametric contradiction to agency theory, that structures designed to increase the monitoring and control of management will be associated with lower company performance. Thus, CEO duality (the unification of the CEO and the chair roles in one person) and a board dominated by inside directors – recognized for their depth of knowledge, access to current operating information, technical expertise and commitment to the firm – should produce the best results.

While stewardship theory rightly considers the impact of intrinsic motivation in human behavior, which agency theory disregards, it goes to the opposite extreme when assuming that only intrinsic motivations influence managers' actions, therefore making it more desirable to allow them act with autonomy. While selfishness is not the rule in business, neither is altruism.

Research intended to support stewardship theory has focused on the composition of boards of directors and on CEO duality, postulating the superiority of a board comprising insiders and of CEO duality. However, data does not seem prescribe stewardship theory, nor does prescribe agency theory. A meta-analysis of fifty-four studies on the performance effects of board composition shows that the proportion of internal versus independent directors has no significant effect on corporate performance. Another meta-analysis, in this case of thirty-one studies on CEO duality, also found no significant impact on performance in any way (Dalton et al., 1998).

Stakeholder salience within stewardship theory

Unlike agency theory, stewardship theory brings the concept of the firm as a community into the picture, in which constructive, loyal and collaborative behavior is more the norm than the exception. Thus, managers will, in general, acknowledge the salience of shareholders and intend to pursue their benefit if they are entrusted to do so. Implicit in this perspective is the understanding that employees also have a high salience, as the attitude of owners and managers toward them will encourage the expected cooperative behavior.

Stakeholder theory

The corporation has relationships with numerous constituent groups ("stakeholders") that affect and are affected by its decisions (Freeman, 1984). These groups include the company's customers, suppliers, employees, owners and local communities, among others. Management must keep the relationships among stakeholders in balance and harmony. When these relationships become imbalanced or inharmonious, the survival of the firm is in jeopardy (Evan & Freeman, 1988). Stakeholder management is fundamentally a pragmatic concept (Freeman, 1999). Even though they might not explicitly refer to the concept, all managers practice stakeholder management when they strive to satisfy, not maximize, the interests of groups that influence the organization. As Evan and Freeman (1988) stated, "Management bears a fiduciary relationship to stakeholders and to the corporation as an abstract entity. It must act in the interests of the stakeholders as their agent, and it must act in the interests of the corporation to ensure the survival of the firm, safeguarding the long-term stakes of each group."

Donaldson and Preston (1995) identify three different uses of stakeholder theories that are frequently combined and confused:

1   Descriptive describes the nature of the firm and explains how managers manage in practice ("how the world really is").
2   Instrumental identifies the connections or lack thereof between stakeholder management and the achievement of traditional corporate objectives ("how means are linked to ends").
3   Normative interprets the function of the corporation, including the identification of the moral or philosophical guidelines of the operation ("how the world should be").

Jones and Wicks (1999) agree with these distinctions and state that the social science vision of stakeholder theory (descriptive and instrumental approaches) and the normative ethics vision (normative approach) cannot be complete without the other. For this reason, they propose a convergent stakeholder theory that combines normative and instrumental elements. Freeman (1999) argues that Donaldson and Preston's distinction tends to separate the discourse of business from the discourse of ethics: "Stakeholder is an obvious literary device meant to call into question the emphasis on 'stockholders.' The very idea of a purely descriptive, value-free, value neutral stakeholder theory is a contradiction in terms."

Advocates of stakeholder theory criticize the idea of shareholder value maximization as the ultimate objective of the firm, deeming it "morally untenable" (Donaldson & Preston, 1995) and in violation of the Kantian principle of respect for all people since it implies that treating the other stakeholders as a means to an end (Evan & Freeman, 1988). Stakeholder theory realistically describes how managers manage, and it explicitly acknowledges the importance of the firm's different constituencies, beyond shareholders. However, the instrumental relationship advocated by stakeholder theory is not actually observable, because the motivation of managers when acting is not observable either. Who can really know whether managers who care for their employees do so out of respect for them as people or because they believe their behavior will benefit overall financial performance?

From a theoretical standpoint, we would like to highlight the work developed at IESE by Prof. Juan Antonio Pérez López (1993) and his followers, who defend the instrumental value of a stakeholder aware approach. They root their analysis in the value premises characterizing the intellectual tradition of Aristotle and Saint Thomas Aquinas. Pérez warns us against the perils of selfish self-interest since it leads to inconsistency in human relationships (i.e., the inability to sustain relationships among agents in the long run).

Stakeholder salience and stakeholder theory

While stakeholder theory certainly widens the range of actors (and things) that can potentially be linked to organizations as holders of a "stake," the challenge of responding to who or what *really* matters to managers in their daily work led to different interpretations.

Frooman (1999) approached the issue from the perspective of resource dependence theory (RDT) (Pfeffer & Salancik, 1978), arguing that stakeholder influence strategies (and their associated salience) will depend on the existing balance of power within the organization. He identified four stakeholder influence strategies:

1 Direct (i.e., through allies) withholding (to withdraw support)
2 Indirect withholding
3 Direct usage (to support under conditions)
4 Indirect usage

He also identified a series of firm-stakeholder relationships (Figure 11.1):

- High interdependence
- Low interdependence
- Firm power
- Stakeholder power

In an attempt to provide a comprehensive view of stakeholder identification which transcends the implications of individual theories, Mitchell, Agle and Wood (1997) established that in order to find out "who or what really counts," it is necessary to evaluate the relative presence or absence of three attributes in the relationships between stakeholders and managers.

This framework led the authors to identify classes of stakeholders based on their possession or attributed possession of one, two or all three of the referred aspects: (1) the stakeholder's *power* to influence the firm, (2) the *legitimacy* of the

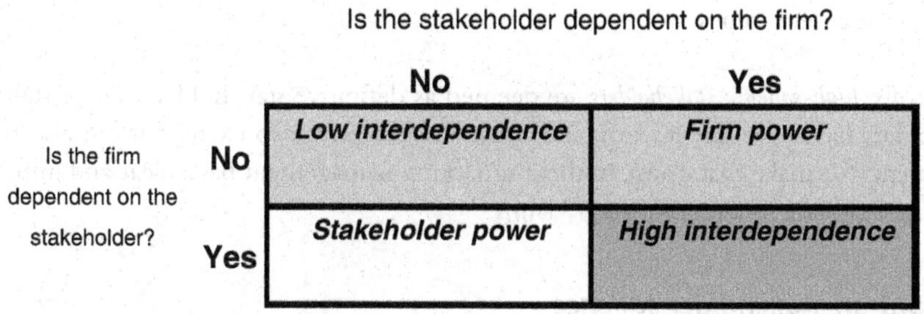

		Is the stakeholder dependent on the firm?	
		No	**Yes**
Is the firm dependent on the stakeholder?	**No**	*Low interdependence*	*Firm power*
	Yes	*Stakeholder power*	*High interdependence*

FIGURE 11.1 Stakeholder Influence Strategies

Source: Frooman (1999, p. 199)

stakeholder's relationship with the firm and (3) the *urgency* of the stakeholder's claim on the firm.[1]

Mitchell, Agle and Wood (1997) urge that these attributes have three features that must be acknowledged to understand the dynamism of the phenomenon of stakeholder salience. Stakeholders may gain or lose salience for the firm's managers for three reasons:

1   Stakeholder attributes (power, legitimacy and urgency) are variable through time.
2   Stakeholder attributes are not an objective reality but rather a socially constructed one.
3   Consciousness of possessing an attribute on behalf the stakeholder may or not be present.

The attributes of power, legitimacy and urgency led Mitchell, Agle and Wood (1997) to develop a typology of stakeholders.

Low-salience stakeholders can be categorized as follows:

Dormant stakeholders have the power to impose their will on the firm, but such power remains unused due to the lack of a legitimate relationship or an urgent claim.

Discretionary stakeholders possess the attribute of legitimacy but lack power or an urgent claim. They are usually the focus of CSR actions as recipients of corporate philanthropy.

Demanding stakeholders are like "mosquitoes buzzing in the ears" of management. They make noise, but not enough to sustain a stakeholder claim.

Mid-salience stakeholders can be categorized as follows:

Dominant stakeholders are powerful and legitimate; their influence is high.

Dangerous stakeholders lack legitimate claims, but their power and urgency mean that they are likely to exert strong pressure on the firm.

Dependent stakeholders have urgent and legitimate claims, but no power, so they must rely on the guardianship of other stakeholders or influence from management values.

Finally, *high-salience stakeholders* are deemed as definitive stakeholders. These stakeholders have not only a legitimate claim and the power to exercise it but also the urgency to make that claim. In these situations, management has a clear and immediate mandate to attend to their claims.

Data on stakeholder salience

Agle, Mitchell and Sonnenfeld (1999) explored how CEOs from a sample of S&P 500 and other big firms rate the salience of five stakeholders based on their recent interactions with each of them. The results enable ranking the salience of these stakeholders as follows:

1   Customers
2   Employees
3   Shareholders
4   Government
5   Community

Stakeholder salience in Latin America

In this section, we will explore the issue of stakeholder salience in the context of Latin America. This region is composed of countries classified as emerging markets. Among the frequently used criteria to define emerging markets are low income levels, relatively underdeveloped capital markets and, on a more positive note, the potential for strong economic growth as a result of pro-market policies.

A closer look at the realities of emerging markets illustrates a weak (or a lack of) rule of law, thorny government bureaucracy, economic vulnerability and volatility, and less-than-functional labor and goods markets. These circumstances undermine the competitiveness of emerging markets and impact the power, legitimacy and urgency of stakeholder claims in numerous ways, as described by Mitchell, Agle and Wood (1997). They also trigger the need for developed institutions to facilitate the coexistence and collaboration among the different economic agents.

The Global Competitiveness Report published by the World Economic Forum (WEF) underscores this reality, as depicted in Table 11.1 Nearly all Latin American countries, with the exceptions of Chile and Uruguay, rank poorly in most of the categories defined as key competitiveness benchmarks. As Table 11.1 illustrates, the three categories that rank the lowest in the sample are the efficiency of the labor market, the quality of institutions and the efficiency of the goods markets.

On the other hand, market size and higher education appear to be relative strengths, in addition to the existence of relatively strong financial markets in several countries. Table 11.2 reflects quite clearly the shortcomings of Latin American countries in their institutional development and underlines the widespread institutional voids, as characterized by Khanna and Palepu (2010).

Our work aims to determine whether these underlying characteristics in emerging markets affect the way managers grant salience to different stakeholders or whether, on the contrary, they grant status to stakeholders following patterns that are similar to their counterparts in developed economies.

The study

Data was collected through a survey given to Latin American CEOs between 2008 and 2016. Therefore, our study is based on a rather unique sample of 538 CEOs from medium- and large-size local enterprises and multinational firms with

TABLE 11.1 World Competitiveness Index 2016/2017 Ranking Position of Selected Latin American Countries in Core Competitiveness Benchmarks (Position in Sample of 138 Countries)

	Argentina	Brazil	Chile	Colombia	Mexico	Peru	Uruguay	Venezuela	Mean
Institutions	130	120	35	112	116	106	32	138	99
Infrastructure	85	72	44	84	57	89	47	121	75
Macroeconomic environment	130	126	32	53	51	33	94	135	82
Health and primary Education	63	99	71	90	74	98	56	91	80
Higher education and training	40	84	28	70	82	80	48	53	61
Goods markets efficiency	135	128	44	100	70	65	63	138	93
Labor market efficiency	130	117	52	81	105	61	121	138	101
Financial market development	127	93	23	25	35	26	51	124	63
Technological readiness	69	59	39	64	73	88	36	107	67
Market size	28	8	44	35	11	48	87	41	38
Business sophistication	88	63	56	59	45	78	82	136	76
Innovation	81	100	63	79	55	119	83	128	89
Overall competitiveness	**104**	**81**	**33**	**61**	**51**	**67**	**73**	**130**	

Source: The Global Competitiveness Report 2016/2017. Klaus Schwab. World Economic Forum.

TABLE 11.2 World Competitiveness Index 2016/2017 Ranking Position of Selected Latin American Countries on Indicators Related to Institutions (Position in Sample of 138 Countries)

	Argentina	Brazil	Chile	Colombia	Mexico	Peru	Uruguay	Venezuela	Mean
Property rights	125	80	33	82	84	92	35	138	**84**
Public trust in politicians	129	138	75	128	124	123	18	135	**109**
Irregular payments and bribes	107	111	31	94	103	70	25	133	**84**
Judicial independence	121	79	37	113	105	103	21	138	**90**
Favoritism in decisions of government officials	131	121	53	112	124	100	24	138	**100**
Wastefulness of government spending	134	128	21	96	94	112	99	136	**103**
Burden of government regulation	132	137	68	124	118	134	99	138	**119**
Overall ranking for institutions	**130**	**120**	**35**	**112**	**116**	**106**	**32**	**138**	

Source: The Global Competitiveness Report 2016/2017. Klaus Schwab. World Economic Forum.

operations in Latin America and across diverse business sectors (retail, energy, financial and manufacturing, among others). Table 11.3 shows the main descriptive statistics related to the CEO's profile.

The survey lists twelve stakeholder groups (Table 11.4) and asks CEOs to rank them by importance, distributing a total of one hundred points and allocating more points to those that they consider more important. As observed in our broad list of stakeholders, mere legal compliance no longer suffices for global companies; social actions are also necessary to legitimize their operations. This situation is particularly intense in emerging markets, since bilateral negotiations between powerful stakeholders are necessary to fill institutional voids.

Thus, prioritizing the diverse stakeholder groups and actions to satisfy their legitimate interests requires a top management team with a special sensitivity. For traditional stakeholders – customers, employees and shareholders – considerable attention should be paid to the board of directors, the government (or the

TABLE 11.3 CEO Characteristics

	Unit	Mean	SD	Min	Max
Age	Years	50.29	10.41	26	89
Experience	Years	10.49	10.30	0.17	55
Ownership (1 = yes, 0 = no)	%	32.57			
Gender (1 = male, 0 = female)	%	95.96			
Current position:					
National entrepreneur (owner or partner)	%	33.77			
Director of a national company	%	18.42			
National director of a multinational company	%	31.05			
Foreign director of a multinational company	%	16.77			
Origin of the company (1 = local, 0 = foreign)	%	55.43			

Source: Elaborated by the authors.

TABLE 11.4 Stakeholder Groups

Board of directors
Community
Competitors
Customers
Employees
Environment
Government and regulatory authorities
NGOs
Shareholders
Suppliers
Treasury
Union

Source: Elaborated by the authors.

regulator), the community (to which it must be integrated), the state treasury, suppliers (with whom it is not easy to establish long-term relationships, due to short-term dynamics in emerging-market economies), trade unions (generally combative and anchored in 20th-century-style antagonistic mindsets) and even competitors (many of them quite active in the informal economy, competing unfairly with lower standards in a corrupt system).

We then applied regression analysis to the score and ranking allotted to each stakeholder by the CEO to evaluate how they prioritize stakeholders. We also used several control variables such as gender, age, experience, origin of capital and the CEO's roles within the firm's corporate governance structure to explore whether these contingency factors affect the way they grant salience to different stakeholders.

Results

As seen in Table 11.5, the overall ranking and score indicate that there is a first main cluster of stakeholders – customers, employees and shareholders – which jointly account for almost 50 percent of the attention of CEOs operating in Latin America. In terms of salience, the first three positions in the ranking coincide with the one included in Agle's study of S&P 500 firms (Agle et al., 1999). Customers, employees and shareholders, respectively, were regarded as the most salient stakeholders in both the S&P-based sample and our sample of Latin American organizations.

These three stakeholders constitute what Carroll (1993) and Gibson (2000) deem as primary stakeholders – that is, groups whose support is necessary for the

TABLE 11.5 Overall Ranking and Score

Source: Elaborated by the authors.

firm to exist and to which the firm owes special obligations. Customers, listed first in the ranking, are at the receiving end of the "business model" of the firm. Employees, second in the ranking, constitute the essence of the organization itself, allowing the firm to fulfill its objective while working toward their personal development. Finally, shareholders, third in the ranking (scored almost 35 percentage points lower than customers), are also a central interest group as the company's owners, usually playing a key role in the financing, governance and control of company.

Contingency factors affecting stakeholder salience

The regression models illustrated in Tables 11.6 and 11.7 help shed light on the different rankings and scores that CEOs gave to stakeholder groups based on their profile. Overall, the results indicate a high degree of consistency among the appreciation of CEOs regarding the salience of different stakeholders. Nonetheless, some significant differences could be observed.

We found significant differences in the appreciation of salience with respect to one of the factors that we analyzed: whether or not the CEO is also a controlling

TABLE 11.6 Ordinary Least Square (OLS) Regressions of Stakeholder Scores

	Shareholders	NGOs	Customers	Competitors	Community	Directory
Gender	-0.65	0.50	-0.16	-0.73	0.60	1.44
(=1 male,	(2.03)	(0.47)	(1.60)	(1.12)	(0.86)	(1.27)
=0 female)						
Age	-0.01	0.01	-0.04	-0.02$\star$	0.02	-0.02
(in years)	(0.04)	(0.01)	(0.05)	(0.01)	(0.01)	(0.03)
Experience	-0.04	-0.02	0.06	0.04	0.03	-0.02
(in years)	(0.05)	(0.02)	(0.06)	(0.03)	(0.02)	(0.04)
Origin of capital	-1.10	0.36	-0.22	-0.68	-0.09	0.29
(=1 local,	(1.68)	(0.47)	(1.55)	(0.69)	(0.48)	(1.23)
=0 foreign)						
CEO of national	1.50	-0.37	-3.87$\star\star\star$	-0.42	0.73	2.41$\star\star\star$
company						
(=1 yes,	(1.29)	(0.38)	(1.41)	(0.57)	(0.46)	(0.86)
=0 otherwise)						
National CEO of	0.60	-0.04	-1.83	1.24	1.62$\star\star\star$	-0.58
an MNC						
(=1 yes,	(1.83)	(0.51)	(1.71)	(0.78)	(0.55)	(1.28)
=0 otherwise)						
Foreign CEO of	2.93	-0.50	-2.44	0.07	1.30$\star\star$	-1.09
an MNC						
(=1 yes,	(2.10)	(0.55)	(1.85)	(0.81)	(0.59)	(1.40)
=0 otherwise)						
Constant	14.84$\star\star$	2.03$\star\star$	22.91$\star\star\star$	8.85$\star\star\star$	2.82$\star\star$	8.07$\star\star\star$
	(3.10)	(0.89)	(3.30)	(1.58)	(1.25)	(2.26)

	Employees	Treasury	Government	Environment	Suppliers	Unions
Gender	−0.89	−0.42	0.42	1.39**	0.49	−0.18
(=1 male,	(1.37)	(0.75)	(0.87)	(0.67)	(0.91)	(0.80)
=0 female)						
Age	0.04	−0.01	−0.01	0.03**	−0.02	0.01
(in years)	(0.05)	(0.01)	(0.02)	(0.01)	(0.02)	(0.01)
Experience	−0.06	0.02	0.01	−0.01	0.03	−0.02
(in years)	(0.05)	(0.02)	(0.03)	(0.02)	(0.03)	(0.02)
Origin of capital	1.78	−0.08	1.15	0.37	0.05	−0.64
(=1 local,	(1.11)	(0.54)	(1.12)	(0.55)	(0.84)	(0.72)
=0 foreign)						
CEO of national company	−2.15**	0.00	2.30***	0.40	−1.59**	0.77*
(=1 yes,	(1.09)	(0.43)	(0.56)	(0.41)	(0.69)	(0.47)
=0 otherwise)						
National CEO of a MNC	−2.50**	−0.50	0.82	0.55	−2.01**	1.39*
(=1 yes,	(1.27)	(0.60)	(1.11)	(0.59)	(0.93)	(0.81)
=0 otherwise)						
Foreign CEO of a MNC	−3.64***	−0.27	1.18	1.19*	−2.01**	1.30
(=1 yes,	(1.34)	(0.64)	(1.12)	(0.66)	(0.98)	(0.88)
=0 otherwise)						
Constant	14.91***	5.65***	2.84	0.62	8.55***	4.31***
	(2.75)	(1.14)	(1.83)	(1.16)	(1.53)	(1.27)

Note: *, ** and *** indicate significance at 10 percent, 5 percent and 1 percent levels, respectively. Robust standard errors reported in parentheses.

TABLE 11.7 OLS Regressions of Stakeholder Rankings

	Shareholders	NGOs	Customers	Competitors	Community	Directory
Gender	0.04	1.23**	−0.16	−0.27	−0.46	−0.84
(=1 male,	(0.91)	(0.58)	(0.66)	(0.65)	(0.47)	(0.85)
=0 female)						
Age	0.00	−0.01	0.01	0.02*	−0.01	0.02
(in years)	(0.01)	(0.01)	(0.01)	(0.01)	(0.01)	(0.01)
Experience	0.03	0.01	−0.02*	−0.01	−0.03***	0.00
(in years)	(0.02)	(0.01)	(0.01)	(0.02)	(0.01)	(0.02)
Origin of capital	0.88*	−0.21	−0.22	0.53	−0.37	−0.43
(=1 local,	(0.39)	(0.43)	(0.41)	(0.42)	(0.45)	(0.59)
=0 foreign)						
CEO of national company	−1.12**	0.52*	0.28	0.64*	−0.47	−1.39***

(Continued)

TABLE 11.7 (Continued)

	Shareholders	NGOs	Customers	Competitors	Community	Directory
(=1 yes, =0 otherwise)	(0.40)	(0.30)	(0.23)	(0.35)	(0.31)	(0.37)
National CEO of a MNC	−1.14*	0.14	0.09	−0.44	−0.66	0.75
(=1 yes, =0 otherwise)	(0.47)	(0.46)	(0.40)	(0.46)	(0.48)	(0.63)
Foreign CEO of a MNC	−1.05	0.24	0.18	−0.16	−1.16**	0.46
(=1 yes, =0 otherwise)	(0.54)	(0.50)	(0.47)	(0.50)	(0.52)	(0.70)
Constant	2.86*	9.29***	2.51***	5.34***	10.15***	5.43***
	(1.25)	(0.94)	(0.95)	(0.94)	(0.81)	(1.26)

	Employees	Treasury	Government	Environment	Providers	Unions
Gender (=1 male, =0 female)	−0.59	1.39**	0.62	−1.21*	−0.49	0.26
	(0.53)	(0.56)	(0.58)	(0.66)	(0.59)	(0.77)
Age (in years)	0.01	0.01	−0.01	−0.03**	0.03***	0.00
	(0.01)	(0.01)	(0.01)	(0.01)	(0.01)	(0.02)
Experience (in years)	−0.01	−0.01	0.01	−0.02	−0.01	0.02
	(0.01)	(0.02)	(0.02)	(0.01)	(0.02)	(0.02)
Origin of capital (=1 local, =0 foreign)	−0.07	0.02	−0.82	−0.93*	−0.36	0.49
	(0.20)	(0.45)	(0.54)	(0.48)	(0.58)	(0.66)
CEO of national company	−0.22	0.64*	−0.80**	−0.33	1.00***	−0.45
(=1 yes, =0 otherwise)	(0.20)	(0.33)	(0.36)	(0.34)	(0.33)	(0.40)
National CEO of an MNC	−0.06	1.18**	0.03	0.24	1.54***	−0.63
(=1 yes, =0 otherwise)	(0.22)	(0.47)	(0.56)	(0.52)	(0.59)	(0.70)
Foreign CEO of an MNC	−0.06	0.67	−0.70	−0.22	1.63**	−0.69
(=1 yes, =0 otherwise)	(0.24)	(0.52)	(0.59)	(0.54)	(0.64)	(0.77)
Constant	3.08***	6.34***	8.92***	12.49***	5.08***	8.13***
	(0.78)	(0.94)	(1.05)	(1.02)	(0.97)	(1.26)

Note: *, ** and *** indicate significance at 10 percent, 5 percent and 1 percent levels, respectively. Robust standard errors reported in parentheses.

Source: Elaborated by the authors.

owner of the firm. CEO owners exercise a higher degree of control over the firm and normally embody the roles of up to three different stakeholders: owner, manager and board member. Data from studies on the agenda of the CEO (see Chapter 151) show that CEO owners have a different understanding of their role as CEOs from their non-owner peers, a fact reflected in the way they prioritize their agenda (Caldart, Carrera & Cornejo, 2017). While they diligently oversee the operations of the business, they feel less controlled and are not inclined to give formal explanations to anyone. CEO owners evaluate and weigh risks differently from other top managers and, understandably, feel less threatened by losing their jobs compared to CEO non-owners.

Furthermore, we find that CEO owners grant a significantly higher salience to customers, employees and suppliers than their non-owner counterparts. CEO owners grant less stakeholder salience to shareholders and the board of directors.

This result deserves some further analysis. It could be argued that the CEO owner is, by definition, the controlling shareholder and therefore the leader of the board of directors. As such, they may be less inclined to perceive these stakeholders as third parties with power over the firm, resulting in their lower salience. This implies that without a mechanism that empowers these stakeholders in the case of unwillingness on the part of the CEO owner, the legitimate and maybe urgent claims associated to minority shareholders and their representatives on the board are at risk of being systematically disregarded. These results are consistent with the scores of the World Competitiveness Index (Table 11.8) regarding indicators related to the use of power in business firms. Data on the indicators related to the effectiveness of boards, protection of minority shareholders and delegation of authority indicate that Latin American countries rank rather low in several cases. This is particularly clear in the cases of Venezuela and Argentina across all three indicators but also Brazil, Chile, Colombia, Mexico and Uruguay on at least one indicator.

TABLE 11.8 Ranking of Selected Latin American Countries in the World Competitiveness Index ranking (Position in Sample of 135 Countries)

	Argentina	Brazil	Chile	Colombia	Mexico	Peru	Uruguay	Venezuela	Mean
Efficacy of corporate boards	92	89	36	31	53	33	60	70	**58**
Protection of minority shareholder interests	129	94	36	70	71	54	40	132	**78**
Willingness to delegate authority	93	39	70	53	67	65	101	116	**76**

Source: *The Global Competitiveness Report 2016/2017*. Klaus Schwab. World Economic Forum.

Another significant finding is the highest salience granted by foreign CEOs of multinational corporations (MNCs) to the community (which is also better ranked) and the environment. These results may indicate the ever-increasing need to manage the corporate reputation of foreign companies in developing countries, where the context is more complex and less predictable. Consequently, these managers need to actively integrate into the communities where they operate and pay attention to the environment to avoid the frequent backlash that arises in some countries against MNCs. In other words, the liability of foreignness (Zaheer, 1995) might be more acute in Latin America.

CEO non-owners of national companies pay more attention to boards (the institutions that nominate them and have the power to remove them), the government (as it can influence the continuity of the company through regulatory upheavals) and unions (which also can block their role as the head of the company and negatively impact their performance). National CEOs from MNCs also see unions as potential blockers of their management and coincide with foreign CEOs in their interest to heed the complaints from the communities where they operate.

Finally, we found some differences related to the age of the CEO. The older CEOs get, the greater the importance they give to the environment, and the lower the importance they give to competitors. This result might imply that as CEOs become more senior, their attention shifts from more day-to-day aspects, like the ongoing competitive struggle, toward more governance-related issues, such as CSR. Finally, we found that female CEOs also grant a relatively higher salience to the environment.

Conclusions

In this chapter, we examined the issue of stakeholder salience, which received a lot of attention and sparked quite a bit of theoretical controversy. Since we are not aware of previous studies on stakeholder salience in Latin America, we decided to explore how CEOs in this region grant salience to their stakeholders. Our findings show that, overall, Latin American managers appear to grant salience following patterns that are similar to their S&P 500 peers. Yet a deeper analysis shows that different profiles of Latin American CEOs seem to have differences of appreciation for the salience of diverse stakeholders.

Notably, the view on salience from CEO owners appears to suggest that the institutional voids widespread in Latin America influence the attitudes of CEOs toward stakeholders. They seem to disregard stakeholders such as minority shareholders and board members who might hold urgent and/or legitimate claims but wield no real power to push their agendas. In addition, MNCs seem to be more inclined to grant salience to stakeholders such as the community and the environment, reflecting their need to go the "extra mile" to overcome the liability of foreignness, which is more acute in most Latin American countries.

These results, confirmed by data on competitiveness from the WEF, suggest the need to strengthen corporate governance practices in Latin America in order to empower minority shareholders and strengthen the professionalism of boards of directors, two factors that would certainly help attract much-needed foreign direct investment to the region.

Note

1 Urgency exists when two conditions are met: (1) the relationship or claim is time-sensitive and (2) the relationship or claim is important to the stakeholder.

References

Agle, B., Mitchell, R. and Sonnenfeld, J. (1999). "Who Matters to CEOs: An Investigation of Stakeholder Attributes and Salience, Corporate Performance and CEO Values." *Academy of Management Journal*, 42(5): 507–525.

Barnard, C. (1938). *The Functions of the Executive*. Boston, MA: Harvard University Press.

Baumol, W. (1959). *Business Behavior, Value and Growth*. London, England: Macmillan.

Benegas Lynch, A. (1994). *Fundamentos de Análisis Económico*. Buenos Aires, Argentina: Abeledo-Perrot.

Berle, A. and Means, G. (1932). *The Modern Corporation and Private Property*. San Diego, CA: Harcourt, Brace and World Inc.

Burton, P. (2000). "Antecedents and Consequences of Corporate Governance Structures." *Corporate Governance*, 8(3): 194–203.

Caldart, A., Carrera, A. and Cornejo, M. (2017). "How CEOs Understand and Execute their Agenda: Evidence from Latin America." *IESE Insight*, (32): 44–51.

Carroll, A. and Bocholtz, A. (1993). *Business & Society: Ethics and Stakeholder Management*. Cincinnati, OH: Western Publishing.

Dalton, D., Daily, C., Ellstrand, A. and Johnson, J. (1998). "Meta-Analytic Reviews of Board Composition, Leadership Structure, and Financial Performance." *Strategic Management Journal*, 19, 269–290.

Donaldson, L. (1990). "The Ethereal Hand: Organizational Economics and Management Theory." *Academy of Management Review*, 15: 369–381.

Donaldson, L. and Davis, J. H., (1991). "Stewardship Theory or Agency Theory: CEO Governance and Shareholder Returns." *Australian Journal of Management*, 16: 49.

Donaldson, T. and Preston, D. (1995). "The Stakeholder Theory of the Corporation: concepts, Evidence and Implications". *Academy of Management Review*, 20(1): 65–91.

Eesley, C. and Lenox, M. (2006). "Firm Responses to Secondary Stakeholder Action." *Strategic Management Journal*, 27(8): 765–781.

Eisenhardt, M. (1989). "Agency Theory: An Assessment and Review." *Academy of Management Review*, 14(1): 57–74.

Evan, W. and Freeman, R. (1988). "A Stakeholder Theory of the Modern Corporation: Kantian Capitalism." In: Beauchamp, T. L. and Bowie, N. E. (eds), *Ethical Theory and Business*. Upper Saddle River, NJ: Prentice Hall.

Freeman, R. (1984). *Strategic Management: A Stakeholder Approach*. Boston, MA: Pitman Publishing.

Freeman, R. (1999). "Divergent Stakeholder Theory." *Academy of Management Review*, 24(2): 233–236.

Freeman, R. and Reed, D. (1983). "Stockholders and Stakeholders: A New Perspective on Corporate Governance." *California Management Review*, 25: 88–106.

Frooman, J. (1999). "Stakeholder Influence Strategies." *Academy of Management Review*, 24(2): 191–205.

Ghoshal, S. (2005). "Bad Management Theories Are Destroying Good Management Practices." *Academy of Management Learning & Education*, 4(1): 75–91.

Ghoshal, S. and Moran, P. (1996). "Bad for Practice: A Critique of the Transaction Cost Theory." *Academy of Management Review*, 21: 13–47.

Gibson, K. (2000). "The Moral Basis of Stakeholder Theory." *Journal of Business Ethics*, 26(3): 245–257.

Jensen, M. (1986). "Agency Cost of Free Cash Flow, Corporate Finance and Takeovers." *The American Economic Review*, 76(2): 323–329.

Jensen, M. C. and Meckling, W. H. (1976). "Theory of the Firm: Managerial Behavior, Agency Costs and Ownership Structure." *Journal of Financial Economics*, 3: 305–360.

Jones, T. and Wicks, A. (1999). "Convergent Stakeholder Theory." *Academy of Management Review*, 24(2): 206–221.

Khanna, T. and Palepu, K. (2010). *Winning in Emerging Markets: A Roadmap for Strategy and Execution*. Boston: Harvard Business Review Press.

Magness, V. (2008). "Who Are the Stakeholders Now? An Empirical Examination of the Mitchell, Agle, and Wood Theory of Stakeholder Salience." *Journal of Business Ethics*, 83: 177–192.

Mitchell, R., Agle, B. and Wood, D. (1997). "Towards a Theory of Stakeholder Identification and Salience. Defining the Principle of Who and What Really Counts." *Academy of Management Review*, 22(4): 853–886.

Muth, M. and Donaldson, A. (1998). "Stewardship Theory and Board Structure: A Contingency Approach." *Corporate Governance*, 6(1): 5–28.

Parent, M. and Deephouse, D. (2007). "Case Study of Stakeholder Identification and Prioritization by Managers." *Journal of Business Ethics*, 75(1): 1–23.

Pérez López, J. A. (1993). *Fundamentos de la Dirección de Empresa*. Madrid, Spain: Rialp.

Perrow, C. (1986). *Complex Organizations: A Critical Essay*. New York, NY: McGraw-Hill.

Pfeffer, J. and Salancik, G. R. (1978). *The External Control of Organizations: A Resource Dependence Perspective*. New York: Harper & Row.

Selznick, P. (1957). *Leadership in Administration*. Berkeley, CA: University of California-Berkeley Press.

Sen, A. (1998). "Freedom and Choice: Concept and Content." *European Economic Review* 32: 269–294.

Simon, H. (1946). *Administrative Behavior*. New York, NY: The Free Press.

Walsh, J. and Seward, J. (1990). "On the Efficiency of Internal and External Control Mechanisms." *Academy of Management Review*, 15(3): 421–458.

Westremius, A. and Barnes, L. (2015). "Managing Complex Business Relationships: Small Business and Stakeholder Salience." *The Journal of Developing Areas*, 49(6): 481–488.

Zaheer, S. (1995). "Overcoming the Liability of Foreignness." *Academy of Management Journal* 38(2): 341–363.

12

RISK MANAGEMENT

The role of the board of directors

Iván Díaz-Molina

> There is a daunting lack of transparency in reporting, and it is not readily apparent who holds the risk or what concentrations of risks exist.
> — *Charles Prescott, Fitch Rating, 2003*

This quote appeared in a report on financial derivatives risks published in 2003 by the CSFI (CSFI, 2003), when complex financial instruments were the key concern of bankers, regulators, customers and other stakeholders. Why did these entities do nothing about risks despite dire warnings from the market from as early as 2003? Did they lack the resources, knowledge or tools to take action and prevent the causes of the 2008 financial meltdown? Certainly not – all means necessary to avoid the crisis were available. CEOs, top management teams (TMTs) and boards did not avert the crisis because of specific factors that were related to the falls of Enron, WorldCom and Parmalat. These cases tell compelling stories about why organizations should consider comprehensive risk management.

While the situations of these companies may seem extreme, and therefore unlikely to be experienced by other organizations, there are many reasons firms should implement risk management. Most importantly, it creates value. A study (Farrell & Gallagher, 2015) on 225 public and private organizations based in Australia, Canada, the United Kingdom, the United States and other countries found that companies with an advanced implementation of risk management methodology (RMM) were valued at up to 25 percent more than those without RMM tools. The authors found that the most relevant factor from a valuation perspective related to TMT engagement and the resultant enterprise risk management culture throughout the firm. Also, rating agencies are incorporating the level of risk management at the organization as a rating criterion (Standard & Poor's Rating Services, 2015). In a study including companies from energy, financial services, banking and insurance sectors, Gates, Nicolas and Walker (2012) concluded that the implementation of an enterprise risk management (ERM) methodology leads to increased management consensus, better-informed decisions, better communication with management regarding risk-taking and increased management accountability. All of these improvements in turn lead to improved performance.

This chapter highlights the common elements of risk management that CEOs, TMTs and boards of directors should focus on to avoid excessive risk in their organizations. First, we introduce the ERM approach and provide a detailed description of the methodology based on an actual example of an electricity utility firm. Second, we present general criteria and key elements of the ERM capability maturity model (CMM) as an implementation tool. Finally, we describe an example of ERM implementation in the mining industry.

Enterprise risk management

To handle risks efficiently, companies must carry out many repetitive and connected tasks and procedures, which together form a complex system. However, firms have traditionally not acknowledged such complexity at the time of managing risks. Instead, risk management has been handled separately and independently within each functional area (finance, operations, etc.), an approach that did not allow for the identification of potential overlaps and inefficiencies. A more comprehensive way to handle risks is introduced here, the ERM methodology. This methodology is associated to several broader frameworks, including the COSO risk management framework (COSO, 2013), the ISO 31000 standards (NTC-ISO, 2011) and the ERM guidelines by FERMA (FERMA, 2003). These methodologies share common elements but have minor differences. For the purposes of conceptual clarity, we will describe a generic ERM model here.

In addition to the benefits of a comprehensive risk management program that we have already mentioned, which primarily relate to financial or performance enhancement, there are other benefits that come with implementing an ERM model:

1   Aligning risk profile and the strategy
2   Connecting growth, risk and the rate of return
3   Enhancing and integrating responses to risk events
4   Minimizing surprises and operational losses
5   Identifying and managing risks across the entire organization
6   Exploiting opportunities
7   Improving capital allocation

ERM system implementation starts with the decision to incorporate risk management into the strategy and culture of the organization. At the strategic level, risks should be related with the firm's strategic goals, and the proper tools for identifying risks should be implemented. The successful implementation of ERM also depends on the robustness of corporate values. The organization should not only outline such clearly defined values but also communicate them and ensure that they are clearly understood and followed by all personnel. Since it is impossible to control the actions of the entire staff, the organization should define relevant values and limits.

The most significant challenge to ERM implementation is corporate culture. In general, people tend to believe that risk management is somebody else's job, namely the internal audit team, the risk manager or the safety, health and environment (SHE) manager. Yet, risk management is the responsibility of everyone in the organization, from the board of directors to entry-level workers. If cultural change does not take place, the best possible scenario would be halfhearted, partial ERM implementation.

The enterprise risk management process

The stages of the process are shown in Figure 12.1. For a more detailed review of the process, see Diaz–Molina (2009).

For a better understanding of the ERM process, let's look at a Chilean utility firm as an example. In 2011, Saesa, a utility company located in southern Chile, decided to implement an ERM[1] system. At the time, management perceived that risk was not adequately taken into account in decision-making processes, as risk management practices were fragmented and isolated in silos. With the help of an external consultant, an ERM project was designed in two phases (see Figure 12.1).

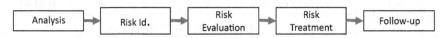

FIGURE 12.1   ERM Process Stages

Source: Author.

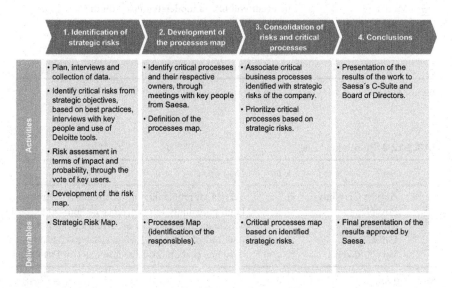

FIGURE 12.2   Phase A – Strategic Risk Map and Critical Processes

Source: SAESA.

Phase A: The first goal was to identify companywide risks and build a risk map. To ensure that risk identification was a bottom-up effort, the company established work groups at all levels of the organization to identify systematic (process-based) and non-systematic risks. With the aid of the consultant, risks were cataloged, quantified and ranked. In the final stage of this phase, the list of risks and the risk map was submitted to top management and the board of directors. The board was required to define the company's risk appetite by selecting and determining the final ranking of the company's risks.

The identification of critical risks was developed based on best practices and interviews with key people in the firm. The critical risk assessment was performed on a qualitative basis and conducted in conjunction with top management.

Risk ranking: Saesa defined the probability of occurrence and the impact of an event based on criteria defined by industry best practices and conclusions from an ad hoc expert panel. A list of the criteria and assigned indices is included in Tables 12.1 and 12.2. The company classified the critical risks identified during the project according to the following scale:

TABLE 12.1 Impact Scale

	Scale	Value	Description	MMUSD
	Catastrophic	5	The event will have a catastrophic effect. (Financial losses with a large impact to the firm).	>5
	Significant	4	The event will have significant effects. (High losses, with an important impact at company level and significant at unit level).	3 - 5
Impact	Moderate	3	The event will have a moderate impact on the company.	1 - 3
	Minor	2	The event will have minor effects on the business units..	<=1
	Insignificant	1	No significant effects	

Source: SAESA.

TABLE 12.2 Probability Scale

	Scale	Value	Description
	Almost Certainty	5	Very High probability of occurrence (>=90%)
	Possible	4	High probability of occurrence (>=66<90%)
Probability	Moderate	3	Moderate probability of occurrence (>=31<66%)
	Unlikely	2	Low probability of occurrence (>=11<31%)
	Very Unlikely	1	Very low probability of occurrence (>=1<11%)

Source: SAESA.

- Risk impact multiplied by the probability between 19 and 13.5: **High risk**
- Risk impact multiplied by the probability between 13.49 and 8.5: **Medium risk**
- Risk impact multiplied by the probability between 8.49 and 1: **Low risk**

Figures 12.3 and 12.4 list the top-ranking risks identified by the company.

Phase B: With input from Phase A, a companywide risk management policy was drafted with the aid of the consultant and presented to the board for approval. The policy had to reflect the utility's risk appetite as defined by the board in Phase A.

Once the policy had been approved, an action plan was developed to address those risks within the limits imposed by the board. Options were to terminate, transfer, accept or act on the risks. At the end of Phase B, an action plan was submitted for consideration and approval of the board of directors (Figure 12.5).

Figure 12.6 shows the original risk map after Phase A was completed in 2011. Highlighted in the graph are the critical risks as defined by the board of directors. Figure 12.7 shows the same risk map as of 2014, when many of the critical risks had been mitigated (i.e., Risk #1 in 2011 becomes #19 in 2014; Risk #2 becomes #1 but with a lower probability of occurrence). Yet, new risks were identified in 2014 (i.e., MoP transfers, a regulatory risk – nonexistent in 2011, #2 in 2014) and included in the analysis.

ID	Risk	Impact	Probability	Total	Risk classification
1	Increased energy loss in the networks.	4.7	4	18.8	●
2	Delay in the start of projects, failure to obtain proper permits, easement and concessions.	4.5	4.1	18.5	●
3	Non-compliance of the subcontracting law.	3.8	4.2	16.0	●
4	Dependence of critical services contractors	4.4	3.4	15.0	●
5	Strikes or protests by contractors	4.5	3.3	14.9	●
6	Work related accidents for non-compliance with established procedures.	4.4	3.3	14.5	●
7	Non-compliance with SEC regulations and applicable rules or laws established to govern the business activities of the company.	4.4	3.2	14.1	●
8	Increased fixed costs in developing the company's activities.	4.1	3.4	13.9	●
9	Services provided by contractors do not have the expected quality.	3.9	3.5	13.7	●

Legend:

● High risk (19–13.5)　　● Moderate risk (13.49–8.5)　　● Low risk (8.49–1)

FIGURE 12.3　Classification of Critical Risks Identified

ID	Risk	Impact	Probability	Total	Risk classification
10	Reduced profits.	4.4	3.1	13.6	●
11	Incomplete strategic objectives, due to lack of coordination among management.	4.2	3.2	13.4	●
12	Failure of business information systems in critical processes of the company.	4.6	2.9	13.3	●
13	Critically limited competencies on company personnel for the continuation of technical-operational activities and businesses.	3.7	3.3	12.2	●
14	Incorrect billing to massive and large clients, regulated or not.	4.2	2.9	12.2	●
15	Inadequate design of contracts, which lead to loss or negatively impact the company.	4	3	12.0	●
16	Failure in the continuous delivery of services in electric power for extended periods of time.	4.2	2.6	10.9	●
17	Inadequate collection for energy sales, other sales and big energy and retail clients.	3.7	2.9	10.7	●
18	Untimely delivery of information on fixed assets to accounting.	2.7	3.9	10.5	●

FIGURE 12.4 Classification of Critical Risks Identified (Cont.)

Roles and responsibilities

Successfully implementing an ERM system relies not only on a clear commitment from the TMT and the board of directors but also on whether they clearly understand their roles during the ERM implementation process and its operation. Some specific roles are nondelegable by board members, whereas others should be assumed by the TMT.

The role of the board of directors

The role of the board of directors regarding the ERM system can be separated into two major components:

1 The definition of the reference framework:

  a Define and communicate the values of the organization. Such values must be clearly communicated and understood by the all the member of the organization. Such communication can be accomplished through workshops, documents and seminars, among other means.

  b Issue a code of conduct. The company should distribute the code to all members of the organization and implement necessary training to ensure its understanding and adoption. The company should offer such training on a continuous basis.

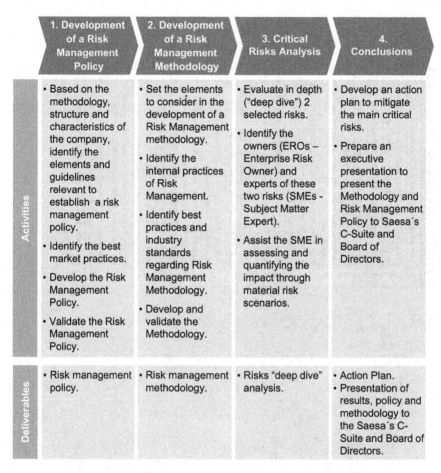

1. Development of a Risk Management Policy	2. Development of a Risk Management Methodology	3. Critical Risks Analysis	4. Conclusions
Activities • Based on the methodology, structure and characteristics of the company, identify the elements and guidelines relevant to establish a risk management policy. • Identify the best market practices. • Develop the Risk Management Policy. • Validate the Risk Management Policy.	• Set the elements to consider in the development of a Risk Management methodology. • Identify the internal practices of Risk Management. • Identify best practices and industry standards regarding Risk Management Methodology. • Develop and validate the Methodology.	• Evaluate in depth ("deep dive") 2 selected risks. • Identify the owners (EROs – Enterprise Risk Owner) and experts of these two risks (SMEs - Subject Matter Expert). • Assist the SME in assessing and quantifying the impact through material risk scenarios.	• Develop an action plan to mitigate the main critical risks. • Prepare an executive presentation to present the Methodology and Risk Management Policy to Saesa's C-Suite and Board of Directors.
Deliverables • Risk management policy.	• Risk management methodology.	• Risks "deep dive" analysis.	• Action Plan. • Presentation of results, policy and methodology to the Saesa's C-Suite and Board of Directors.

FIGURE 12.5   Action Plan

    c   Define how to address the organization's risks (policies) and how to implement the ERM.

2   Oversight of the organization's risk management policy

    a   Oversee the ERM implementation and secure the necessary resources.
    b   Periodically oversee risk management practices.

The role of the top management teams and employees

The TMT is in charge of implementing the ERM within the organization and guaranteeing that each member becomes an agent of risk management within their area of responsibility. The team is also responsible for implementing self-evaluations to determine the ERM goals' compliance level, implement corrective measures if necessary and inform the risk management office (RMO).

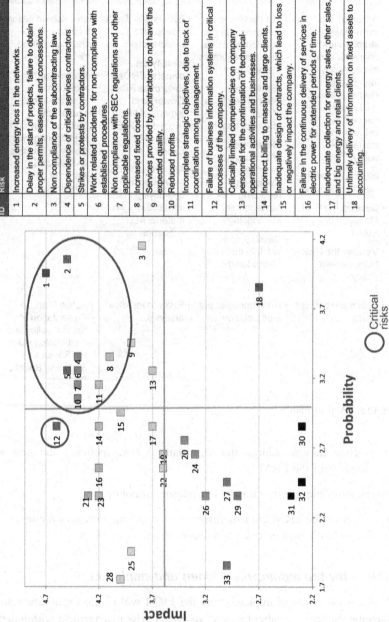

ID	Risk
1	Increased energy loss in the networks.
2	Delay in the start of projects, failure to obtain proper permits, easement and concessions.
3	Non compliance of the subcontracting law.
4	Dependence of critical services contractors
5	Strikes or protests by contractors.
6	Work related accidents for non-compliance with established procedures.
7	Non compliance with SEC regulations and other applicable regulations.
8	Increased fixed costs
9	Services provided by contractors do not have the expected quality.
10	Reduced profits
11	Incomplete strategic objectives, due to lack of coordination among management.
12	Failure of business information systems in critical processes of the company.
13	Critically limited competencies on company personnel for the continuation of technical-operational activities and businesses.
14	Incorrect billing to massive and large clients.
15	Inadequate design of contracts, which lead to loss or negatively impact the company.
16	Failure in the continuous delivery of services in electric power for extended periods of time.
17	Inadequate collection for energy sales, other sales, and big energy and retail clients.
18	Untimely delivery of information on fixed assets to accounting.

FIGURE 12.6 Risk Map (2011)

ID	Risk
1	Project delay and higher costs related to concessions and community
2	Mop trnsfers
3	Changes in regulatory framework
4	Serious or fatal accident - company employees and/or contractor staff
5	Serious or fatal accident of a third party caused by negligence and/or deficiencies in facilities
6	Non-compliance with environmental standards
7	Failure to meet the financial goal projected for 2018 in terms of "other unregulated businesses"
8	Loss of supply in Sub-Transmission due to lack of backup
9	Failure to recognize assets in IV - NRV
10	Quality of Services Technical Standard – Distribution (Dx)
11	Exposure to fines and image deterioration due to prolonged outages
12	Forest fires due to alleged responsibility of the company
13	Loss of business opportunities (projects) due to low competitiveness (included in risk 7)
14	Corporate communication strategy (lack of a proactive and reactive agenda for internal, external communications, institutional realtions ans CSR)
15	Failure to comply with the Subcontracting Law
16	Non-compliance with technical standards for Gx and Tx
17	Dependence on critical personnel
18	Shortage of and/or dependence on contractors
19	Higher losses energy
20	Security (vandalism against strategic facilities)
21	Incorporation of PMGD in NRP
22	SERNAC (Consumer Protection Agency) Oversight Role
23	Non-compliance of other regulations
24	Structure not in line with fulfillment of present and futur strategic objectives
25	Maturity Model (Vision 2020)
26	Rebalancing of compensations in DX
27	Competition zones (loss of supply to customers)
28	Billing errors on a massive scale
29	Lack of a contingency plan in case of earthquakes
30	New public policies associated to HR
31	Business continuity
32	Leakage of information (confidentiality)
33	Robbery at facilities or while moving valuables that theatens people's safety
34	Unsafe facilities (e.g., firewall)
35	Management of new contractor firms
36	Centralized management of complaints by SEC

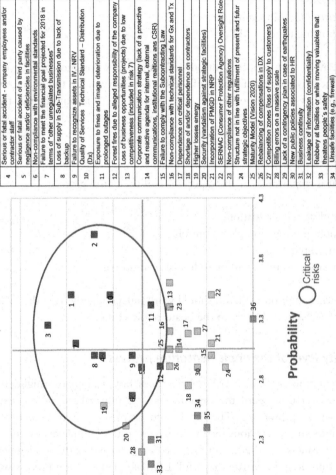

FIGURE 12.7 Risk Map (2014)

Risk management office

This unit, usually placed in the controller's area, is responsible for the following functions:

1   Monitoring self-evaluations
2   Analyzing KPI
3   Controlling mitigation plans
4   Reporting to the TMT

When RMM isn't properly introduced, employees commonly believe that risk management is the responsibility of the RMO. Everyone in the organization must understand, as soon as possible in the process, where responsibilities for specific tasks fall.

Internal audit office

This unit is responsible for the supervision of the entire process:

1   Sampling self-evaluations
2   Sampling mitigation plans controls
3   Controlling tests
4   Reporting to the board or audit/risk committee

The internal audit office (IAO) should work independently from the management structure and report directly to the board of directors.

Maturity level of the implementation process

Implementation of final ERM policies does not happen overnight. It requires numerous iterations until the organization has internalized new behaviors and decision-making processes. The timeline for implementation of an ERM model, as described in the previous section, is based on the complexity of the organization, the business and the levels of resources committed to the implementation. In general, one should estimate that a full ERM implementation process would take between three to five years.

A risk management maturity model is the appropriate methodology for implementation of an ERM in the organization (Diaz-Molina, 2008). As an illustration, Figure 12.8 depicts the maturity level of ERM implementation at Saesa in 2015. Even though the organization had been working on ERM implementation since 2011, its overall maturity level was 2.68, or roughly in the middle of the scale. As referred above, the cultural change associated to the implementation of a risk management maturity model requires time.

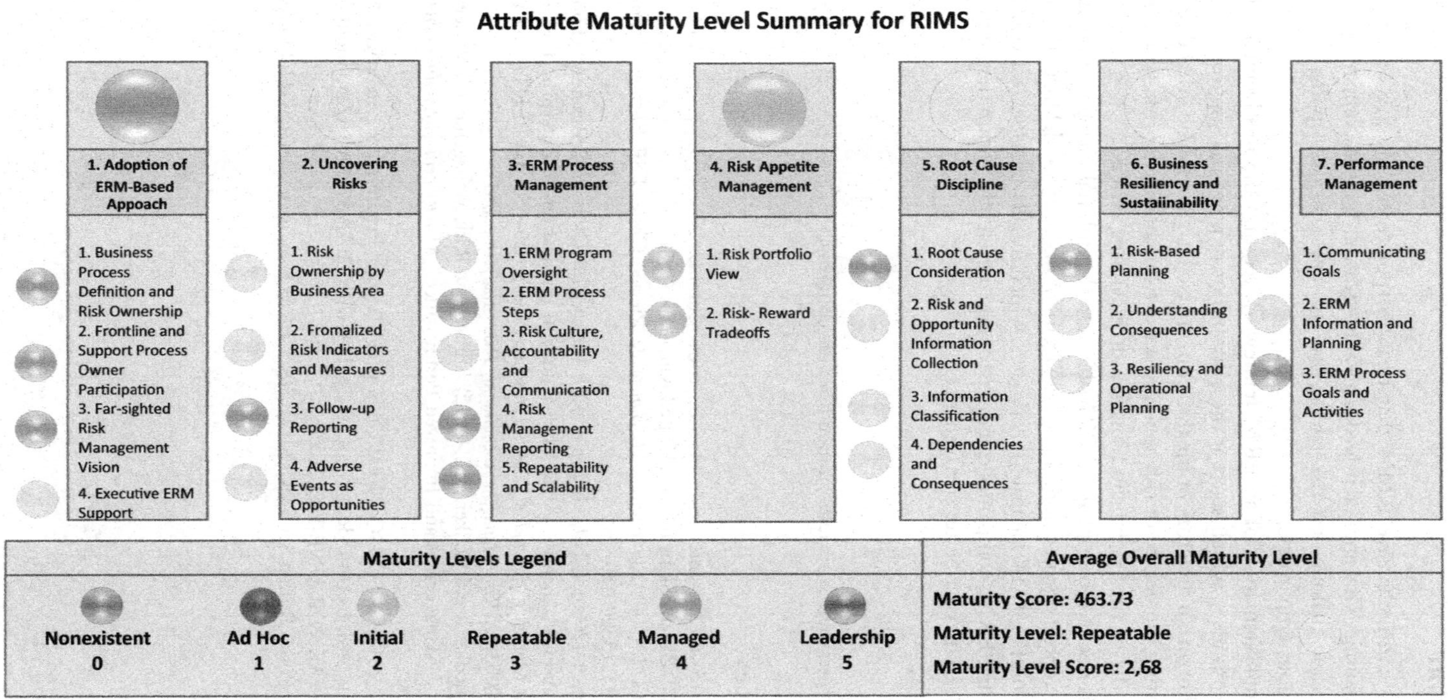

Attribute Maturity Level Summary for RIMS

1. Adoption of ERM-Based Approach	2. Uncovering Risks	3. ERM Process Management	4. Risk Appetite Management	5. Root Cause Discipline	6. Business Resiliency and Sustainability	7. Performance Management
1. Business Process Definition and Risk Ownership	1. Risk Ownership by Business Area	1. ERM Program Oversight	1. Risk Portfolio View	1. Root Cause Consideration	1. Risk-Based Planning	1. Communicating Goals
2. Frontline and Support Process Owner Participation	2. Fromalized Risk Indicators and Measures	2. ERM Process Steps	2. Risk- Reward Tradeoffs	2. Risk and Opportunity Information Collection	2. Understanding Consequences	2. ERM Information and Planning
3. Far-sighted Risk Management Vision	3. Follow-up Reporting	3. Risk Culture, Accountability and Communication		3. Information Classification	3. Resiliency and Operational Planning	3. ERM Process Goals and Activities
4. Executive ERM Support	4. Adverse Events as Opportunities	4. Risk Management Reporting		4. Dependencies and Consequences		
		5. Repeatability and Scalability				

Maturity Levels Legend

Nonexistent 0	Ad Hoc 1	Initial 2	Repeatable 3	Managed 4	Leadership 5

Average Overall Maturity Level

Maturity Score: 463.73
Maturity Level: Repeatable
Maturity Level Score: 2,68

FIGURE 12.8 Saesa. Maturity Level of ERP Implementation (2015)

Conclusion

ERM is a comprehensive RMM that treats corporate risks in a systematic and integral manner. This approach leads to value creation for the company through better decision-making, less risk-taking, less risk-coverage overlapping and more risk-conscious employees.

The implementation of an ERM framework requires the involvement of the entire organization, which starts at the bottom but requires full support from the TMT and board of directors. Some decisions are exclusive of the board of directors, such as setting the degree of risk appetite of the firm, setting the risk management policy for the company and allocating resources, among others.

Time is needed to implement ERM because the cultural change required will involve the entire organization. A risk management maturity model helps the board directors and the TMT navigate this process, which usually takes several years. Yet by embracing ERM, companies can operate more efficiently within their expected risk profile, achieving better performance.

Note

1 Example presented with authorization from the company.

References

COSO. (2013). COSO Internal Control Executive Summary.

CSFI. (2003). Banana Skins Report. United Kingdom: CSFI.

Diaz-Molina, I. (2008). *Introducción al Manejo de Riesgos*. Chile: ESE Business School, ii, S1889183715300015.

Diaz-Molina, I. (2009). *ERM – Enterprise Risk Management*. Chile: ESE Business School.

Farrell, M. and Gallagher, R. (2015). "The Valuation Implications of Enterprise Risk Management Maturity." *Journal of Risk and Insurance*, 82(3): 625–657. doi:10.1111/jori.12035

FERMA. (2003). *A Risk Management Standard: Risk Analysis*, p. 881.

Gates, S., Nicolas, J. and Walker, P. L. (2012). "Enterprise Risk Management: A Process for Enhanced Management and Improved Performance." *Management Accounting Quarterly*, 13(3): 28.

NTC-ISO. (2011). NTC-ISO 31000 Gestión del Riesgo. Principios y Directrices. NTC. https://global.ihs.com/doc_detail.cfm?gid=UMJETEAAAAAAAAAA&input_doc_number=AENOR UNE-ISO 31000

Standard & Poor's Rating Services. (2015). *S&P's ERM Framework*. McGraw-Hill Financial.

13

FAMILY-OWNED FIRMS

The role of the board of directors, family council and family office

Josep Tàpies

Conventional corporate governance instruments – boards of directors, executive committees and shareholder assemblies – are not enough in family-owned companies. When ownership is in hands of a family, new dimensions emerge, and emotions must be managed with the highest degree of professionalism. Just like traditional corporate governance instruments, family-owned businesses require two additional structures to manage the family dimension: the family council, aimed at managing the emotional component of family-run firms, and the family office, dedicated to managing financial resources that are no longer tied to the core business.

In this chapter, I will explore the common dynamics at play in family enterprises and why they require a special governance system. In doing so, I will briefly review the history of family-owned governance systems and their common characteristics examine in depth the main features of family councils and family offices.

Governance systems of family-owned enterprises

The historical foundations of modern-day governance structures in family firms can be traced back to the Roman Empire, when regulations first appeared relating to the management of family patrimony. Under Roman law, the *pater familias* was the ultimate authority on familial property, which comprised not only things – land, houses, livestock and other properties – but also people, including slaves and, later on, tenant farmers.

Far from pursuing personal aims, the *pater familias* exercised an institutional role that reflected the family's objectives and advocated for their common good. In this sense, the Roman inheritance process facilitated the transfer of family wealth and fostered the transcendental nature of the family line and its patrimony. The family patrimony was largely nontransferable and expected to remain within the family sphere.

Property regulations also contemplated the possibility of assigning part of the family patrimony to specific social projects and charitable pursuits. The Justinian Code built on this practice by granting a separate legal status for patrimony allocated for social aims, which eventually evolved into the family foundations of today.

Indeed, family-owned businesses may be the oldest form of business organization, although their governance frameworks have logically evolved since Roman times. Today, family enterprises require an effective governance structure to ensure the long-term sustainability of the firm while fostering harmony and unity to ensure that the family is an asset – and not a threat – to the company's continuity.

In the early stages of a family-run business, the efforts and vision of the founder – often implicated in every aspect of the business – are the primary drivers of its success. However, as the company grows and incorporates new generations and other family members, it requires a solid governance structure that separates the rational nature of business from the emotional landscape of familial relationships. If not addressed and properly channeled, family dynamics can lead to an emotionally charged atmosphere that undermines day-to-day management, critical thinking and corporate strategy.

As Figure 13.1 illustrates, family-run businesses must reconcile the interests of three overlapping domains – ownership, family and business – and the areas where they intersect. This requires open lines of communication and shared decision-making within and across these dimensions.

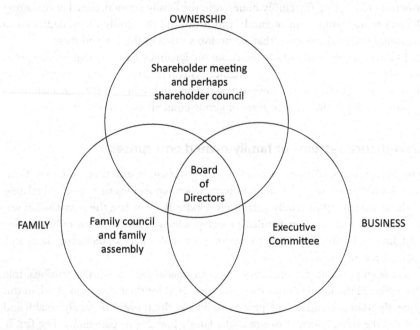

FIGURE 13.1 Basic Governance Structures in the Family Enterprise System

Source: John A. Davis, 2007.

The corporate governance structure of family firms doesn't differ from non-family-owned companies, as we can see in Figure 13.2: a general manager leads the venture, guided by a board of directors that oversees and approves matters of strategic significance. Annual general meetings convene shareholders and provide updates on the organization's progress, previous and future initiatives and fiscal results from the previous year. Using Figure 13.2 as a guide, the difference lies in everything pictured to the left of the corporate governance structure: family members and a family governance structure with its own unique areas of operation.

The family governance structure counterpoises the corporate governance branch. A family council sits at the helm and oversees any matters that might overlap and affect business operations. The council carries out this endeavor in coordination with the board of directors, which is the dotted line or nexus at which business and family spheres connect.

At least once a year, the family council also hosts an important meeting: the family assembly. This event gathers family members to inform them of the company's progress and, more importantly, to cultivate a sense of community that transcends the immediate corporate domain. Hence, the assembly welcomes members who work in the firm and those who don't hold shares or participate directly in its operations.

By inviting members of the wider family network, the family assembly acts as a crucial bridge to the business, underscores the family legacy and keeps the door open for future alliances. The words of thought leader Baba Dioum on the need to preserve the planet are equally applicable to the legacies of family-owned

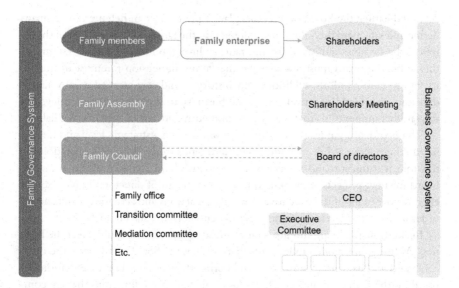

FIGURE 13.2 Governance Structures in Family Enterprises

Source: Author.

businesses: "In the end, we will conserve only what we love; we will love only what we understand and we will understand only what we are taught" Dioum, 1968).

The board of directors in family enterprises

The board of directors is undoubtedly one of the most important business governance structures in the family enterprise. Serving as both mediator and mentor, the board works actively to ensure alignment between the corporate and family structures. The board of directors carries out the following functions, among others:

- Defining and promoting the vision, mission and values that will guide the family enterprise.
- Balancing the interests of shareholders with corporate objectives and family expectations.
- Ensuring that the company fulfills its legal obligations.
- Counseling the CEO and executive team on strategic, long-term issues and helping them gain a holistic view of the business.
- Hiring, evaluating and, if necessary, firing the CEO.
- Encouraging assertiveness during board meetings, since many families often try to avoid hot-button topics.
- Building bridges across the family, shareholders and corporate governance spheres.
- Self-assessing the board's performance.
- Building an atmosphere of trust among board members.

As noted earlier, the board of directors plays a pivotal role in helping the company define and safeguard the values that will reign in the family enterprise, which should reflect the owning family's ideals and radiate throughout the corporate culture. In this sense, the board must always keep the family dimension foremost in mind – its family culture, ideals, traditions and history – and stay attuned to any family dynamics that could negatively affect the business. In short, they strive to leverage the family's influence so that it acts as a competitive advantage and not as a liability.

The board also guides the executive committee on a strategic level and helps it see the big picture while avoiding any interference in the business's operations. In this role, it stimulates and motivates new initiatives and acts as a reliable sounding board for new projects, ideas and concepts. The board of directors should exercise effective oversight of the executive committee's actions and activities at all times, in order to serve the interests of company shareholders and stakeholders.

In addition, the board monitors family-related aspects that could affect the business. Although no single model exists that outlines the board's activities – the owners, board and executive committee will define their responsibilities and authority based on the firm's unique characteristics – there are some functions that are common to all boards of family enterprises. In its role as mediator, the board maintains regular communication with the family council to stay abreast of the family's desires, interests and expectations and to ensure that they concur with the firm's strategic outlook. It also mentors family members, evaluates the performance of the CEO and senior management team and actively participates in generational succession processes so that the baton is passed to the right person at the right time.

Many families tend to avoid conflict and perpetuate certain interpersonal dynamics. For this reason, the board stands sentry to encourage members to be assertive and forthright, and it guides them in making the most opportune decisions for the sake of the firm and its key stakeholders.

Family council

The family council addresses the emotional dimension of family-run firms and promotes initiatives that enhance the family's well-being across financial, intellectual and personal realms. Moreover, the council aims to foster a sense of trust, pride and belonging in the family and to instill a sense of purpose that transcends the company's core business (Tàpies & Chiner, 2008).

Jaime Augusto Zóbel de Ayala is the CEO of the Ayala Corporation, a large conglomerate founded in the Philippines in 1834. He captured this sense of transcendence when he explained, "It is important to teach each new generation, early on, the difference between ownership and stewardship. Ownership is a right of possession. Stewardship is a fiduciary role. It is holding the institution in 'trust for' the next generation. We feel, as a family, that this institution has been passed on to us for our care and not for us to dissipate or do what we will with it for our personal gain" (Reyes, 2012).

Like the board of directors, the council aims to ensure that family members positively contribute to the company's long-term success, albeit far more directly. The council's composition depends on a series of factors, including its degree of development, the life stage of the firm, the existence of a family constitution and the circle of family members involved, since the dynamics between parents and children, for instance, differ significantly from those among siblings or cousins.

Core functions of family councils

The family council's functions, core values and guiding principles are articulated in the family constitution. More than a detailed written document, the family constitution – or family protocol – is the fruit of lengthy debates, countless hours of reflection and hard-earned family consensus. It goes beyond regulating business-family relations to form part of a wider framework aimed at fostering peaceful coexistence between the family, the company they own and the people who straddle both spheres.

By nature, the family constitution should be a flexible and living document that adapts to the evolving structure, dynamics and processes of the business family and ensures that the family and business realms progress in parallel. The relationship between these two domains is too intertwined to treat them as "islands unto themselves," immune from interference: business decisions affect the family in the same way that certain family decisions will inevitably affect the business.

Tailored to the distinct characteristics and circumstances of the company, family constitutions establish well-defined criteria regarding familial and personal matters and provide clarity regarding roles and responsibilities. The development and implementation of this essential charter undoubtedly elevates the degree of rigor in family business practices. The family constitution also transmits the family's common heritage, beliefs and ideals, which translate into the vision, mission and values that guide the corporate governance structure.

The vision statement is the "shared dream" of the family enterprise, painting a picture of how it envisions itself in the future. Beyond short- or medium-term objectives, the vision statement conveys the organization's larger sense of purpose and a clear sense of direction to guide both current and future generations. The entire family should share this vision, hence the importance of articulating and communicating it.

The mission expresses the raison d'être of the family enterprise and how it will interrelate with players in the larger circle of the business operation. Rather than a mere descriptive exercise, the mission should reflect the firm's interests, differentiating features and unique value proposition. In combination, these concepts come to represent the family enterprise's distinctive insignia.

The bedrock of any family business is its value system, which in family-owned companies is shaped directly by the imprint of the founding family. The company's values confer a sense of identity and remain inalterable over time as they are transmitted from generation to generation. They take on particular relevance during leadership transitions.

Key advantages of family councils

Family councils aim to facilitate communication and transparency between the family and corporate governance structures, although the challenge typically lies in their implementation, not in their design. The need for family councils is widely recognized, so some of its core advantages deserve to be outlined here.

First, family councils clearly delineate the issues that should remain in the family sphere and those that pertain to the corporate structure. Family-owned businesses sometimes find this practice difficult, but establishing well-defined boundaries between corporate and family spheres is critical for avoiding conflicts later on.

Second, they offer an objective vantage point by incorporating external consultants to appraise and assess children and other family members. When familial and corporate lines overlap, maintaining impartial viewpoints and effectively managing core processes like performance appraisals when comments are taken as personal attacks, can pose a challenge. The inclusion of external advisors mitigates the risk of these potentially damaging situations.

Third, family councils take an active role in formulating training plans, career objectives and evaluation systems. Objective benchmarks are important to avoid the sink-or-swim model or what-worked-for-my-parents-will-work-for-my-kids approach that prevails in some family-owned firms.

Fourth, family councils encourage accountability among family members in a variety of ways and provide a forum for those who work outside the organization, thus encouraging their sense of belonging.

Fifth, they offer a formal framework for family issues without the legal and commercial constraints typical in corporate governance contexts. In general, family councils are responsible for establishing criteria and objectives; planning family council meetings, preparing an agenda of action items; and chasing action items to drive initiatives forward. In this regard, family councils may benefit from the guidance of an experienced external advisor, especially during the initial stages.

Sixth, family councils provide a platform to leverage the expertise of older generations, who can share their knowledge, offer career guidance and educate younger family members about the business. Younger generations, in particular, benefit from these insights as they grow up and at the onset of their university studies.

Lastly and perhaps most importantly, family councils build trust among their members and establish open channels for communication, promoting dialogue and ensuring that everyone has a voice.

Steps to successfully implement family councils

- Successful implementation starts with communication. The family council should be founded once a level of communication and transparency has been reached that transcends hidden agendas and taboo subjects. There must be an open forum for expressing opinions.
- It requires mutual respect. The family council is a channel to voice opinions about concrete family issues, not a forum for everyone to state their opinions on unrelated matters, invade each other's space or judge their professional performance. Clear boundaries must be set from the beginning to define the scope of issues that are up for debate within the family council. The corporate structure of the business and family and business hierarchies must be respected.
- Family councils must reach a consensus or vote. Family council members should not feel that differences of opinion or opposing viewpoints are detrimental. Consensus should be sought, but if that is not possible, a vote must be taken, and the outcome must be accepted. The family council becomes stagnant and ineffectual if it is unable to reach accords and make decisions.
- Success requires professionalism. Business families must move past the notion that family relationships are incompatible with professional ones, or that only non-family members are capable of acting professionally. Family members who serve on the family council should act professionally to scrupulously fulfill their duties. Talent among family members should be developed and put to use in the family business. Self-esteem and healthy pride in the family are necessary to successfully effectively carry out the duties of a family council.

- Family councils must take preventive actions. No family is immune from conflict. In family enterprises, divergences often emerge when the founder or first generations believe that the same management approach that overcame initial hurdles will be equally effective to navigate future challenges. Unfortunately, this is rarely the case. Issues that impact the family require unique solutions that reflect the company's current reality.
- Family councils need formal mechanisms. As the composition of the family network evolves – one generation ushers in the next or siblings or cousins join the scene – formal mechanisms to share information and make decisions become increasingly necessary. Talking business around the dinner table can be useful, but strategic issues normally addressed by the family council, like generational successions, need to be treated with greater formality and rigor.
- Family councils need to be evaluated for ongoing improvement. No one should fear evaluating others or being evaluated. If this is the case, fostering the culture of hard work and rigor becomes difficult. Performance metrics are the only way to guarantee continued improvement. Education and training processes should be demanding in terms of quality, standards and degree requirements.
- Family councils need clear objectives and priorities. From the outset, the family council should be clear about the wants and needs of family members. What does everyone expect in terms of dividends, social recognition, employment opportunities and power sharing? These aspects must be deliberated and discussed.
- Family councils require continuity. Holding sporadic meetings isn't enough to ensure continuity. Family councils should establish a calendar of regular meetings to guarantee a forum for analysis and collective decision-making, which requires time and effort. Members should be honest, consistent and rigorous in preparing meetings, with their corresponding agendas, minutes and action items.
- Prospective family council member must be able to communicate their past grievances. Grievances need be addressed and resolved before creating a family council, to prevent any latent acrimony or hostility from contaminating the atmosphere or filtering down to the next generation. Although forgetting is difficult, forgiveness is always possible.

The family office

The family office is in charge of managing, building and sustaining wealth for current and future generations of the business family. It organizes and administers family resources that are no longer tied up in the core business, in addition to other services that enhance the well-being of family members (Tàpies & Chiner, 2009).

Some family offices limit their range of services to financial management, consulting and insurance services, whereas others manage investments that, in time, can become holdings or investment corporations in their own right. In some cases, they even grow to become as important as the initial family business.

Depending on its size and complexity, the family office is usually provided with a legal structure, independent governing bodies, an executive team and professional staff. Ideally, it should be led by seasoned professionals capable of providing multidisciplinary consulting services and adequate information on different fields to support the family's decision-making process.

The team should avoid conflicts of interest when determining the family's objectives, balancing the needs of individual family members with those of the collective whole. Most members of a business-owning family consider the family office a useful service. As a customized entity, it responds to the family's needs in different domains and fosters their sense of belonging in a shared project.

Origins and evolution of family offices

Several scenarios may prompt business families to diversify their economic assets: the sale of the family company; excess liquidity in corporate operations that need to be separated from the core business; periods of abundant and recurring dividends; or the important influx of liquidity generated after the company goes public.

In the early stages of family-run firms, family offices are often contained within the domain of company and headed by trusted employees. However, as new generations enter the scene and family wealth increases, the need for greater professionalization and a broader portfolio of services also increases. Figure 13.3 illustrates the evolution of how family wealth is managed from the time the business is founded until the incorporation of subsequent generations.

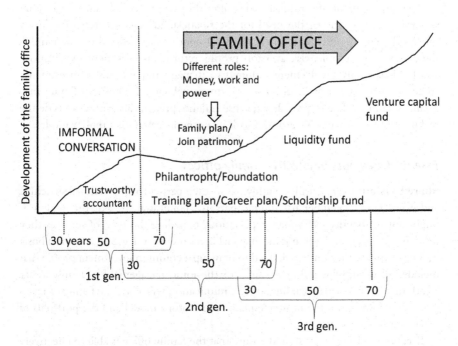

FIGURE 13.3 Evolution of Family Wealth Management

Source: Author.

The decision to establish a family office separate from the business marks a critical juncture in the life of a family business, especially when it moves from the initial stage of a founder-dominated firm to a larger, well-structured family enterprise. Establishing the foundations of a family office provides a platform for members to develop a strategy grounded on sound business principles and establish a hub for financial services, accounting, tax consulting and training services that serves the entire family and introduces other initiatives such as scholarship funds and philanthropic ventures.

As in the corporate domain, the need will arise to establish merit-based criteria and professional objectives for new members who join the family office to optimize its efficiency and ensure the highest level of professionalism. In time, the family office should ideally generate its own income and serve as a source of profits to increase the family wealth.

When is the timing right to establish a family office?

There are different times in the life of a family business when the creation of a family office is recommended. The first is when members of a generation mutually agree to the joint management of their common assets. They define a decision-making process and clear criteria with two main objectives: securing the future preservation of the wealth, on one hand, and the family business's capability for creating value in the future, on the other.

The development of surplus liquidity after the sale of a core business is another scenario that may trigger the need for the financial advisory services of a family office. The family office will design an investment portfolio based on the family's joint investment profile, risk aversion profile, return-on-investment expectations and level of family involvement required to manage and administer investments. In addition to advice on traditional investment vehicles, the business family may require a family office to provide expertise on entrepreneurial ventures outside the realm of their core business or lower-risk investments based on a rentier model.

Essential elements in effective family offices

Shared vision: Every business family has its own particular generational structure, and every family member has unique personal circumstances. For this reason, is important to identify everyone's expectations regarding the type of services they need. If the idea is to develop joint financial investment services and common business investments, the family will need to draw up a common investment profile that includes all what, why and how issues for the joint management of family assets. Working together with open lines of communication will allow the family to reach a precise definition of the most adequate family office model and the portfolio of services it will provide.

Strategy: The strategy should ensure that the family office is able to effectively deliver the services specified by the family. In the case of investment services, the strategy should include investment characteristics and conditions. In addition to asset allocation, details concerning the liquidity fund, namely the amount and conditions approved, should be given to support the liquidity policies agreed on by family shareholders.

A basic dividend policy must also be drawn up and maintained, although this may limit the amount of funds invested or nature of investments that can be made. The harmony and security of the family are more important than profitability. These goals should be formulated with medium- and long-term timelines and followed with unwavering discipline, avoiding short-term decisions that could be impacted by market volatility.

In the case of business investments, it's important to establish clear parameters regarding the degree of family involvement in their governance and management.

Standards and procedures: Criteria must be set regarding the ownership structure, governance and management of the family office. The governing bodies and management bodies must be clearly defined, along with the necessary requirements for family members' participation.

Professionalism and meritocracy should prevail, with the utmost level of selectivity based on objective evaluation systems and solid career planning services. A permanent evaluation process should include comparisons with benchmarks and relevant market criteria. Thus, the family office should form part of a family governance system that has been ratified in the family constitution, serving as a means to achieving specific goals defined by the family.

Implementation and launch: At this stage, precise tools for control and reporting need to be implemented to ensure accountability to the owner family and build trust in the family office project. In this respect, adequate information must be provided to monitor and analyze the activities and movements of the investment portfolio and ensure that it adheres to the family's wishes in terms of risk profiles, investment vehicles and involvement levels.

Areas of activity

The family office may play different roles and employ a variety of tools depending on the family's interests, which generally relate to the areas of financial management and human and intellectual capital. Figure 13.4 provides an overview of different domains of activity of a family office with concepts that will be developed later in the chapter.

In terms of financial capital, the family office structures and manages accumulated family wealth and coordinates its possible diversification into different investment vehicles, from low-risk patrimonial investments to financial or business investments with higher levels of associated risk, such as venture capital and private-equity funds. In all cases, the investment portfolio should reflect the family's common investment profile.

Ultimately, the family office should aim to minimize the costs from the transfer of ownership to the next generation and selling off shares among family members

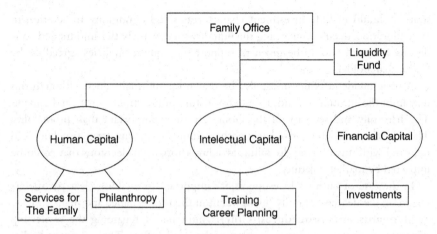

FIGURE 13.4 The Family Office: Areas of Activity

Source: Author.

or to third parties. A set of norms and liquidity mechanisms can allow for adequate preventive management of family members' expectations and possible liquidity needs

Career planning committee

This committee fosters family talent by promoting the human and intellectual development of family members, including those with formal roles in the family business, those with aspirations to join and others whose professional ambitions lie elsewhere. It facilitates training programs and ongoing learning and strives to provide any necessary resources to help family members fulfill their roles in the governing bodies, both in the family and in corporate governance structures. To this end, the career committee also selects and coordinates the services of external professionals for family members, such as mentors or coaches. Scholarship funds toward specific studies or coursework may also be available to support the continuous growth and development of family members.

The committee plays a key role in supporting younger family members and guiding them toward a particular professional path. The committee may arrange for tests to assess their skills and abilities to complement the efforts made by their immediate circle and career service counselors.

Philanthropy and family foundations

In the context of the family business, philanthropy denotes activities carried out by family members voluntarily and as a group (as opposed to individually) with the aim of giving back to society.

Philanthropic initiatives are effective at fostering family harmony across different generations and uniting members around a common cause. They also have the dual benefit of bolstering the personal growth and development of participating members while having a positive impact on the community.

The family's philanthropic activities should not be confused with the CSR initiatives related to business operations, although they can be provided a legal structure to channel their areas of operations and safeguard their continuity, if necessary.

Philanthropic ventures require time, dedication and valuable resources. For this reason, the project should be close to the family's heart and chosen in consensus. It should spark interest in all family members and match their family values so that, in time, it becomes an enduring legacy passed on to future generations. Finally, the project should establish clear objectives and mechanisms to ensure the highest degree of professionalism and effectiveness based on tangible and measurable results.

Venture capital funds

This fund supports entrepreneurial ventures of family members who do not work in the family business, helping them design a business plan, carry out a professional feasibility study and gain access to the necessary resources. Because it provides professional assessment, the fund also prevents family members from dedicating their time to projects considered unviable.

The fund can provide a unique learning experience for young family members by allowing them to sit on a board of directors, albeit a small one, and participate in decisions regarding investments, divestments, management and monitoring. Their involvement gives them a glimpse into the inner workings of a board of directors and helps them prepare for the future if they eventually serve in the family business structure.

Each generation must establish its own family business model and promote entrepreneurship for the next generation. The venture capital fund is a solid instrument toward achieving this goal.

Liquidity funds

This fund is created to finance the purchase of shares from family members in need of liquidity. It is established and governed by an agreement among family shareholders and managed by the family council.

Family businesses tend to be closed-off networks due to their intentions to maintain most of the capital in the hands of the family. As a result, family members often set up pacts or arrangements, and third-party shareholders from outside of the family are usually permitted only for specific, justifiable reasons.

Liquidity mechanisms involve different methods and varying degrees of obligation with respect to other shareholders and/or the company itself. A company's obligation to provide liquidity to its shareholders is directly proportional to the conditions and limitations that affect shareholders when requesting that their liquidity needs be met. The end objective is to protect the company and secure its continuity while discouraging sales to external shareholders, especially during economic downturns or other endemic problems that could jeopardize the viability of the company.

Conclusion

The evolution of a family-run firm tends to follow a similar pattern: the first generation is owner-driven, impelled by the vision, efforts and passion of the founder. In the next stage, the company grows and integrates other members of the family, evolving from a sole proprietor or small-business structure to a family business. If the firm continues to prosper, it will progress from a family business to a family enterprise. Bear in mind, however, that the odds are not in its favor: less than 14 percent of family-owned firms continue to operate into the third generation, and only 5 percent remain active long enough for the fourth generation to take the helm.

What differentiates consolidated family enterprises from those that close shop after one or two generations? Indeed, economic gains are essential but they aren't the only factor that ensure a family firm's long-term continuity: the journey from family firm to family enterprise, one with a lasting legacy, requires more than merely hitting growth targets or reaching strategic objectives. If family firms are to progress past the second generation, they must inculcate a family legacy grounded on a shared culture, values and vision.

With each passing generation, the bloodlines among family members become more diluted, and over time, all family relationships change and evolve. However, for family-owned businesses, the imperative is to make concerted efforts to instill their shared history from one generation to the next to avoid a situation like the one faced by the Bancrofts.

Firms that are fixated solely on making money will have only fleeting success, although this single-minded focus isn't typical of family-run firms. Turning a profit is certainly important, but it is far from their only incentive. Family-owned firms that stand the test of time are grounded on solid governance structures and aspire to a more transcendental, less quantifiable incentive: the pride of making history.

BOX 13.1 FAMILY ENTERPRISES: REAL-WORLD SUCCESS STORIES

Cargill leads into its sixth generation

Founded in 1865, the US-based agricultural trading giant Cargill has successfully balanced corporate interests and family objectives for six generations. Around a hundred family members – descendants of the Cargill and MacMillan families – hold 90 percent of the company's shares, while employees and management control the remaining 10 percent in stock ownership plans.

Executive Chair Greg Page expressed the importance the company gives to balancing the business and family spheres: "We are going to have the shareholders that we deserve . . . so we need to be proactive to get their emotional as well as their financial attachment to the business. It's a two-way street" (Tàpies, San Román & Gil, 2016).

Robust governance structures have enabled Cargill's ongoing success as a privately held firm, more than 150 years after its foundation. The company's board of directors has seventeen members, comprising six family members, six independent advisors and five Cargill executives. In addition to a highly professional board, Cargill has a clearly defined dividend policy: the company is allowed to invest 80 percent of annual earnings back into the business, and the rest is paid as dividends (Meyer & Hume, 2015).

In 2011, Cargill again proved its management dexterity when its largest shareholder, the Margaret A. Cargill Foundation, wanted to diversify its holdings, a large portion of which comprised by Cargill stock. To allow the foundation to liquidate its shares while avoiding the need to go public, the company spun off its 64 percent stake in the fertilizer company Mosaic and transferred US$12 billion in Mosaic shares to the foundation and other family shareholders. The operation demonstrated an innovative approach to procuring liquidity for shareholders: selling off shares of a subsidiary while maintaining control of the parent company.

Cargill executives claim that the company has survived and flourished thanks in part to its corporate structures as many of its rivals have either gone public or been acquired.

Merck: 350 years as a family business

Merck is a German multinational that operates in the chemical, pharmaceutical and life sciences sectors, with operations in seventy countries and 50,000 employees around the world. Founded in 1668, it is the world's oldest chemical and pharmaceutical company and among the largest pharmaceutical companies in the world.

The pioneering spirit of the Merck Group is evident, not only by its continual, strategic growth but also by the adroit governance of its corporate and family spheres. The company started off as a pharmacy that was passed from one generation to the next until 1827, when it began the industrial-scale production of alkaloid, plant extracts and other chemicals, elevating the pharmacy to a new level.

As part of its international expansion strategy, in the late 1800s, the company began sending Merck descendants abroad for their university degrees and apprenticeships to broaden their horizons and their awareness of foreign cultures. By the 1900s, the company was present on five continents. In 1920, Merck formed its first board of directors to ensure the best possible leadership and reduce its dependence on family members as the only source of management talent. From that time on, people from outside the family could opt for executive positions, and the board would oversee decisions relating to "important matters," although the leadership position would be reserved for a family member.

Merck is a model of family business. In 2005, it was in the hands of two hundred family members, of which around 130 were partners in the company. The corporate doors are open for both Mercks by bloodline or by marriage, which has benefited the business by allowing talented outsiders to join the firm.

The Merck family members are closely involved in the development of the company and strive to create a sense of belonging from one generation to the next. To become a partner in Merck is considered more of an honor than an obligation, although family members and outsiders alike must prove their worth. As its mission states, "We at Merck do what we say and then measure ourselves on this basis" (Tàpies & Neumann, 2006; Tàpies, San Román & Gil, 2016).

References

Dioum, B. (1968). Triennial Meeting of the General Assembly of the International Union for the Conservation of Nature and Natural Resources (IUCN), New Delhi, India.

LL. Reyes, M. A. (2012). The Zobel Family Council: Ensuring the Next Generation of Leaders. *The Philippine Star*. www.philstar.com/business/787816/zobel-family-council-ensuring-next-generation-leaders (17 November 2016).

Meyer, G. and Hume, N. (April 2015). Cargill Guards Private Life in 150th Year. *Financial Times*. www.ft.com/content/ec6f88c2-e4ec-11e4-bb4b-00144feab7de (14 November 2016).

Tàpies, J. and Chiner, A. (March 2008). *The Family Council: Organization and Functions, Technical Note SMN-0660-E*. Barcelona: IESE Publishing.

Tàpies, J. and Chiner, A. (April 2009). *The Family Office, Technical Note SMN-0669-E*. Barcelona: IESE Publishing.

Tàpies, J. and Neumann, F. (October 2006). *Balancing Family and Business Needs at Merck KGaA, Case Study DG-1505-E*. IESE Publishing.

Tàpies, J., San Román, E. and Gil, A. (2016). *100 Families That Changed the World: Family Businesses and Industrialization*, pp. 169–172. Barcelona: Fundación Jesús Serra.

14

GENERAL MANAGEMENT AS FIRM OWNERSHIP CHANGES

Marta Elvira and Luis Manuel Calleja

> Having first-rate people on the team is more important than designing hierarchies and clarifying who reports to whom.
> — *Warren Buffett, CEO of Berkshire Hathaway*[1]

This chapter examines the relationship between a firm's ownership and its general management in cases where the CEO remains even through ownership changes. A firm's institutional configuration comprises the governance activities in place to diagnose, choose and implement its financial, legal and corporate contours, which serve to organize the entrepreneurial project, its funding and the political interests, ensuring the company's sustainability in the long term.

This institutional configuration influences other governance areas such as the firm's business model, management structure and professional commitment (Valero & Lucas, 2011). Similarly, an essential aspect of effective governance consists of selecting the most appropriate partners and choosing the CEO to run the enterprise – hence, the importance of having an effective relationship between owners and managers.[2]

In recent years, we have observed an increasing number of acquisitions in which new company owners decide to maintain existing top management teams. This chapter explores the trend and advances a conceptual approach for management and board of directors in these situations.

To understand this phenomenon, we will first describe three case studies of companies in different countries: Berkshire Hathaway, UFINET Telecom and USP Hospitals. Although these businesses reflect different regions, industries, structures and activities, our analysis points to some common characteristics that may contribute to their long-term success through multiple ownership changes.

Building on the foundations and evidence presented in the first part of the chapter, we then explore a theoretical framework to understand these situations, an underlying business policy model and the relevance of various ownership models. To that end, we describe different kinds of firm owners and their influence on top management continuity. We conclude with recommendations to advance work on this topic.

An increasingly common phenomenon

In an environment characterized by economic uncertainty, technological advances and industry integration, changes in company ownership are becoming increasingly common. In many of these cases, company management is often left in place. This trend is worth studying in light of its rising prevalence and the limited body of research to date.

According to the data from the Madrid Stock Exchange, shareholders of listed companies have evolved as shown in Figure 14.1.

Figure 14.1 shows the large number of nonresident shareholders, even during the financial crisis period. Because future changes in reference shareholders are likely for most large companies listed on the Spanish stock exchange, with buyers mainly from outside Spain, local management teams might remain at the helm even as shares change hands.

Among unlisted companies, frequent mergers occur and new companies go public. In Spain, growth in these trends surpasses European and world averages: 38 percent of unlisted companies' operations were associated with going public in 2014 (Thomson Reuters Annual Report, 2015). We are particularly interested in unlisted companies run by financial investors who, a priori, are top candidates for retaining managers, given certain performance conditions. Data suggest that half of them are nonresident financial investors and that 80 percent retain their management after the transaction.[3]

Similar trends appear outside of Spain. The development of "common ownership" – in which the same companies are the owners of businesses competing in the same

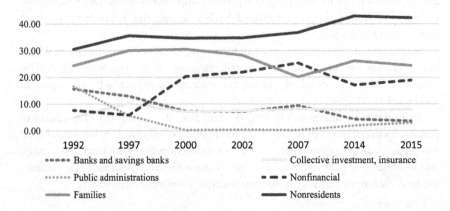

FIGURE 14.1 Shareholders of Listed Companies on Madrid Stock Exchange

sector – is relatively new. Until recently, BlackRock and Vanguard were rarely listed among the top ten shareholders of any company. In 2016, along with State Street, they owned stock in 88 percent of the companies on the S&P 500. In fact, the concentration of common ownership has almost doubled in the past two decades in the manufacturing, construction, finance and service sectors (Anton et al., 2016). The same study indicates that as of 2015, BlackRock is the largest shareholder in one out of every five US corporations listed on the stock exchange, and Fidelity is the largest shareholder in one out of every ten public companies, often owning at least 10 to 15 percent of shares (Anton et al., 2016).

The Economist (2016), citing Bain's numbers, reports similar data: "the share of America's midsized companies controlled by private equity tripled between 2000 and 2013; for large companies it increased more than fivefold." The impact that private equity has on firm performance is mostly attributed to increased focus: "Private-equity funds, the boards they put in place and the top managers who work for them all tend to concentrate on underlying performance to the exclusion of almost everything else. Public companies face a mountain of often incomprehensible or conflicting regulatory demands that are not relevant to performance; that delisting has risen in step with such demands seems unlikely to be a coincidence."

Investors consider many factors before backing a firm – from country risk to growth, interest rates and the company's fundamentals.[4] These considerations help explain the rising number of operations in which managers are maintained, even after ownership has changed hands. They also reflect the shift toward nonresident/ international investors who depend to a greater extent on local management.

Insights from three case studies

To better understand this phenomenon, we draw on three company cases that speak to its global reach: Berkshire Hathaway, UFINET Telecom and USP Hospitals.[5] Berkshire Hathaway, the US financial holding company, illustrates most clearly how new owners may choose to not get involved at all in the daily operations of an acquired company. On the other end of the spectrum is UFINET, the Spanish/ LATAM cable operator, which exemplifies a managerial team remaining through ownership changes. Finally, in the USP Hospitals case, the founding team plays the role of entrepreneur, board or managerial team of the conglomerate, depending on the evolving phase of the company. We analyze these companies over time to identify dimensions of governance that emerge only in the long term.

BOX 14.1   BERKSHIRE HATHAWAY: THE ROLE OF THE CHAIR (LYNCE & CALDART, 2012)

The organizational model of Berkshire Hathaway (BH) is based on a simple and straightforward decentralization of all business management responsibilities.

Following this principle, Warren Buffett entrusts his CEOs with authentic and unique "ownership" over these responsibilities. Buffett, with the support of Charlie Munger, the vice-chair, makes all BH's investment decisions and picks all capital allocations.

Each year, Buffett uses the conglomerate's annual report to explain investment and managerial decisions. In it, Buffett describes how he and Munger mostly work on capital investments and provide support for the CEOs of their businesses. The company's policy of granting autonomy gives executives the ability to make operational decisions and send BH the resulting profits.

This decentralization principle is so important that the responsibility for finding possible synergies among firms falls on the companies' CEOs, without the involvement of BH's corporate center.

"Our subsidiaries' collaborators have the feeling that their business is much more important than BH. In the end, they do not need any support from the corporation," explains Buffett. Such decentralization is possible thanks to clear policies that leave room for discretionary actions (flexible criteria with strict application). Supervision applies to how CEOs define, develop and use such policies.

Buffett believes that CEOs should work for pleasure rather than for material needs: "My task is to select good, high-level managers who have demonstrated their ability. But this is only the beginning because if we do not have the capacity to retain them, we do not get continuity in our business. Most of them do not need their salaries, although sometimes they get checks worth millions of dollars. We depend on their work and their knowledge, and that is why we must create the right conditions and be sure that they work with the same motivation as when they managed their companies. And this cannot be achieved with contracts!"

BOX 14.2 USP HOSPITALS: THE ROLE OF MANAGEMENT (SAN JOSÉ & ROURE, 2007)

The Spanish healthcare company USP Hospitals has acquired twenty-one hospitals while retaining most managers in the original healthcare centers. USP Hospitals' senior management team had worked together before creating and building the company together.

Gabriel Masfurroll, president of USP Hospitals, recalls that "we knew where to go, how to do it: we had the crew, but we were missing the boat." Upon the creation of the conglomerate, they put all their savings into the new venture.

Over the years, ownership has changed from a US venture capital firm to shareholders in the stock market, then to an investment fund. The company's approach to working with management teams of acquired hospitals, however, has remained constant.

According to Masfurroll, "Each acquired hospital has a managing director with a team that meets weekly with the functional director at USP – the person in charge of purchases or the infrastructures, etc. – of the subject to be addressed in the meeting."

Masfurroll is an entrepreneur who has developed a solid management team. His job includes many managerial tasks, though he increasingly focuses on the corporate agenda. He is virtually a "one-person show," due to limited board influence. In 2012, the firm was acquired by another Spanish healthcare company, which in turn was acquired by the German group Helios in 2016. Throughout these shifts, most hospital directors remained in their roles.

BOX 14.3   UFINET TELECOM: THE INTERACTION BETWEEN MANAGEMENT AND THE BOARD OF DIRECTORS (ELVIRA & CALLEJA, 2016)

The multinational telecommunications company UFINET, headquartered in Spain, has operations in Guatemala, Honduras, El Salvador, Nicaragua, Costa Rica, Panama, Colombia and Mexico and has a presence in Miami, New York, London and Frankfurt. It changed ownership three times before 2017 while retaining the same CEO and manager for Latin America.

Iñigo García del Cerro, UFINET's CEO, explains how the firm's activities have varied depending on the owner. For instance, after it was acquired by a multinational utility company, it became a small division. Given that the new owner was from a different sector, García del Cerro spent much of his time explaining their business to the rest of the enterprise. "If talking to someone who was from the planning department who would say 'I need your investment forecast for the next two years,' I had to explain to him that my business did not work that way at all."

In contrast, when UFINET was bought by the investment fund Cinven, meetings with the board drastically changed. Previously, these meetings focused on bookkeeping and milestone presentations. The new board, however, employed part of its efforts on strategic issues and high-level decisions: "Now the typical presentation of milestones and summary – which was most important in the previous period – is limited to a page and a half. Operational issues are not that relevant. We stress the financial part – numbers, KPIs, etc. – and the strategy part, to which most of the meeting time is devoted. It might include new growth opportunities, new countries to invest in, and even potential M&As. We did not devote any time to this before."

Having briefly described the cases, we now point out some common themes that emerge from all of them. Table 14.1 describes these features: a high level of trust between the owners and managing team; effective, long-lasting top management teams that have stayed through ownership shifts; and change in managerial work methods, viewed as learning opportunities.

TABLE 14.1 Selected Features of the Relationship between the Top Management Team and the Board of Directors: Some Evidence from the Cases Described

High level of trust between owners and managing team

Strong trust among all the parties involved in these processes appears to be a key ingredient for the long-time success of changes of property. If the new owners do not believe in the managerial team's experience and ability to lead the new phase of the company, it does not make sense for this team to remain in the enterprise. In the end, absence of trust will negatively impact not only the relationships among them but also the financial outcomes.

Berkshire Hathaway	• Warren Buffett places an emphasis on integrity and effectiveness in the running of his businesses. What he calls the "newspaper test" is one way this is determined: "We have the ability to work with possible financial losses. But we cannot be exposed to the loss of credibility. That is why I ask our CEOs to self-evaluate their actions so that they can be published by an astute, not-known reporter on the front page of their local newspaper and be read by their relatives, friends and neighbors" (Lynce and Caldart, 2012).
UFINET	• Jose Antonio Tazón, chair of UFINET – the company bought by the investment fund Cinven – supervised the management team's activity only by suggesting ideas, lines of action and anticipating possible problems, without interfering in the day-to-day activities.
USP Hospitals	• While searching for their first venture capital fund, the USP team chose the "Americans" over the "British," although the latter made a better offer. As Juan Pedro, a member of the team, explained, "In Don, we saw a person willing to follow this project" (San José and Roure, 2007).

Effective, long-lasting top management teams who remain through ownership changes

In every case studied, we find some common characteristics among the teams, including the time the team has been together and the similar backgrounds among team members. They work as a team, as a complementary and synergistic group.

Berkshire Hathaway	• All members of the board of directors had been chosen by Buffett, who emphasized that all of them were friends and all had been chosen for both their ability to manage businesses and their human qualities. • Regarding the managing directors of the acquired companies, BH was proud of not having lost a CEO to the competition in forty years. (In 2011, David Sokol, his successor in pectore, was removed for betraying Buffet's confidence.)

UFINET	• According to Iñigo Garcia del Cerro, "(UFINET) had a culture in which most of our people had been with us for many years. We have many employees who started as interns and are still here" (Calleja et al., 2016). That includes the current CEO and top VPs. And this happens in a high-tech industry with a high level of rotation.
USP Hospitals	• The entrepreneurial team was the same even before the start of USP, although it added managers of some of the hospitals that they acquired. Hospital directors have mostly stayed as executives, even after USP was acquired by Quirón and, more recently, by the German group Helios.

Change in managerial work methods, viewed as learning opportunities
In most cases, a change in the ownership of a company includes shifts in managerial tasks. Multiple examples of this appear in the cases. Interestingly, although these changes imply additional work, the management team views them as opportunities to improve the company's way of doing things.

Berkshire Hathaway	• Buffett encourages every business acquired, or in the process of being acquired, to maintain their share of the company and ownership of the company's sustainability. "Proceed as if the company were 100 percent owned by you, which was the only asset of your family and could not be sold in the next 100 years" (BH is an exception). This acts as an external control that conditions management actions" (Lynce and Caldart, 2012).
UFINET	• "With Gas Natural – which acquired UFINET from Union Fenosa – we started to have real corporate processing . . . This system provided seriousness and management capacity, and I think we have learned a lot from it. We had a clearly defined method to present projects, whereas before we used more casual methods. In Gas Natural Fenosa, we had our procedures fit for a large multinational," explained Iñigo (Calleja et al., 2016).
USP Hospitals	• According to its president, Gabriel Masfurroll, USP Hospitals' IPO "was an exciting and very sobering process. This process and the demands of the US securities authorities forced us to be much more rigorous in all the management, control and information tasks we used. We learned and improved. This is a more serious, rigorous and transparent way of working."

Source: Authors.

We note three clear drawbacks to our sampling procedure: the number of cases is small; some cover a long time period; and the role of management is at best ambiguous. Moreover, the political nature of a firm's institutional configuration, coupled with its strongly situational-cultural nature, challenges quantitative analysis because statistical averages in the corporate sphere are not as representative as in those related merely to management.[6]

The case studies used are descriptive, not decision based, and are grounded on in-depth interviews with the people in charge. What matters is the choice of the different sectors and institutional sizes and configurations: hospitals, services and manufacturing, high-tech and low-tech; listed, family-owned, MBO holdings and private equity. Also represented are organic and inorganic growth, diversifications, M&As and spinoffs. These different archetypal aspects affect management more than the number of cases or other considerations.

The longitudinal aspect reflects our interest in observing sufficiently long periods of time to be able to discern correlations between corporate changeovers, financial outcomes and management actions. It allows us to observe under what conditions the management team has changed or what kind of ownership affects it over a given time frame. For example, at USP Hospitals, we observe the conditions for its acquisitions after ten years of initial development as a start-up.

Studying this topic is difficult because of the variety of hierarchical or organizational positions associated with the figure of "general manager," which dilutes the concept (Stein & Gallego, 2013). We propose referring to the aforementioned business policy model, with the figure of a "vertex person" or "company politician" at the helm. This person – and not a structural position –has the owner's de facto trust to hold the most power in the organization, however limited, regardless of their specific title within each structure.[7] In fact, that is how Spanish legislation, consistent with European laws, refers to the specific labor relationship of top managers with owners (see Real Decreto, 1985).

We thus observe empirically what intuition suggests: when ownership changes occur – especially when the new owner is a foreign financial institution – managers with the closest ties to the first owners leave, whereas those who deliver sound performance remain. Likewise, when shares change hands, the new shareholders might place some of their trusted people in key positions, but lines keep operating with their prior managers.

The evidence also suggests that these changes are beneficial for companies and society at large. Those harmed by certain changes in control – if anyone – are the managers and board members, not the economy in general (Fernández & Bonet, 202).[8]

Likewise, there are cases in which the initial owners sell a company that does not meet their objectives; the new investors retain the same management; and within a short time period, the company achieves the expected results. This happened at USP Hospitals while it was acquiring clinics. In this case, USP's executive director kept the management teams of the acquired clinics with optimal outcomes and kept even executive managers of hospitals that were not doing well due to inadequate owners. Some of them even became part of the parent company's organizational structure.

The reasons for this change in performance within such a short period are not investments or economies of scale but rather timely decisions made by the board following the needs of the business and the positive change in both internal and external expectations. For this to happen, a decisive factor is personal and professional trust between owners and management after a fine diagnosis of the causes of poor performance. For example, UFINET's relatively young managers expressed surprise when they were told that relationships did not always exhibit such mutual trust in processes of ownership changeover.

Conceptual framework

Thus far, we have established the pervasiveness of changes in company ownership in firms where top management teams remain. The nature of a company certainly goes beyond its contractual aspects: a company is a sociopolitical, economic and labor organization built on trust, which has intelligible meaning over periods of time. Based on this perspective, we can better understand the phenomenon, predict behaviors and suggest certain considerations for management effectiveness.

A contract clarifies responsibilities and penalties when expectations are not met, but it is not the main factor behind responsible action; security, even legal security, is a limited academic matter. At first glance, the case in which a firm changes ownership but keeps the top management intact may be seen as an exception in agency theory. This theory explains a company's governance as a contract among shareholders (the principals in the relationship) and administrators and directors (the agent) in which the administrators seek to maximize their personal benefit at the expense of the shareholders whom they supposedly serve. This shareholder-manager relationship assumes asymmetrical access to information, with the administrators having a clear edge over the shareholders, who are dependent on the former for access to information (Holmstrom, 1981, 1994, 1999).

With information asymmetry at the core, agency theory essentially posits two potential problems. First, firm management is inefficient, and there is an inherent risk in the company's profits compared with its potential profitability. Second, even when management is effective at running the company and generating optimal earnings, part of the shareholders' profits may be being diverted due to opportunistic behavior.

Although a change in ownership and the retention of the management team might be regarded as a specific case of agency theory, the phenomenon challenges either of the two dilemmas referred in the previous paragraph. In this case, the company is not getting the expected results with a given management and owner, but shortly after changing ownership (while retaining the management), it delivers good outcomes.

Owners tend to adapt their expectations to the characteristic of the business at hand, not simply arbitrary results.[9] We surmise that agency theory fails to include basic aspects of a company, like earned trust; its political – and not merely contractual – nature; and the fact that a company is a working environment for people, among many others.[10] The influence of management is obvious, but the influence of ownership is not as clear, which suggests the need to consider aspects in addition to agency theory, such as trust, and to give a more prominent role to the person at the top of the company structure.

On the underlying business policy model and the variety of management roles

We observed a diversity of managerial roles from the BH, UFINET Telecom and USP Hospitals cases. All sensible, realistic models of corporate management stress the importance of alignment and the absence of contradictions between business and organization. In particular, the business policy model developed by professors Valero and Lucas (2011) additionally underscores the nature of managerial action (Table 14.2). This dovetails with Aristotelian practice in several ways, such as the fact that good leadership is not about merely following the rules, regulations or laws. It requires going beyond the rules. Furthermore, policy is more important than ethics since policies make possible the ethics of many. It also fits the conditions of metaphysics, which requires sustainability for a company's survival over time.

TABLE 14.2 Underlying Business Policies and Management

The "vertex person" – more than the "general manager" – is considered the one who in fact holds the greatest power in the company, even if such power is limited. And even if it does not correspond to a specific structure and position but rather to a broader set of roles that are performed.	*Not focusing on job and position titles but the contents and the provision of sufficient power.*
The need for the different partners or owners to summon enough initiative, money and proper use of power in the conviction that a serious dearth of any of the components cannot offset the abundance of the others.	*The contribution of the managers who remain is primarily their proven and successful know-how, while the new financial owners provide money and power.*
Alignment understood as coherence and harmonization – not just balance – among the different areas of governance and operations.	*The lack of business-partner alignment tends to lead to more management changes.*
A logical relationship between the areas of government and their parts such as to produce self-reinforcement. Hence, the evidence that not every partner is suitable for every business and vice versa.	*Either by forcing a trustworthy manager of the property but inadequate to the business, either by having a manager appropriate to the business but without the trust of the owner.*
Corporate concerns meant as those aspects, and only those aspects, in which the partners peacefully agree, not a mere balance of forces stemming from monetary contributions or legal issues of business.	*A lack of sufficient agreement tends to entail a lack of definition of the main executive's mandate, and this leads to a higher number of serious management errors.*
The distinction between the list of executive tasks and those of governance as determined by the board; the need to follow them and keep them up to date, regardless of whether the president and the management are occupied by the same or different people.	*The proper distribution of management-governance tasks and their flexibility allows for taking care of both the short term and the longer corporate term.* *This accordingly allows for better and more focused operational and financial results.*

For example, this business policy model stresses that the most important thing in managing change is managing what should not be changed.

This responsibility for the immutable – the DNA, in today's parlance – befalls an institution's governing bodies, especially the board and particularly its chair. Meanwhile, what can be changed is the responsibility of the top management team.

Regarding the relevance of ownership types

The cases used as illustrations show that there are many ways of running a business, depending on the type of ownership. An additional example is the case of Oscar Mayer (OMSA), with successive changes in ownership – fifteen times in thirty years – while retaining management and with chairs who are focused on their boards, investor relations and the stock market. The separation of executive and governing functions is clear, and the autonomy of the general manager (Damián Frontera) depends heavily on some of the conclusions of this study, in addition to solid performance, including financial outcomes. OMSA was then acquired by the meat company Campofrío and successive firms before being acquired by the Mexican firm Sigma: the board's chair and most of the top management team remained.[11]

For this reason, we analyzed different kinds of owners [12] and their influence on managers' continuity, particularly in the case of "financial investors." A categorization of owner types follows (Valero & Lucas, 2011):

- Multinational or large shareholder base
- Family-owned company: more specific than "families"
- Entities "without shareholders": public administrations, savings banks and so on
- Listed companies
- Management owns part of the capital
- Financial investors

Within the general tendency of changes in company control, we focus on the growing segment of investors that is important because of its implications for company management. Given their diversity, we care about how top management's work might be affected not so much by the owners' general push for profitability but by their specific interests, be they liquidity, earnings, dividends, negotiability, value, speculation, time frame, growth, security, stability, taxation, prestige, following "traditions" or work, in addition to profitability.

Firms must ensure a good fit between their business and financial partners. The contributions regarding entrepreneurial initiative, money and the positive use of power are the three basic components of the institutional configuration of the company.

Management and ownership: key recommendations

Changes in ownership mean changes in certain company policies, although the new key shareholder may be a financial institution and thus should not extensively affect the company's modus operandi. The acquisition decision usually follows a firm's positive performance at the time, plus the ease of certain critical changes. While changes might appear small, they are felt substantially in the day-to-day management of firms. Even if we refer to them as "policies," we should clarify that policies as such tend not to change: what changes is their interpretation, adaptation or application.

Recommendations regarding management

As the UFINET case illustrates, a change of ownership typically includes changes in the established managerial practices of the company. The most frequent, immediate and significant differences in management and managers relate to policies:

- *Reporting policies* include issues, frequencies, hierarchical levels and levels of detail; suggestions, objectives, policies and leeway in interpreting them; priorities and kinds of participation; and delegation.
- *Treasury policies, especially managers' expenses* include not only what's related to liquidity as a goal or to costs and expenses but also changes in procedures for managers' travel spending, ordinary expenditures and so on.
- *Different purchasing policies* include suppliers, purchasing processes, decision makers, economic conditions and so on.
- *Sales policies* include priority segments, price policy, economic conditions, growth and so on.
- *Compensation policies* include changes in bonuses, incentives and so on – especially if these reflect objectives and priorities that differ from those in place before the purchase. Mismatch or misalignment is common in the first few years.
- *Different time frames* include redefinitions of short, medium, and long term in the new situation.
- *Risk management policies* include changes in the risk appetite of the new owners; what activities to avoid; in what areas risk needs to be reduced; and what risks should be shared with third parties.
- *Debt policy* is especially related to growth and dividends policy.
- *Internal promotion policy* may have a greater impact than salary on the company's future.
- *Policies on ethical standards* include, as happens with risk preferences, differences in attitudes, sensibilities and values, which can affect policies.

Managing change while retaining executives implies some critical skills for general management, including adaptability, learning and formalizing new roles and responsibilities. However, the two-fold status of executive and board member is noteworthy, not just because the individual attends plenary meetings but also because they may adopt increasingly long-term responsibility beyond the stay of the owners, a responsibility which otherwise belongs to the board both collectively and individually. The process of adaptation seems easier from an executive standpoint than from a board membership perspective.

The new short, medium and long terms and the risk appetite may be more noticeable in financial decisions, especially in the budgeting process or when refining the company's strategy. Debt, promotion and the ethical tone will affect companies deeply and slowly.

Here it might help to consider the general stages of learning on the job when a new manager takes charge (Gabarro, 1985). Although these phases are not always present or in the sequence suggested by Gabarro, being familiar with the patterns should help general managers and board presidents navigate the initial working stages.

1 Taking hold: frenzy, "the big stuff"; relevant functional aspects
2 Immersion: calm, depth; aspects of governance
3 Reshaping: maximum activity; getting feedback on what was done
4 Consolidation: overall evaluation of how the company is doing; loose ends
5 Refinement: new opportunities; end of "learning"

The cases of BH, UFINET Telecom, SA and USP Hospitals also show how the degree of work/task changes may vary depending on who the new owner is. All the successful managerial teams we studied saw change as a learning opportunity for improving executive action with the new ownership conditions.

Recommendations for the board of directors

Various caveats for governing change should be noted, which are the responsibility of the new board. USP Hospitals provides an example of the role that the board of directors plays in the change of ownership and what should be done to increase the success of the company under the new structure.

The order in which the recommendations are followed should be based more on the importance and consequences than on what the board members might "feel." Such recommendations are as follows:

- Reviewing, along with the executive team, the strategic or value creation plan.
- Reviewing the new composition of the board and considering whether it should include any of the executives as full members.
- Reviewing governance affairs and execution matters; the frequencies that these bodies meet; and the specific information systems.
- Reviewing the key points of reporting with top management.
- Redefining a permanent board agenda and eventually creating a committee to lead its implementation.

The value creation plan or strategic plan should not take more than two or three months to develop. It often builds on that which the company had at the time of purchase, which in turn tends to match the purchase book.

Vital board participants are the chair and the independent members. Owner board members and the executive board members should be evaluated most carefully. A typically debated issue is the appropriateness of independent board members, often from a legal perspective, in the quest for balance, auditing and the defense of minority shareholders. In the cases discussed here, the focus is on how these members can cooperate to ensure that the joint efforts of all the directors on the board lead to positive performance and governance.

The decisive role of the chair

When examining the cases in which a company changes ownership and retains the same general management, we find a relationship that is not only not conflictive, as agency theory suggests, but also mutually beneficial. For instance, as the chair, the magnate and philanthropist Warren Buffett has stated, "We delegate to the point of abdication," making this an essential part of the business model (Buffett, 1999). This positive formulation assumes that the company is being efficiently managed, that it is earning profits in line with its potential and that fund generation management follows the owners' wishes.

The chair is responsible for the smooth operation of the board of directors, both legally and operationally (Calleja & Rovira, 2015). This figure is not someone who merely monitors and coordinates. When stating that the essential aspect of being the chair is to "chair," we are assuming a degree of power and unique authority to be the leader, to occupy the leading place, to organize: to bring order and lead, if needed, and to do, make and impose, to have special influence and to personify the institution.

If agreement exists among the owners regarding the business model and performance expectations, the board of directors can work *collegially*, not merely on the basis of balances and democratic arithmetic. In collegial governance, the chair plays at least two roles: the statutory role assigned to the chair – which can vary widely – and the discretion and flexibility needed to carry out the role. Underlying both roles is the wide variety of collegial forms and the need to enlist the participation of a wide variety of people and circumstances.

If governance is presidential in style or based on personal decisions, the "dictator" will assume all the responsibility alone. If it is a democratic or rules-bound kind of governance, the chair must follow the rules of the game and ensure they are obeyed. But collegial governance requires conditions similar to the paradigm of the traditional good governor. It is a purely political job, neither despotic nor technical like the others cited, with a few particularities worth mentioning. When management remains after the change in ownership, collegial governance is needed paradigmatically, along with a consequent high degree of delegation.

The person chosen to lead a *progressive* board of directors – in the terminology of Ram Charan (Charan, 2005) – whose rules encompass, for example, the combination of experience and knowledge of all the board members through discussion[13] should meet a number of general qualifications:

- Have the respect of the board members and the management team
- Generate balanced trust between the board and the CEO
- Be independent but at the same time supportive of the CEO
- Be managerial and exercise good communication skills
- Be strong and make no concessions to one's own or others' egos

In any event, the chair should be trusted by the owners, the shareholders and the board, and they should have the approval of the holding company, if there is one. The activities of a chair vary greatly according to how close they are to the chair's executive activity. In the cases of José Antonio Tazón at UFINET and Oscar Mayer, the role of the chair is removed from managerial execution. Warren Buffett at BH, on the other hand, takes part in management.

In the cases evaluated, we observe the following characteristics of the board chair (Calleja & Rovira, 2015):

- *Mental clarity in distinguishing different things*

  - Profound, natural identification with the organization's mission: goals, principles, methods.
  - Distinguishing debate from execution and the political aspects from the technical ones.

- *Getting board members to participate and decide*

  - Getting people to participate; getting them to think; knowing how to get others to speak and how to get them to listen to one other; asking good questions.
  - Summarizing agreements and disagreements.

- *Avoiding the abuse of power and excessive control*

  - Use of influence more than power.
  - Decisions on the kind of control to exert in a peaceful agreement with the management.

The value of external or independent board members

The contributions of independent or external board members are appreciated because of their contrast with those accepted by non-independent ones. A new board usually includes former managers and new advisors of the investor, who may agree to neutral elements. It is an exacting job, requiring a vision not blurred by management or execution. Our study had no access to people serving as independent board members, largely because they participate discretely and always outside the board – that is, their job is primarily done before or after plenary meetings.

In the minutes of many of the cases, we can see objectivity in the diagnoses, even a certain cool-headed judgment as if things had nothing to do with the board and would not affect them, especially when weighing risks and making judgments about people's capacities. The influence of independent board members and the good sense of the chair can be felt.

According to Lucas Tomás, we can distinguish contributions, from the viewpoint of the practical implementation of cooperation as an independent board member (Lucas Tomás, 2009):

- Diagnosing: *what and why; underlying causes*
- Suggesting initiatives: *business, management, corporate*
- Warning about dangers: *three to five most critical risks*
- Providing ideas for the future: *anticipation*

Concerning the implementation of cooperation, some recommendations follow:

- *Invitation*: diagnosing before joining

  Understanding the company's business
  Prestige more than money

- *Work*: before, during and after plenary board meetings

  Overall goals and criteria: "*red lines*"
  Stating disadvantages respectfully
  Criterion of "*the bearable truth*"

- *Leaving*: willing to say "I can leave it at any time"

Demanding: "heroic" courage

Beyond the cited references, for the cases we are considering, we deduce some critical characteristics: diagnosis before joining the board; warning about the most critical specific risks and dangers; understanding the company's specific business (more than being a "good professional"); and setting out goals and overall criteria as red lines. Among these, understanding the business is paramount.

How to advance in these situations

Overall, our initial findings regarding management and governance emphasize a general management framework that would transcend contractual relationships and avoid determinism, with learnings at different levels:

- *About top managers*: Understanding the general manager as the individual who in fact holds power in the company, even if such power is limited and does not correspond to a specific structure and position but rather to a broader set of roles that are performed.[14]

- *About the nature of partner contributions*: The central importance of finding partners who will together provide enough initiative, money and power to drive the company forward in unison.
- *About alignment*: Understood as coherence and harmonization – not just balance – among the different areas of governance and operations. Clearly, not every partner is good for every business and vice versa.

From these findings, we draw some initial practical recommendations for the effective governance of these situations:

1   Adapting the owner to the business or vice versa is a governance task that profoundly conditions the work and stability of the firm and its management. Conducting the adaptation process is the chair's responsibility.
2   General management should have "good results" and learn and adapt to the requirements, interests and styles of the new owner – their "corporate business."[15] The owner must get to know and understand the *business* of the acquired company.
3   The general manager's role in communicating and teaching is decisive and requires clarity and political savoir-faire. On the part of the new owner, the figure of the chair of the board is critical to understand the business, make it function properly and support and encourage the general manager to take the most suitable courses of action.
4   The general manager has to find personal ways of respectfully stating inconveniences within the board (Lucas Tomás, 2016), while the chair has to be old enough and experienced enough to tell the general manager in private that they're making a fool of themselves, but without losing mutual respect (Wong, 2011).
5   Finally, the responsibility for the company's future also reaches the general manager since they are the "permanent" part of the business, meaning that their responsibility should go beyond the short-term results that may be demanded by the board of directors. The distinction between the list of executive tasks and those of governance need to be redefined and updated in line with the ownership stage.[16]

Conclusion

Companies commonly experience changes in ownership while maintaining the top management team. Overall, the case analyses suggest that a merely contractual approach is inadequate for offering practical recommendations to managers. The nature of the firm goes beyond contractual relationships: it is a sociopolitical, economic and trust-based work organization that is best understood over relatively long periods of time. Taking a long-term perspective, we have provided criteria to help managers lead companies through different ownership phases. In our conclusions, we have stressed the relevance of general managers for the long-term survival or sustainability of organizations.

Although some research has tended to focus on the position and responsibilities of general managers, we have approached the question from the angle of organizational theory, which identifies the general manager as the person embodying the owners' trust and the person who holds the greatest power in the organization, limited as that may be. We have evaluated several case studies about companies that have experienced changes in ownership while maintaining their top management teams.

Our initial findings suggest that changes in ownership naturally imply changes in partners, though this no longer means the substitution of the executive teams running organizations, especially when they are performing well and the investors are adequate in size and age, history and transnational experience. Still, these top managers have seen their behavior and roles evolve according to the type of ownership in the organization. In this chapter, we have described different types of owners and their effects on top management actions, with a particular focus, but not exclusively, on financial investors as owners.

Changes in ownership typically involve adaptation, especially in certain policies, even if the new shareholder is a financial institution. Because the executive team has to lead through organizational transformation and change initiatives, critical abilities for general management include adaptability and learning and formalizing new roles and responsibilities. Also, a dual condition affects executive members on the board: on the one hand, they attend plenary meetings; on the other hand, they accept long-term responsibility for the continuation of the firm, irrespective of the time that each owner remains with the company. Paradoxically, this concern for the sustainability of the company is typically a responsibility of the board, collectively or individually. Additionally, we have addressed how ownership changes affect work functioning and provide some guidelines to navigate the transition successfully.

Overall, we trust that our case analysis and managerial recommendations will help top management teams and boards navigate the increasingly common situations of a change in firm ownership.

Notes

1 Cunningham, L. (2013). *The Essays of Warren Buffett: Lessons for Investors and Managers.* Hoboken, New Jersey: Wiley.
2 See "The Government of the Business Enterprise." A. Valero and J. L. Lucas (2012) on company policy. EUNSA, 8th edition. *Business:* Governance area of the company that refers to the choice of the supply of goods and services that are offered to obtain a profit in exchange for them; *Management structure:* Governance area of the company that tries to gather the right people and entrusts them with particular parts of what has to be done to carry out the company's business; *Professional community:* Governance area of the company that seeks to ensure that the people who form the company work in the pursuit of the business and coexist internally with professionally sound criteria.
3 Annual report on the stock market 2015. National Securities Market Commission. www.cnmv.es/DocPortal/Publicaciones/Informes/Informe_Anual_2015.pdf
4 The fundamentals include the managers' know-how, especially in new technologies or specific niches.

5 The cases presented in this chapter are based on the AESE case DG-A-1081, "Warren Buffett and Berkshire Hathaway"; IESE case SM-1640, "UFINET Telecom, SA Alineando la Dirección General con la Propiedad"; and IESE case E-106, "USP Hospitales," (A), (B) and (C). The authors have also examined IIST DGI-86: OMSA Alimentación, SA Additional cases cited are derived from press articles.

6 We suggest that the reader consult "Appendix B: The Research Agenda," in Ram Charan's (2005) classic, *Boards that Deliver*, which illustrates the most suitable and unsuitable methods for corporate and institutional-level issues.

7 A vertex person: the person who has the greatest power in the company, even if it is small. With similar responsibilities and powers, this person is also called an "enterprise politician." See A. Valero and J. L. Lucas (2011).

8 See "Fusiones, Adquisiciones y Control de las Empresas" by P. Fernández and A. Bonet.

9 In fact, despite the pervasiveness of agency theory rhetoric in depicting corporate America's behavior in recent decades, scholars argue that the phenomenon reflects "performativity" (Jung & Dobbin, 2016). Management followed some of agency theory's recommendations to increase initiative and risk-taking (stock options, de-diversification, debt financing and outsider board members) without simultaneously incorporating risk-monitoring prescriptions (including executive equity holding and independent boards) (Dobbin & Jung, 2010). Despite being associated with two major recessions, the shareholder value model of the firm promoted by agency theory appears alive and well.

10 "Valero and Lucas (2011) considered that the firm should be seen as a political community and organized and governed as such. By 'political' they do not mean "public" or forming part of the state. In the Aristotelian-Thomist tradition, the notion of political community can be understood in the sense of a human group pursuing a common end, formed by free individuals that have some participation in the shaping of their common good. We hold that firms might be considered and organized as political communities of a certain kind and, therefore, that political wisdom is needed to guide them to the achievement of their common good by free cooperation." See R. Calleja and D. Melé. "Political Wisdom in Management and Corporate Governance," *Philosophy of Management*, 15(2), 99–119, 2016.

11 Campofrío was purchased by Smithfield Foods – a leader in processed pork in the United States. In 2008, Smithfield merged its European subsidiary with Campofrío and the state-owned company COFCO acquired 5 percent of Smithfield. In 2013, the Chinese company Shuanghui purchased Smithfield Foods – it now owns the American participation of the company. In 2014, the Chinese company shared Campofrío with the Mexican company Sigma. In June 2015, Sigma bought its stake from Shuanghui and became the 100 percent owner of Campofrío.

12 Having a greater and direct influence on management than the classification of the regulator, this allows a study approach based on archetypes, not on statistical techniques designed for quantitative analyses.

13 The conditions for belonging to the family-owned company category go beyond the ownership of shares by one or more families – for example, having gone through the succession process.

14 This does not mean that everyone has to think alike. On the contrary, on "progressive" boards the goal is to identify opportunities and complement different viewpoints to reach collegial solutions. On "ceremonial" boards, the rule is to listen and be quiet, whereas on "liberated" boards, it is to speak out regardless of the circumstances.

15 The different denominations and positions found in the cases over time were director general, general manager, president, chair, CEO and COO, among others.

16 The corporate business is the one held by the owners on the occasion of the principal, the core business of the company. This allows them to make new investments in businesses other than the original. An example would be shareholders of a shopping center: in addition to the retail business, a subsequent real estate business is possible due to revaluations of the occupied land.

References

Antón, M. Ederer, F., Giner, M. and Schmalz, M. (2016). Common Ownership, Incentives and Top Management Incentives. IESE Business School Working Paper.

Calleja, L., Elvira, M., and Isaac, S. (2016). Ufinet Telecom S.A. Aligning General Management with Owners. IESE, SM-1640.

Calleja, L. M. and Rovira, M. (2015). *Gobierno Institucional. La Dirección Colegiada.* Pamplona, Spain: EUNSA, Chapter 2.2.

Buffett, W. (1999). *Berkshire Hathaway Inc.: An Owner's Manual.* www.berkshirehathaway.com/ownman.pdf.

Charan, R. (2005). *Boards That Deliver.* San Francisco, CA: Jossey-Bass.

The Economist. (2016, October). Private Equity: The Barbarian Establishment. The Economist. https://www.economist.com/briefing/2016/10/22/the-barbarian-establishment

Elvira, M. (2001). "Pay Me Now or Pay Me Later: Analyzing the Relationship Between Bonus and Promotion Incentives." *Work & Occupations*, 28: 346–370.

Elvira, M. and Calleja, L. M. (2016). Ufinet Telecom, SA Alineando la Dirección General con la Propiedad, IESE Case Study SM-1640.

Gabarro, J. (1985). "When a New Manager Takes Charge." *Harvard Business Review*, 63(3): 110–123.

Holmstrom, B. (1981). "Contractual Models of the Labor Market." *American Economic Review*, 308–313.

Holmstrom, B. with G. Baker and M. Gibbs. (1999). "The Internal Economics of the Firm: Evidence from Personnel Data." *Quarterly Journal of Economics*, 109(4): 881–919. https://doi.org/10.2307/2118351, accessed in November 1994.

Holmstrom, B. (1999, January) "Managerial Incentive Problems: A Dynamic Perspective" *Review of Economic Studies*, 66(1): 169–182.

Jung, J., and Dobbin, F. (2016). "Agency Theory as Prophecy: How Boards, Analysts, and Fund Managers Perform Their Roles." *Seattle University Law Review*, 39: 291–320.

Lucas Tomás, J. L. (2009). Los presidentes son convenientes. Nota Técnica II San Telmo, original 1991, revisada en 2009: DGIN-06.

Lucas Tomás, J. L. (2016). El Papel del Consejero Independiente. Paper Delivered at the 17th International Meeting of Professors of Business Policy, Instituto Internacional San Telmo (San Telmo International Institute).

Lynce, L. and Caldart, A. (2012). "Warren Buffett and Berkshire Hathaway," *AESE Case DG-A-1081.*

Morera, E. (2010). *Responsabilidad: Concepto Jurídico y Sus Singularidades.* Barcelona, Spain: Ariel.

RD 1382/1985. (1985). *Real Decreto Ley del 1 de Agosto por el que se regula la relación laboral de carácter especial del personal de alta dirección.* Spain: Ministerio de Trabajo y Seguridad Social.

Ricart, J. E., Álvarez, J. L. and Gifra, J. (2007). *Los Accionistas y el Gobierno de la Empresa: Análisis de la Situación Española.* Barcelona: Deusto.

San José, A. and Roure, J. (2007). USP Hospitales, (A), (B) and (C), IESE Case E-106.

Stein, G., Susaeta, L., Gallego, M., and Cuadrado, M. (2013). "Los consejeros dominicales y la rotación del primer ejecutivo. Evidencias de las empresas cotizadas españolas 2007-2010." *Revista Empresa y Humanismo*, XVI.2, 33–79.

Thomson Reuters (2015). *2015 Annual Report.* New York.

Valero, A. and Lucas Tomás, J. L. (2011). *Política de Empresa*, pp. 131–138. Pamplona, Spain: EUNSA.

Valero, A. and Lucas Tomás, J. L. (2018). *Business Policy: An Approach on Corporate Management*. Fundación San Telmo, Seville. Annex A, 113–120.

Wong, S. C. Y. (2011). "Boards: When Best Practice Isn't Enough." *McKinsey Quarterly*. https://www.mckinsey.com/featured-insights/leadership/boards-when-best-practice-isnt-enough

PART 4

Integrating principles, strategy, organization and governance

15

THE AGENDA OF THE CHIEF EXECUTIVE OFFICER

Adrián A. Caldart, Alejandro A. Carrera and Magdalena Cornejo

The work of the GM is arguably the most important of all of those developed within an organization. The actions of the GM will likely have the highest impact on the rest of the corporate structure: on an individual level, with regard to members' specific roles, and on a corporate level, since they shape the social environment in which people spend a significant portion of their lives. From another perspective, it can be argued that the prosperity of a country strongly depends on the quality of the people running its main business firms.

Despite the importance of the role of the GM, research on the topic suffers from substantial gaps. First, the most celebrated theoretical contributions were developed from the beginning of the 20th century until the 1970s. While certain aspects of the GM agenda undoubtedly transcend time, it is far from prudent to simply assume that the role of a GM in 2018 will have the same scope, complexity and dynamism as that of a GM in the 1970s.

Contemporary GMs face a new reality that differs significantly from the one that confronted their peers half a century ago. It is characterized, among other factors, by the widespread availability of information (and highly sophisticated technologies to analyze it) and increased complexity and dynamism in competitive landscapes in a large number of industries, as well as the growing importance of environmental sustainability and social commitment in the corporate strategy of most businesses.

Current literature on the work of the GM reflects two main currents. On one extreme is popular literature, characterized by a broad, comprehensive perspective that is essentially anecdotal and lacking a solid empirical background. On the other extreme is academic literature, which approaches the topic with the required rigor but without vocation for comprehensively addressing the agenda of the GM, with a few exceptions (Hart and Quinn, 1993; Glick, 2011).

In this chapter, we aim to make a contribution to the development of contemporary knowledge on the work of CEOs. To this end, we will first review the classic academic contributions within this field and discuss recent work that aspires to shed light on the work of contemporary CEOs. Second, we will complement this work by presenting the results from a survey given to CEOs from firms operating in Latin America. The survey is based on a model of the CEO agenda (Carrera, Caldart & Cornejo, 2011; Carrera, Caldart & Cornejo, 2012, 2014) and examines how CEOs determine their agenda ("understanding") and the core issues that occupied their time during the year preceding the survey ("execution").

The need to better understand what GMs do (and should do) is particularly urgent in light of the numerous corporate "mega-scandals" over the last fifteen years in Europe, Asia and North America stemming from egregious managerial misjudgment, negligence and, in some cases, completely unethical and unlawful behavior on behalf of the GMs in the exercise of their duties.

Examples abound of organizations and industries rocked by corporate scandal, including Enron (Kenneth Lay), Hyundai (Chung Mong Koo), Computer Associates (Sanjay Kumar), the global financial system that triggered the worldwide 2007 crisis and more recent cases of Turing Pharmaceuticals (Martin Shkreli), Toshiba (Hisao Tanaka) and Wells Fargo (John Stumpf). These cases clearly illustrate the prolonged periods of deficient leadership that reigned in these firms and the failure (or at least ineffectiveness) of the multiple and supposedly sophisticated internal and external control systems that they were subject to. These reprehensible situations discredited the figure of the CEO globally.

In the wake of these scandals, the matter of CEO compensation was put in the spotlight, especially after information emerged on the multi-billion-dollar variable remuneration packages collected by CEOs of high-profile firms in the years leading up to the economic crisis. Despite the dark clouds on the horizon, many of these CEOs assumed high-risk strategies that, while profitable in times of economic growth, would expose their firms to unbearable financial stress (and even bankruptcy) if the economic outlook went sour. A survey illustrates this point, revealing that 74 percent of Americans considered CEO pay to be excessive.[1] The topic was even highlighted during the 2015 presidential debates of the past US election:

- The average CEO "is now earning 200 times the average hourly wage. Twenty years ago, the ratio was about 40 times. People all over this country are really upset about this" (Hillary Clinton).
- CEO compensation is a "total and complete joke . . . they get whatever they want" (Donald Trump, who served as a CEO for more than thirty years).

The agenda of the CEO in management literature

The study of the CEO agenda attracted the attention of several highly renowned intellectuals within the academic field of management. In Henri Fayol's seminal work *Administration Industrielle et Générale*, the French engineer and pioneer of organization theory established that the roles of the top executive of the firm comprised (long-term) *planning, organizing* (process and assignment of mandates to collaborators), *leadership* (to motivate and oversee), *coordination* (to harmonize organizational life) and *control* (to verify and confirm). This approach, reaffirmed shortly thereafter by Luther Gulick, was developed significantly by Chester Barnard in 1938 in his celebrated book *The Functions of the Executive*. In his work, Barnard established that the CEO must also "formulate and define the purpose of the organization."

This notion acknowledges the role of the CEO as the main link between the firms they lead and the external environment in which they operate in order to fulfill their overriding objectives. In 1957, Phillip Selznick introduced an important idea: the vital role of the CEO as the promoter and protector of corporate values. In this sense, the CEO also assumes the role the "institutional leader" in the firm.

The "real work" of the general manager

Henry Mintzberg made in his 1968 doctoral dissertation an extraordinary contribution to the study of the CEO agenda, which he later developed as the foundation of his 1973 book *The Nature of Managerial Work*. After developing well-structured observations on the work of five general managers over the course of a week, Mintzberg concluded that the nature of the general manager's function is far from highly ordered and well planned. Instead, it encompasses a large range of fragmented activities performed in conditions of high pressure, constant interruptions, great uncertainty and ambiguity. CEOs are essentially relational and experiential, as opposed to exacting and analytical. The descriptive work of Mintzberg had a high impact, and his list of ten roles of the general manager remains a first-order reference till this day (Table 15.1).

John Kotter published in his 1982 book *The General Manager* the results of his research based on interviews and observations of fifteen US general managers.

TABLE 15.1 Roles of the General Manager

Information Roles	
Monitors	Seek and acquire work-related information
Disseminators	Communicate/disseminate information to others in the organization
Spokespersons	Communicate/transmit information to outsiders
Interpersonal Roles	
Figureheads	Perform social and legal duties, act as symbolic leader
Leaders	Direct and motivate subordinates, select and train employees
Liaisons	Establish and maintain contacts within and outside the organization
Decisional Roles	
Entrepreneurs	Identify new ideas and initiate improvement projects
Disturbance Handlers	Deal with disputes or problems and take corrective actions
Resource allocator	Decide where to apply resources
Negotiators	Defend the interests of the firm

Kotter classified his interviewees according to their performance, using both financial and qualitative measures. He concluded that successful general managers shared similar behaviors in their daily work:

- They spend more than 75 percent of their time with other people.
- They are proficient in an array of topics that transcend those directly related to their business.
- They rarely make important decisions during conversations.
- They ask others lots of questions.
- Most of their agenda is unplanned or evolving, even when it is an intensely planned agenda.
- They work around sixty hours a week.

The role of the general manager today

The importance of CEOs for the organizations they run and the high economic, social and reputational costs when their leadership falls short of the mark underlines the need for research that reexamines the "classics" and provides answers on the sphere of work of contemporary CEOs and their conception and execution of this role.

An important step in this direction is the work of Margaret Glick (2011), who reexamined the role of the general manager originally identified by Mintzberg through a set of personal interviews and surveys of a broad sample of general managers. Her results confirm that there are roles that remain as current as when Mintzberg included them in his 1968 research, but others lost importance. Specifically, Glick concluded that today's general managers tend to delegate the roles of negotiator and spokesperson and that, in general, the "information roles" have lost relative weight since the 1970s.

The research carried out by Bandiera, Prat and Sadun (2014), based on interviews of CEOs in several different countries, reveals that CEOs spend 74 percent of their time in formal and informal interactions, confirming the findings from Mintzberg and Kotter, and the remaining 26 percent of their time is spent alone. In addition, Prat found that firms in which CEOs devote more time to internal work perform better than those in which the CEOs dedicates more time to work outside the realm of the business.

From a European perspective, the work of IESE Professors Joan Enric Ricart and Jaume Llopis[2] stands out. Their study, based on in-depth interviews of more than twenty general managers from prominent European firms or European subsidiaries of global firms identified a set of priorities that appears to be common among modern-day general managers:

- Anticipate and prepare the firm for the future by building clear, long-term and client-focused strategies.
- Constantly adapt or "reinvent" the firm's business model.

- Create an effective executive team, and continuously develop and maintain it.
- Create a solid foundation that supports, integrates and coordinates organizational efforts in the form of principles, corporate values and institutional purposes.

In particular, the "reinvention" of the business model as a top priority of general managers did not appear in the classic works on the topic. This is a new reality stemming from the tectonic technological changes underway in an increasing number of industrial sectors, which have allowed innovative business models to flourish and challenge what used to be considered enduring business "truths." These shifts are reflected in Ford Motor Company's decision to diversify its business into "transportation services," General Motors' investments in the ride-sharing service Lyft Inc and the disruptive effects of newcomers like Uber and eCooltra.

The agenda of the chief executive officer: data from Latin America

In this section, we will build on the aforementioned research on the work of 21st-century CEOs by outlining the findings and insights from research on the agendas of CEOs based in Latin America.

We gathered data through survey-based interviews of 180 CEOs operating in Latin America between 2012 and 2015. Data collection was based on a conceptual framework on the agenda of the CEO, developed inductively and validated empirically in previous works (Carrera, Caldart & Cornejo, 2011, 2012; Caldart, Carrera & Cornejo, 2014), as seen in Figures 15.1 and 15.2. We asked CEOs about the tasks that they consider characteristic of their job function ("understanding") and those that they actually performed during the year preceding the survey ("execution"). In this way, we can perceive gaps between rhetoric and reality and determine whether these gaps are contingent on the CEO profile. In short, our objective is to find out whether there are likely "blind spots" affecting how CEOs perform their roles.

FIGURE 15.1   Agenda of the CEO. Three Processes

248   Adrián A. Caldart et al.

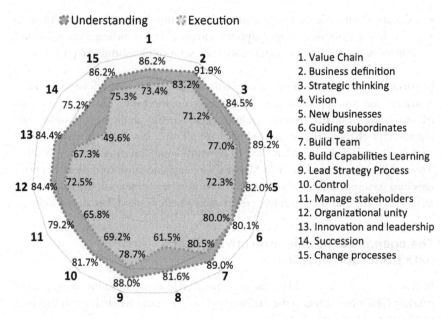

FIGURE 15.2   Agenda of the CEO. Understanding vs. execution of tasks

Using music as a metaphor, the roles of CEOs could be considered as the complete set of musical notes. The CEOs interviewed since the start of this project, in 1999, acknowledge that all the notes – the framework tested in the survey – are relevant for their work. Yet when it comes time to use these notes to create their melodies, CEOs rely on different subsets and combinations. Next, we examine this reality with to identify these differences and discuss their implications for the governance of business firms.

We analysed the differences (gaps) between the tasks that CEOs consider *they focus on* and *those that they actually executed* taking into account contingency factors related to the CEOs themselves or to the firms they lead. We studied the impact of factors such as the CEO's degree of experience on the job, the nationality of the firm (local or foreign) and whether the CEO is also the owner of the firm or not. Finally, the third viewpoint relates to understanding what proportion of "what is done" results from planned work and what proportion instead derives from an emergent agenda.

Methodology

Figures 15.1 and Table 15.2 summarize the conceptual framework that underlies the data collection. It conceives the CEO agenda as a set of fifteen tasks clustered around three processes that, while clearly different, must be treated consistently (Valero & Lucas, 1991). These areas are defined as the *business process, management process* and *institutional configuration process*, as illustrated in Figure 15.1.

The business process underpins the firm's development through the definition, understanding and operation of the business and aims to effectively reach corporate objectives. The management process comprises the organization's activities and learning processes, which enable it to develop the capabilities required to conduct its businesses. Finally, the institutional configuration process focuses on creating the suitable institutional conditions that will allow the firm to grow in accordance with organizational needs.

Within each of these processes, our previous research led to the identification of specific tasks that make up the CEO agenda, as seen in Table 15.2.

TABLE 15.2 The Agenda of the CEO

Business Process	Management Process	Institutional Configuration Process
1. Have a clear understanding of the value chain where the company operates and of the competencies and resources demanded by the industry for being successful. ("VALUE CHAIN")	6. Guide subordinates' actions. ("GUIDING SUBORDINATES")	11. Organize the coexistence and interaction with the different stakeholders in a harmonious way. ("MANAGE STAKEHOLDERS")
2. Define effectively which businesses the company will focus its activities on and the business operations it will carry out. ("BUSINESS DEFINITION")	7. Selecting collaborators and delegating responsibility. ("BUILD TEAM")	12. Promote and take care of the organizational unity. ("ORGANIZATIONAL UNITY")
3. Develop and promote strategic thinking among the people who belong to the organization. ("STRATEGIC THINKING")	8. Develop the organization's learning skills. ("BUILD CAPABILITIES")	13. Promote innovation and leadership development. ("INNOVATION AND LEADERSHIP")
4. Create and develop a vision for the company. ("VISION")	9. Lead the strategy formulation process. ("LEAD STRATEGY PROCESS")	14. Select and develop its successor. ("SUCCESSION")
5. Promote and develop new businesses. ("NEW BUSINESSES")	10. Lead the strategic and operational control. ("CONTROL")	15. Promote change processes in the organization. (CHANGE PROCESSES)

Source: Adapted from *Política de Empresa: El Gobierno de la Empresa de Negocios* by A. Valero y Vicente and J. L. Lucas Tomás, 1991, Pamplona, Spain: EUNSA.

We asked a sample of 180 CEOs to assess the tasks included in Table 15.2 through two main prisms:

1   The extent to which they considered these tasks part of their CEO agenda ("understanding").
2   The extent to which they executed these tasks during the previous year ("execution").

For this purpose, we used a Likert scale from 1 (Very Low) to 7 (Very High). The dependent variable in the analysis is the level of understanding/execution of the fifteen different dimensions of the CEO's work. This level of understanding/execution is classified as low, medium or high.

Even though our descriptive analysis of the full sample indicates a medium to high level of understanding and execution along these different dimensions, we also examined the potential impact of the CEO's profile on the probabilities of understanding or executing those tasks.

The dependent variable Y represents the levels of understanding or execution for each of the fifteen tasks. We then developed statistical models[3] that enabled us to estimate the probability that a CEO has low, medium or high levels of understanding and execution for the tasks on the agenda, based on the following factors:

- Experience (measured in years of tenure in the position of CEO in their current firm or other firms)
- Origin of capital (= 1 if the firm is local, = 0 if the firm is foreign)
- Duality (= 1 if the CEO is also the owner, = 0 if not)
- Education
- Current position
- Age

Table 15.3 summarizes some characteristics of the CEOs included in the sample. In addition, we analyzed the intensity of execution of the different tasks, assessing the significance of differences for diverse CEO profiles.

TABLE 15.3 Levels of Understanding and Execution

Likert Scale	Y
1	1 (low)
2	1 (low)
3	2 (medium)
4	2 (medium)
5	2 (medium)
6	3 (high)
7	3 (high)

Source: Elaborated by the authors.

Research findings

General analysis

As shown in Table 15.4, the best understood among the three areas is the business process. The management process comes in second, with a narrower gap between understanding and execution, while the institutional configuration appears in third place as the least understood and with the largest gap between understanding and execution.

Table 15.4 illustrates the values of understanding and execution at the task level. Represented graphically in Figure 15.2, these results indicate only one task that doesn't have a gap between understanding and execution ("what is said and what is done"), namely that of "guiding subordinates" (business process). For the remaining fourteen tasks, we perceive a gap that shows in all the cases a higher value for understanding than execution.[4] This gap is quite narrow for the tasks of "build team," "business definition" and "lead strategy process." On the other extreme, we find the tasks of "succession," "build capabilities" and "innovation and leadership" have the highest gaps.

The task "succession" is not only the one with the largest gaps but also the least prioritized ("understood") by CEOs, followed by "build capabilities learning" (8th) and "promote innovation and development of leaders" (13th).[5] At the other end of the spectrum, the tasks for which we observe the lowest gaps, aside from the aforementioned, are "guiding subordinates" (6th), "build team" (7th) and "business definition" (2nd).

Segmented analysis

The multinomial logit estimations of the level of understanding and execution are presented in Table 15.6. For the sake of brevity, only tasks that show significant differences between subsamples are reported.

CEO owners vs. CEO non-owners

Data show that while CEO owners and CEO non-owners have a similar understanding of the tasks their agenda comprises, CEO owners execute tasks related to the management and institutional configuration processes with a far lower intensity.

When we frame the analysis to the task level, we observe that the aforementioned relative lack of attention to the task "succession" is even more pronounced in the case of CEO owners. Moreover, these "dual-role" CEOs also seem to disregard the task of "manage stakeholders." This task is one of the least understood and executed by CEO owners and one that shows a larger gap between understanding and execution compared to CEO non-owners. A third task rather neglected by CEO owners is "strategic thinking," even though they consider it an important part of their agenda. On the other hand, there are some tasks that CEO owners

TABLE 15.4 Understanding and Execution (in Percentage): Mean Differences by Process (Und. = Understanding, Exec. = Execution)

	Overall		Ownership				Origin of Capital				Experience			
			Owner		Non-owner		Local		Foreign		Until 5 Years		More than 5 Years	
	Und.	Exec.	Und.	Exec.	Und.	Exec.	Und.	Exec.	Und.	Exec.	Und.	Exec.	Und.	Exec.
			(a)	(b)	(c)	(d)	(a)	(b)	(c)	(d)	(a)	(b)	(c)	(d)
Business	86.8***	75.4	87.8***	76.6	86.1***	74.7	87.6***	77.2**[(d)]	85.3***	72.6	87.0***	74.8	86.6***	76.0
Management	84.1***	74.0	85.2***	71.8	83.4***	75.3	85.0***	73.6	82.6***	74.6	85.3***	76.0*[(d)]	83.1***	72.3
Institutional configuration	81.9***	66.1	81.1***	61.5	82.4***	68.9***[(b)]	81.6***	65.0	82.3***	67.9	82.5***	66.7	81.4***	65.6
Total	**84.2***	**71.8**	**84.7***	**70.0**	**84.0***	**73.0**	**84.7***	**71.9**	**83.4***	**71.7**	**85.0***	**72.5**	**83.7***	**71.3**

Note: *, ** and *** indicate significance at the 10 percent, 5 percent and 1 percent levels, respectively, between understanding and execution. Mean differences between different types of CEO are indicated with a letter corresponding to each column.

Source: Elaborated by the authors.

TABLE 15.5 Level of Understanding and Execution (in Percentage): Mean Differences by Dimension (Und. = Understanding, Exec. = Execution)

| | Overall | | Ownership | | | | Origin of Capital | | | | Experience | | | |
| | | | Owner | | Non-owner | | Local | | Foreign | | Until 5 Years | | More than 5 Years | |
	Und.	Exec.	Und. (a)	Exec. (b)	Und. (c)	Exec. (d)	Und. (a)	Exec. (b)	Und. (c)	Exec. (d)	Und. (a)	Exec. (b)	Und. (c)	Exec. (d)
(1) Value chain	86.2***	73.4	85.5***	72.7	86.6***	73.9	86.6***	75.3	85.5***	70.4	87.0***	73.8	85.6***	73.2
(2) Business definition	91.9***	83.2	93.7***	87.0**(d)	90.9***	81.0	92.1***	84.3	91.6***	81.5	92.7***	81.8	91.3***	84.4
(3) Strategic thinking	84.5***	71.2	82.6***	67.0	85.7***	73.7	84.6***	72.3	84.5***	69.3	85.2***	71.1	84.0***	71.3
(4) Vision	89.2***	77.0	91.8***/*(c)	78.6	87.6***	76.1	91.0***/*(c)	77.7	86.3***	75.8	90.7***	78.8	88.0***	75.6
(5) New businesses	82.0***	72.3	85.5***/**(c)	77.7**(d)	79.8v	69.0	83.9***/***(c)	76.2***(d)	78.8***	66.0	79.6***	68.4	83.8***	75.5
(6) Guiding subordinates	80.1	80.0	82.8	78.8	78.5	80.7	82.1*(c)	79.7	76.9	80.5	80.7	80.2	79.7	79.8
(7) Build team	89.0***	80.5	91.6***/**(c)	79.2	87.4***	81.3	89.7***	79.0	87.8***	83.0	89.3***	84.5**(d)	88.7***	77.3
(8) Build capabilities learning	81.6***	61.5	82.1***	56.7	81.3***	64.4**(b)	82.5***	61.9	80.3***	60.7	83.2***	62.3	80.4***	60.8
(9) Lead strategy process	88.0***	78.7	88.2***	78.6	87.9***	78.8	88.2***	79.3	87.8***	78.7	89.6***	81.4	86.7***	76.5
(10) Control	81.7***	69.2	81.1***	65.8	82.1***	71.3	82.5***	68.1	80.5***	77.7	83.8***/*(c)	71.8	80.1***	67.1
(11) Manage stakeholders	79.2***	65.8	76.9***	57.8	80.6***(b)	70.8***(b)	79.5***	65.1	78.6***	71.0	81.4***/*(c)	68.8	77.3***	63.5
(12) Organizational unity	84.4***	72.5	85.9***	70.4	83.5***	73.7	85.5***	70.8	82.8***	67.0	84.5***	76.6**(d)	84.4***	69.1
(13) Innovation and leadership	84.4***	67.3	83.2***	65.1	85.1***	68.6	83.1***	66.5	86.3***	75.2	85.0***	66.3	83.8***	68.1
(14) Succession	75.2***	49.6	72.9***	44.3	76.6***	52.9**(b)	73.1***	49.7	78.6***	68.5	73.8***	44.1	76.3***	54.1**(b)
(15) Change processes	86.2***	75.3	86.3***	69.7	86.1***	78.6**(b)	86.7***	73.0	85.3***	49.6	87.9***	77.9	84.8***	73.2
Total	84.2***	71.8	84.7***	70.0	84.0***	73.0	84.7***	71.9	83.4***	71.7	85.0***	72.5	83.7***	71.3

Note: $\star$, $\star\star$ and $\star\star\star$ indicate significance at the 10 percent, 5 percent and 1 percent levels, respectively, between understanding and execution. Mean differences between different types of CEO are indicated with a letter corresponding to each column.

Source: Elaborated by the authors.

TABLE 15.6 Multinomial Logit Estimates

Works	Level of Understanding						Level of Execution			
Dimensions:	(4) Vision		(10) Control		(14) Succession		(3) Strategic Thinking		(11) Stakeholders	
	Medium	High	Medium	High	Medium	High	Medium	High	Medium	High
Age	0.13	0.18*	0.04	-0.01	0.04	0.06**	0.04	0.08**	0.04	0.08**
	(0.10)	(0.10)	(0.06)	(0.06)	(0.03)	(0.03)	(0.03)	(0.03)	(0.03)	(0.03)
Experience	-0.05	-0.08***	-0.11	-0.09	-0.02	-0.01	-0.03	-0.04	-0.08**	-0.08**
	(0.05)	(0.03)	(0.08)	(0.08)	(0.04)	(0.04)	(0.06)	(0.06)	(0.04)	(0.04)
Level of education	-0.41	0.32	-0.15	-0.17	-0.52	-0.54	0.08	-0.21	-0.58	-0.54
	(0.98)	(0.94)	(0.44)	(0.44)	(0.39)	(0.38)	(0.51)	(0.53)	(0.40)	(0.41)
Owner	17.28***	17.02***	-16.85***	-17.94***	-0.43	-0.13	-1.82***	-2.40***	-1.47*	-1.96**
	(1.42)	(1.26)	(1.29)	(1.39)	(0.68)	(0.70)	(0.69)	(0.69)	(0.86)	(0.83)
Local company	-1.21	0.18	4.24***	4.92***	0.18	-0.65	0.51	1.47*	1.52*	1.69**
	(1.99)	(1.92)	(1.58)	(1.64)	(0.74)	(0.73)	(0.74)	(0.75)	(0.86)	(0.83)
Constant	-1.84	-4.30	16.11	18.72***	1.05	0.80	1.29	-0.31	1.57	-0.27
	(3.22)	(3.00)	(1.62)	(1.57)	(1.38)	(1.38)	(2.14)	(2.19)	(1.79)	(1.82)

Note: *, ** and *** indicate significance at 10 percent, 5 percent and 1 percent levels, respectively. Robust standard errors reported in parentheses. The low level is the base category.

understand and execute with greater intensity than their non-owner peers. Among these, we highlight "vision."

With respect to gaps, we observe that highly experienced CEOs execute the tasks of "build team" and "organizational unity" with less intensity. As expected, less experienced CEOs focus less intensely on the task of "succession" than their more senior peers do.

Local CEOs vs. country managers of foreign firms

Contrary to the case of local CEOs, CEOs from foreign subsidiaries show no gap between understanding and execution on the "control" variable. CEOs from foreign firms also pay relatively more attention to "succession" and consequently show a narrower gap between understanding and execution on this task.

Both CEOs from local and international firms rate the importance of "change processes" on the same level. Yet at the level of execution, country managers from foreign firms devote far less attention to this task.

Conclusion

Our findings reveal that while there is considerable consensus among CEOs on the roles that make up their job definition ("understanding"), there is less uniformity when it comes to "combining the musical notes" that constitute the agenda they actually execute. These differences relate to several factors, including the nature of the roles, the firms' external and organizational environments and the CEOs' personal characteristics.

CEO owners seem to prioritize tasks related to business process, such as the search for new businesses, over those related to management and institutional configuration processes. Data on execution suggest that in owner-led firms, strategic decisions tend to be more centralized, and processes aimed at building strategic capabilities are less relevant than in firms run by CEO non-owners. In addition, the strong position of CEO owners within the governance structure of the firm makes them less sensitive to the interests of other stakeholders and less prone to promote organization-wide change processes.

This perceived bias of CEO owners toward major business decisions and their apparent disdain for the long-term factors of building corporate capabilities and a sound governance structure exposes their firms to potentially serious dangers. For instance, an untimely inability of CEO owners to carry out their duties could cause uncertainty in the governance structure in the absence of a solid succession plan. Similarly, disregard for the development of organizational skills, coupled with the lack of concern for change processes, exposes the firm to management gaps that might prove difficult to remedy with quick fixes. Therefore, these CEO owners are advised to take it upon themselves to nominate board members and/or hire external consultants focused on these topics and equipped to challenge the CEO owner's dominant logic.

On the contrary, CEO non-owners tend to focus more intensely on management processes and on reconciling the agendas of the firm's various stakeholder groups. Local CEO non-owners tend to be the most inclined to engage the firm in change processes. In particular, CEOs who operate MNC subsidiaries demonstrate a higher degree of management formalization and reporting practices than do their local counterparts. This is reflected by the strong emphasis they put on management control. Succession is another issue that subsidiary CEOs pay more attention to than do their local peers. Again, corporate processes influence the actions of the CEO, whose tenure periods tend to be briefer than those of their local counterparts.

As in the case of CEO owners, CEOs of foreign firms tend to disregard the development of change processes. "Business as usual" seems to be their guiding principle. That said, anecdotal evidence suggests that foreign country managers are more inclined to emulate this conservative behavior than are their local peers. The difference can be attributed to local country managers having a greater attachment to the country and are therefore more committed to growing the subsidiary to develop their own career path. Foreign country managers, on the hand, are more likely to envision another international assignment on their future career path.

Differences in the level of experience in the position also explain variations in the way CEOs execute their agendas. "Junior" CEOs prioritize change processes more than their "senior" peers do. This might be associated with the need of new CEOs to make their mark in the organization. Similarly, "juniors" pay more attention to building their team and promoting organizational unity, tasks that senior CEOs have probably already developed in the past and now pay little attention to.

From a conceptual standpoint, CEOs seem to be clear and in agreement on the content of their job. Yet when it comes to moving from concept to action, they tend to lean toward topics related to operations while neglecting the institutional elements of their job, such as promoting a context that supports the firm's long-term sustainability, beyond their tenure. This situation has a dual-effect: first, what we could characterize as their short-term or urgent legacy (i.e., their succession) and, second, their "enduring" legacy linked to developing organizational skills, fostering innovation and cultivating future leaders. These tasks constitute core elements of securing the firm's long-term continuity.

If we compare the agendas of CEO owners and CEO non-owners, we verify that the former consider strategic thinking as a personal and nondelegable task, as opposed to one developed within the firm. On the other hand, it would follow that the agendas of CEO non-owners would require a more consensual approach when performing their job. They are held firmly accountable to the board and major shareholders and must act accordingly. Although the business process is highly important to them, they must also mobilize the organization and achieve goals, tend to institutional aspects (to remain in their post) and promote any change process required by the firm (which, in many cases, justified their appointment).

Differences in CEO agendas stemming from different levels of experience indicate that CEOs learn on the job and that newcomers have inherent priorities associated with their first years of tenure: leading change processes, building their teams and cultivating organizational unity. On the other hand, the emphasis on selecting a successor increases as CEOs spend more years in the post. In short, we can state that their emphasis on different tasks has dynamics that are significantly associated with the CEO's trajectory.

Upon observing the agendas of CEOs of local firms against those from foreign subsidiaries, it is apparent that they have different perspectives: the former are responsible for 100 percent of the firm's business lines and activities, and therefore take a comprehensive perspective. The latter manage the business areas and activities that their headquarters decided to delegate to them, a circumstance that can lead them to think and act less holistically than their local peers. Their agenda is strongly subject to their geographic location and by the management systems established by the multinational firm. We assume that in the absence of geographic and systems-based factors, some tasks would lose ground in forwarding their agenda in the face of short-term exigencies, as occurs with local CEOs.

Finally, within the common ground constituted by their understood agenda, there are clearly different and contingent, while somewhat predictable, emphases on the execution side and a common disregard for tasks related to the firm's institutional configuration. This should set off some alarm bells for practicing managers, boards of directors, academics and other stakeholders connected with global firms, since in the long run, the quality of the organization's institutional configuration is what ultimately determines the success of the other two processes. The awareness of the systemic relationship among these three processes and actions to ensure harmony among them constitutes a distinguishing feature of effective CEOs.

Notes

1 Rock Center of Corporate Governance at Stanford University (2016).
2 More information on this topic is available in Chapter 1.
3 Logit multinomial models were used.
4 The gaps for the fourteen variables are statistically significant.
5 These results are statistically relevant.

References

Barnard, C. (1938). *The Functions of the Executive*. Cambridge, MA: Harvard University Press.
Bandiera, O., Prat, A. and Sadun, R. (2014). Managing the Family Firm: Evidence from CEOs at Work, NBER Working Paper No. 19722.
Carrera, A., Caldart, A. and Cornejo, M. (2011). "La Agenda del CEO Latinoamericano." *Harvard Business Review América Latina*, 89(5): 94–102.
Caldart, A., Carrera, A. and Cornejo, M. (2012). "¿Cómo cambia la agenda del director general a lo largo de su carrera profesional?" *Harvard Deusto Business Review*, 217: 40–47.
Caldart, A., Carrera, A. and Cornejo, M. (2014). "Liderar una Empresa Local o una Subsidiaria: Distintas Responsabilidades, ¿Distintas Agendas?" *Harvard Deusto Business Review*, 233: 66–75.
Fayol, H. (1916). "Administration Industrielle et Générale," *Bulletin de la Société de l'Industrie Minérale*, 10: 5–164.

Glick, M. (2011). "The Role of Chief Executive Officer," *Advances in Developing Human Resources*, 13(2): 171–207.

Hart, S. and Quinn, R. (1993). "Roles Executives Play: CEOs, Behavioral Complexity, and Firm Performance," *Human Relations*, 46(5): 543–574.

Kotter, J. (1982). *The General Managers*. New York, NY: Free Press.

Mintzberg, H. (1973). *The Nature of Managerial Work*. New York, NY: Harper & Row.

Selznick, P. (1957). *Leadership in Administration*. New York, NY: Harper & Row.

Valero y Vicente, A. and Lucas Tomás, J. L. (1991). *Política de Empresa: El Gobierno de la Empresa de Negocios*. Pamplona, Spain: EUNSA.

PART 5
Cases

16

CASES

The following are summaries of business case studies either cited in the book or related to topics discussed by the contributors.[1]

Fisipe: a high-risk management buy out (Luis Lynce de Faria, Adrián A. Caldart, AESE Escola de Direção e Negócios)

This case tells the story of an acrylic fiber plant built in 1973 in Portugal by the Mitsubishi Rayon Company and by CUF, the most important inorganic chemical group in Portugal. The plant would be located at the Tagus river border near Lisbon and form part of the Barreiro industrial complex.

Fisipe was a supplier to the Portuguese textile industry, which was an important economic engine and stronghold of the country's balance of payments with Europe at the time. After the contract was signed in October 1973, the initial groundwork was laid for the future site, and orders for manufacturing equipment were placed.

Difficult times lay ahead, not only for Portugal as a whole but for the petrochemical sector in particular. The oil crises of 1973 and 1978 and a National Socialist Revolution in 1974, which led to nationalization of the company in 1975, completely upended the vision of the original company owners. At the time, the size of the Portuguese textile market was around 20,000 tons, but the company was protected by favorable tax conditions and a special authorization that limited imports of acrylic fibers. Bayer, Montefibre and Courtaulds were Fisipe's main competitors, all with vast experience in the manufacture and supply of European and overseas markets. Among their most well-known brand names were Dralon, Leacryl and Courtelle.

Plant construction was delayed by a year as a result of these political and economic upheavals. The company's situation was further exacerbated by ongoing claims and strikes by labor unions, which directly impacted the firm's investment value. In the end, Fisipe was forced to increase its social capital.

Finally, in 1984, the company presented its first positive performance results, following an expansion of its productive capacity to 50,000 tons. In 1988, import protections were removed, so Fisipe started to compete in an open market, leading its market share in Portugal to drop to 50 percent in the following years. To offset this decline, the company concentrated its efforts on rapidly building its presence in other European and international markets.

The top management team was kept in place from 1973 to 1997, until Fisipe was privatized once again and returned to the CUF group. During this period, the textile industry was delocalized from Europe to Asia and the production, and consumption of fiber in European markets suffered a dramatic decline, causing more than 50 percent of plants to close shop. Market competition was extreme, and the product ultimately became commoditized.

After an unsuccessful strategy implemented by the CUF group, and without any solution in sight for Fisipe's slipping performance, CUF accepted an MBO in 2005, headed by one of the company's top managers during its first twenty-four years.

Seven years after the MBO, in 2012, the new owners of Fisipe sold the business to the SGL Group, which was interested in the company's technology to produce carbon fibers by using acrylic polymer compounds. How was this company's turnaround possible in such a competitive and turbulent market?

Solancis: competitiveness through innovation and sustainability (José Ramalho Fontes, Pedro Alvito, AESE Escola de Direção e Negócios)

This case briefly describes the history of the company Solancis from 1969 to the present. The firm extracts limestone from its nearby quarries and transforms them to building façade tiles. It has a modern factory with semi-robotized operations located in the Alcobaça district, 100 kilometers from Lisbon. Solancis exports 92.5 percent of its production to France (32 percent) and other EU countries (40 percent), the United States (6.75 percent), China (4.74 percent) and other countries.

The first part of the case succinctly describes the production line, the technologies applied and the demanding sustainability measures carried out in the factory and in the quarries it explores. Many of the company's characteristics are unusual in its sector. The case explores Solancis markets and details target customers, which are generally architecture firms. It also presents the organizational chart, the composition of its HR and its training practices.

The second part of the case focuses on the company's innovative dynamics, presenting different research-and-development projects and innovative EU projects in which Solancis participates in or leads and which involve a network of companies, associations and research centers. The case describes its internal innovation process, from the decision of engagement to the public presentation of its results, and its relationship with the footwear sector and with the technological company CEI.

The different innovations implemented over the previous ten years have transformed the firm's capabilities, offering the possibility of creating more value in its commercial offer. Finally, the case shows what the three current and future challenges are. The economic-financial data of the company show a downward trend in EBIT and net profit, due to investments, despite a rise in turnover.

Solancis is a one-person show. The company's CEO, Samuel Delgado, has both human and environmental values, but it is unclear whether the firm can achieve its full potential market reach. The company is increasing know-how to fortify performance. The CEO believes that innovation has allowed the company to grow and feels confident about the future since the company has significant work. The case examines his agenda for gauging the future of Solancis. His relationship with his two daughters is also an issue discussed in the case.

Minas Conga (Hugo Alegre, PAD Escuela de Dirección)

This case describes the social conflict that took place in 2012 in Cajamarca, Peru surrounding the emblematic cupriferous project Minas Conga. It explores why this region, one of the poorest in the country, rejected the execution of a project that would have led to significant economic benefits, including tax revenues, job opportunities (direct and indirect) and direct social assistance, among many others. It also examines the factors that can influence the onset of social rejection toward a project and the elements that can turn rejection into conflict. This case underlines the need to meet stakeholder expectations and provides a platform for a discussion on legality and legitimacy. Additionally, it provides a framework to reflect on possible strategies that governments and enterprises can implement to gain social legitimacy in extractive projects.

This case revisits the history of the relationship between the main shareholder of Minas Congas and the Cajamarca region, with Yanacocha – one of the most important goldmines in the world – as the main thread. It's a relationship tainted by events that have left a negative impact on the residents of Cajamarca despite the significant business efforts made to support the region's development. Can bad memories be erased with good actions? If so, what's the best approach to achieve this aim?

The town's primary fear was that the project would affect their water sources, thus hindering their agricultural work, the region's main economic engine. Their apprehension opens up the debate on the risk and benefits of extractive activities. As we analyze this debate, we need to take into account the different perspectives of the country as a whole, the region of Cajamarca and the communities in the areas of influence (both direct and indirect). Reality against perception is another interesting area of reflection. What happens when these diverge? What is the cause of these divergences? And finally, what can be done about it? On the other hand, the inability of the Peruvian government to adequately channel the funds generated by mining taxes makes us question the extent to which private enterprises should be involved in community development.

An immensely rich group of participants provides insights into the Peruvian political sphere, including its main opposing players and overriding interests. Who is in favor of and who is against the project moving forward? What are the reasons behind their viewpoints? How should these opposing viewpoints be managed?

Finally, the process undertaken by the government to approve the project and its later objections opens up the discussion about legality and legitimacy. Did the company act ethically to obtain approval, or did they overlook the most important stakeholders? How can the government play the dual role of advocate and arbitrator? The challenges of aligning the divergent interests of the government, business community and residents ultimately proved insurmountable, and conflict ensued. The question we asked was when do differences in opinion lead to conflict, and when does conflict turn into violence? What steps could have been taken to avoid this outcome? Or was it inevitable?

El Tejar Ltd. (Alejandro A. Carrera, IAE Business School)

In 2009, El Tejar Ltd. was poised to become the world's largest and most global large-scale agribusiness company, with operations spanning nearly 1 million hectares. In under two decades, the company had transformed from a family-owned cattle-raising cooperative in the Salado River basin of Argentina into a world-class international farming firm. Widely regarded as a reliable, innovative and entrepreneurial business, it was also a people-centered company that relied entirely on its human potential to attain an admirable growth rate envied by its competitors.

This case provides an opportunity to analyze El Tejar's governance performance and the role of its top management team and president, Oscar Alvarado. The case examines its corporate governance around three main pillars: its business process (BP), its management process (MP) and its institutional configuration process (ICP).

Oscar Alvarado stands out as a top-tier executive who embodies the traits of a true leader. In addition to exploring his personal management style, we examined his views on global organizations and how to lead them. In a rapid process of global expansion, El Tejar faces a significant challenge: at face value, it would appear that El Tejar's growth and expansion capabilities are endless. Where do the company's growth boundaries – if any – lie?

As they search for a possible solution, participants should consider the following questions:

1 What do you find remarkable about El Tejar's short life thus far?
2 What do you think about its sizable growth? How do you explain it? Do you think it is sustainable? Why or why not?
3 Do you recommend that El Tejar accept the capital offered by the US fund FM? Explain your reasoning.
4 What challenges does El Tejar face at this crossroads? How do you envision the future of this company, which likes to plan for the next seven hundred years? Envision what El Tejar might look like in 2020. What recommendations would you make to its top management?

By addressing these questions, participants gain a better understanding of the implications of managing a people-centered company and how this approach impacts its decision-making frameworks. Finally, the class will look into Oscar Alvarado's performance by examining his responsibilities as a manager determined to ensure that his company reaches its objectives and fulfills its overarching mission.

Mercado Libre: the battle for Chile
(Roberto Vassolo, IAE Business School)

By August 2013, Mercado Libre (hereinafter, MELI) enjoyed a leading position in Latin America in terms of traffic and sales, achieving double-digit growth year after year. In this case, Federico Procaccini, general manager of Argentina and the Rest of Latin America (hereinafter, ROLA), following the first eighteen months of his administration, analyzed the situation of countries that did not have a local office and were managed from the parent company.

In particular, 2012 marked a resounding success for Argentina, which ended with spectacular growth and a net turnover of 56 percent. However, within the ROLA countries, the situation in Chile was complex. This country was in the group in which MELI did not have commercial offices and so was managed from the parent company. It was, without doubt, one of the most sophisticated markets in the region. Given the development of Chile's economy and the high level of banking access, MELI faced a sophisticated market.

The company had forged a powerful brand in LATAM based on its location and adaptation of the best commercial practices in a regional scenario that presented great opportunities for an internet-based marketplace provider. However, the company could not capitalize on its reputation in the business to customer (B2C) or "high-stretch" segment of the Chilean market. In this segment, large stores such as Falabella, Paris, Ripley and La Polar dominated. Meanwhile, MELI generated turnover mainly on the basis of consumer to consumer (C2C).

Specifically, the department store chain Falabella had triumphed in Chilean retail. A few years beforehand, the company had launched its own website to sell online. Its business model was strongly anchored in the store and personalized customer service, providing the consumer with a reliable and friendly shopping experience. Procaccini felt that to face this type of competitor, MELI needed a strong investment in product, specifically in the renovation of Mercado Pago. However, he was concerned that this type of investment would compete with resources from larger countries such as Brazil, where the competitive battle was with global competitors such as Amazon.

While there was no strong competitor at the regional level so far, many questions remained in Procaccini's head: What was the strategic value and associated costs of maintaining or modifying the company's presence in Chile? What was the real risk of not being there? What kind of resources would be compromised? What were the key success factors in this industry? What type of client should MELI be serving? Would there be regional consolidation? In a scenario of increasing competitive intensity, what should be Falabella's next step? How was Amazon expected to advance in the region? What threats and opportunities did the traditional retail business model present?

AJE Group: selling drinks to the base of the pyramid (José Luis Nueno, Silvia Rodriguez, Miguel Bazán, IESE Business School, PAD Escuela de Dirección)

This case study describes AJE Group's birth, expansion and internationalization process. It analyzes its foray into the Asian market and the consumer profile in this region as opposed to the company's natural market, South America. The case describes the challenges of a family business turned multinational group: human resource management, financial management and cultural issues.

AJE was established in Peru in the 1980s during a period of upheaval: threats of terrorism and a high inflation rate that reached 6,000 percent. It faced many of the difficult circumstances experienced by Latin American countries as they expanded at that time.

This situation of instability was the foundation for AJE's learning and development in the beverage business. AJE's strategic analysis was simple: their business was directed toward people with few resources. They identified an opportunity in people who could not afford luxury drinks. This determined both the concept and business model: their product, "Big Cola," was not a luxury product but a mass consumption product.

AJE had a clear low-cost strategy, although this did not mean its strategy was to offer a cheap product. Selling at a fair price was a priority. The low-cost strategy was emphasized throughout the value chain, in their suppliers, on the operational side and in the internal team up. It also extended to satisfying their customers' needs. Their skilled competitors felt comfortable managing strategy further up in the pyramid, but that was not where they wanted to compete.

AJE stayed at the base of the pyramid, preferring to have 10 percent of the market in more countries than fight over 20 or 30 percent and even lose money. AJE had a presence in countries such as India and Indonesia, where the average per capita consumption for products such as water was 1 to 3 liters, whereas in Latin America it was more than 80 liters. There was potential for thirty-fold growth over the coming years. That is where AJE's strategy was focused: democratizing beverage consumption by promoting growth in their markets, adding new consumers and not taking a percentage from competitors.

Entering Mexico, the largest market in Latin America, marked a milestone in AJE's expansion, as they had previously mostly entered into small and medium markets in Latin America. Next, they entered Asia.

When AJE sold only cola in Peru, it had a clear platform and a relatively high level of sales. Then, however, products such as sports drinks, juices and waters were added, and thus, the business become even stronger and more consistent. AJE focused on two relevant areas: increasing the market and being profitable. The mission and vision of the company was to be among the top twenty consumer goods companies.

Throughout the process of growth and internationalization, AJE remained a family business. It bridged two generations that grew the company together, going from being a business to being a company and aiming to become a publicly traded company: "an enterprise," in the words of CEO Carlos Añaños.

RBS Group (Cesar Bullara, ISE Business School)

The Sirtosky family, owners of the RBS Group, had seen clouds forming on the horizon for quite some time. As a traditional media group, they not only faced declining readership and advertising revenues but also confronted rising costs of paper and increased competition from online channels.

To address this situation, the board of directors assembled a special task force in 2011 to study the potential impact of internet media on their business lines. Of particular concern was the group's leading newspaper asset, Zero Hora, whose future was in doubt. According to their scenario forecasts, they had only a six-year timeframe to turn things around at the newspaper. As it happened, change occurred much sooner than they expected. In 2012, RBS's corporate revenue had dropped precipitously in the wake of waning advertising income. These disastrous results made it clear that a new strategy was necessary.

RBS CEO Eduardo Sirotsky was the right person in the right place at the right time. He had just attended the 2012 Digital Media Europe, an event organized by the WAN-IFRA (Word Association of Newspapers and News). By the time the event concluded, Sirotsky knew that the internet would play a pivotal role in the future of the publishing industry.

The data supplied by the task force only confirmed what they already knew: the time had come to revamp their business model. At the same time, he knew that a new business model must be supported by changes in the corporate culture and employee mindsets. This was no easy feat in this traditional company: it would require an enormous amount of effort and patience and, most importantly, the expertise of a change-management strategist. For several reasons, Sirotsky didn't think he was the right person to lead this process.

A few months later, RBS Group hired Deli Matsuo as its new vice president of HR to spearhead the cultural change initiative. With a background in electrical engineering and computer science, Deli joined RBS after several successful years as the HR director of Google, where he had led several important global projects in the United States and Asia.

Deli was aware of Sirotsky's vision for the company and of his intent to completely transform the corporate culture. It would demand a titanic effort. Stimulating innovation in traditional business environments requires profound changes in its structures, processes and job designs. It would also affect the company's daily operations. There were several deep-seated traits embedded in the corporate culture that would impede the change process. Chief among them were bureaucracy and lack of accountability.

Babé y Cía: adaptation to the environment of a century-old company (María Fernández, Jaume Llopis, Josep Tàpies, IESE Business School)

The A and B cases of the company Babé y Cía tell the story of a century-old family business that is currently facing a strategic challenge. Case A allows us to analyze the capacity of a family business to adapt to major changes that occurred in the oil industry during the 20th century. Case B illustrates how business-family relationships are managed to avoid conflicts of interest between the two areas.

Case A

Babé was the first oil refinery in Galicia and was founded in 1888 by Evaristo Babé and Gely (1848–1920). The business of the refinery was, at that time, a truly uncertain adventure, in which few visionaries were able to see the potential of what would become the fuel of the 20th century. The company adapted to the progressive changes that were taking place in the international oil sector, a particularly dynamic and strategic industry, and it made strategic shifts, two of which were particularly relevant. The first shift, in 1927, occurred when the initial refinery was expropriated when the Compañía Arrendataria de Monopolio de Petróleos (CAMPSA) was created and the family decided to found another distribution company. Since that date, the new company has had exclusive distribution of oil for the provinces of Pontevedra and Ourense. The second shift, in 1992, was made when the end of CAMPSA's monopoly forced the company to change its business model.

Case B

Since 1887, the company has gone through five generational successions. Traditionally, Babé was a presidential company: the position of president was held by the oldest male member of the family (in any of its branches), but the rest of the family members had little direct relationship with the management of the company.

In 2008, the newly appointed president, Javier González-Babé Ozores, decided to professionalize management. It included the youngest members of the family, both on the board of directors and in the management of the company and external directors with whom it intended to deal with the restructuring of the company. In the area of company management, the family created a board of directors made up of family members and three external professionals, all of whom would act as the highest collegiate governing body. In addition, to manage the relationship between the company and the family, a family protocol was signed in 2010, which provides for the creation of a general meeting of shareholders and a family council.

APA (The Peruvian Poultry Association): a change of paradigm (Alejandro Fontana, PAD Escuela de Dirección)

In recent years, the Peruvian poultry sector has assumed a relevant role in the development of the country. The annual production of poultry meat grew from 400,000 tons in 1998 to almost 1.4 million tons in 2012. During this period of time, however, the key driver for growth in this sector has been the increase in poultry as a source of animal protein, with consumption rising from 19.5 to 39.1 kg/capita. This outcome is also the consequence of a shift in this enterprise association's paradigm: it started to focus on the common good and thus work to assure food safety for the national population.

This case shows that the market sector plays a crucial role in identifying and solving social problems. It is relevant in these solutions because of its ability to identify the actual causes of a problem and because of their creativity and capacity to finance any proposed solution. The case also shows how the sustainability of these solutions demands the participation of other social actors as well: public administration, politicians and civil society.

UFINET Telecom, SA: aligning general management with ownership (Marta Elvira, Luis Manuel Calleja, IESE Business School)

UFINET was established in 1998 within Unión Fenosa Redes de Telecomunicación as a secondary business supporting the utility company. In 2009, the unit merged with Cable Development as part of Gas Natural's acquisition, becoming GNF Telecommunications. Finally, in 2014, UFINET was acquired by investment fund Cinven for €510 million (with €139 million in revenues and €69 million EBITDA). At that point, the business became an autonomous firm: UFINET Telecom, SA.

UFINET's successful growth in Spain, and especially in Central America, is due largely to the effective operational and strategic direction set by the top management team that has led the company from the start. The same team has persisted through three different ownership periods. CEO Íñigo García del Cerro and vice president CEO of LATAM Francisco Javier Lacasa are both telecom engineers whose professional development mirrors the growth of the company: starting with a focus on technical tasks, their roles evolved into that of executives, whether at the head office or leading the expansion into Latin America.

Becoming an independent company owned by Cinven turned out to benefit both organizations because liquidity and knowledge of the industry was accompanied by a respectful governance model. The fund is expected to remain owner for four to six years. UFINET is attractive because of its large margins and cash flow, its business predictability, quality of operations and strong positioning in Latin America.

What are the critical factors determining continuity and success on the top management team throughout the three ownership periods? What changes can be overserved in their leadership styles? What are the roles of chair and the new board? What future paths are possible alternatives for the project – for example, going public or remaining private but with a different ownership structure? When would it be appropriate to present each alternative, and who should do this?

The case illustrates the learning process of general managers and the importance of adapting to changing norms and processes through the different stages of a firm, which grows in two continents as an independent operator of fiber optics. In LATAM, unlike in Spain, the business requires greater flexibility while experiencing 20 to 23 percent growth across thirteen different countries.

At the same time, the general manager role evolves from leading an internal service to the management of a business unit within a gas utility and on to the general management of an independent company owned by the investment fund. Relevant agenda issues shift from executive action to strategic planning and new business opportunities. Knowledge transfer among regions also improves.

The board's chair plays an important role in managing the board's activities while coordinating with general management. The top management team finds it helpful to be governed through wise, deep-level questions, which serve to guide decision-making. Paradoxically, it is the CEO who is responsible for both short- and long-term results, due to the variation in ownership.

Barbuss Global, SA: globalizing a small enterprise (Adrián A. Caldart, IESE Business School)

Barbuss Global was a small firm operating in the insurance recovery sector. It had been led by Mauro Arcucci, a forty-year-old lawyer, since 2002. The insurance recovery business provides a service to the insurance sector by managing the rights of an insurance company to enforce its rights against firms (transport companies, warehouses, etc.) that with its actions could have obliged the insurance company to assume the coverage of a certain claim from any of its clients.

In many situations, the management of such rights represented a challenging task for the insurance firm, because the claim could have been made in a jurisdiction in which the firm did not have operations. In such situations, the insurer frequently outsourced the management of its rights to a law firm or to a firm specialized in managing these legal actions, such as Barbuss Global. In payment for its services, the firm that managed the insurer's rights received a "success fee" equivalent to 15 to 25 percent of the amount effectively recovered.

The year 2015 closed with sales of over $4 million for Barbuss Global. Such an amount represented a significant growth over previous years. The net margin was above 20 percent, the highest in the firm's history. In addition, the firm operated in eight countries and employed fifty-four people.

Mauro and his team attributed the success of the company to its organizational culture, characterized by a strong entrepreneurial spirit, a "can-do mentality" and an imagination at the time of dealing with complicated cases – a capability acknowledged and valued by its customers. Such characteristics enabled the firm to build the reputation that took it from its leadership position in Latin America to become an incipient player in Europe, Africa and Asia.

Yet Arcucci wondered whether the firm would be able to maintain such freshness and dynamism as its size and complexity increased. In addition, Arcucci was reflecting on his own role at Barbuss Global. He entertained the idea of becoming chair and non–executive president of the firm and appointing a new CEO recruited from outside the firm.

In this context, Arcucci and his management team, entirely made up of professionals in their forties, carried out a strategic review to decide the future direction of the firm. This reflection led the team to conclude that Barbuss Global had high growth potential in the Western European market.

But was Barbuss ready for a new CEO in substitution of its founder? Which roles should Arcucci retain as chair and president, and which ones should he delegate to his successor? Should Barbuss seek to become a leading player in Europe or instead focus its energies on Latin America as its core geographic area?

Note

1 Full versions of most of the cases included in this chapter are available at www.iese publishing.com.and http://publishing.iae.edu.ar/

EPILOGUE

Adrián A. Caldart, Joan E. Ricart
and Alejandro A. Carrera

The fifteen chapters in this book touch on different aspects of strategic management, organization theory and corporate governance. Despite the variety of topics and authors, a common thread cuts across all of them.

Our first intention was to respond to calls from academia and management practitioners for a more comprehensive and down-to-earth yet rigorous view of the role of the general manager. The book stresses the need for greater coherence and harmony in the way general managers conduct the broad range of responsibilities that make up their agendas. Only by striking a balance among their roles as *strategists* who set the course, *leaders* who align employees and *politicians* who unite the company's diverse stakeholders will global managers achieve their overriding objective of promoting the long-term continuity and prosperity in their organizations.

Second, we wanted to reflect the voices of prestigious thought leaders on the importance of moral responsibility and ethical behavior as mainstays of the management profession. Throughout the book, the authors have underlined that top-tier business leaders cannot rely solely on instrumental theories, nor can business schools limit their scope to teaching students to effectively execute core business techniques. Top managers must assume their unique and nondelegable role as socially responsible leaders, and business schools must assume their key responsibility in helping them assume this role.

Since their foundations, IESE and its network of associated business schools in Argentina, Brazil, Colombia, Chile, Ecuador, Mexico, Peru, Portugal and Uruguay have stood apart by placing this responsibility at the top of general management agendas. We hope the book that you now hold in your hands offers an insightful intellectual journey and that you find this work as a vivid reflection of such an ideal. This would be our greatest reward.

INDEX